THE LABOUR OF LEISURE

THE LABOUR OF
LEISURE

THE CULTURE OF
FREE TIME

CHRIS
ROJEK

Los Angeles | London | New Delhi
Singapore | Washington DC

First published 2010

Apart from any fair dealing for the purposes of research or private study, or criticism or review, as permitted under the Copyright, Designs and Patents Act, 1988, this publication may be reproduced, stored or transmitted in any form, or by any means, only with the prior permission in writing of the publishers, or in the case of reprographic reproduction, in accordance with the terms of licences issued by the Copyright Licensing Agency. Enquiries concerning reproduction outside those terms should be sent to the publishers.

SAGE Publications Ltd
1 Oliver's Yard
55 City Road
London EC1Y 1SP

SAGE Publications Inc.
2455 Teller Road
Thousand Oaks, California 91320

SAGE Publications India Pvt Ltd
B 1/I 1 Mohan Cooperative Industrial Area
Mathura Road, Post Bag 7
New Delhi 110 044

SAGE Publications Asia-Pacific Pte Ltd
33 Pekin Street #02-01
Far East Square
Singapore 048763

Library of Congress Control Number 2009922163

British Library Cataloguing in Publication data

A catalogue record for this book is available from the British Library

ISBN 978-1-4129-4552-3
ISBN 978-1-4129-4553-0 (pbk)

Typeset by C&M Digitals (P) Ltd, Chennai, India
Printed by CPI Antony Rowe, Chippenham, Wiltshire
Printed on paper from sustainable resources

Mixed Sources
Product group from well-managed forests and other controlled sources
www.fsc.org Cert no. SGS-COC-2953
© 1996 Forest Stewardship Council
FSC

'The First Principle of Action is Leisure,' Aristotle, *Politics*

CONTENTS

List of Figures   viii

1   Positioning Leisure   1

2   The Leisure Society Thesis and Its Consequences   21

3   Roadblocks to Free Time   53

4   Visionaries and Pragmatists   84

5   What Is Wrong with Leisure Studies?   110

6   Multiple Equilibria: A Balanced Approach   118

7   The State   133

8   Corporations   160

9   It's Still Leisure, Stupid   179

Notes   190
References   194
Author Index   204
Subject Index   207

LIST OF FIGURES

1   20 Richest people in the world (2008)   15
2   UK time-use survey, people aged 16 and over   24
3   US time-use, people aged 15 and over (2005)   25
4   Distribution of religious faith in England and Wales   64
5   Distribution of religious faith in the USA (2001)   66
6   NRPA top 10 books on leisure and recreation   106

1
POSITIONING LEISURE

This is the sixth book that I have written on the subject of leisure. Its predecessors are *Capitalism and Leisure Theory* (1985), *Ways of Escape* (1993), *Decentring Leisure* (1995), *Leisure and Culture* (2000) and *Leisure Theory* (2005). The books were neither planned nor written as a sextet; nor would I wish them to be read as such. Each can be read as a stand-alone volume. To a lesser or greater degree all six are concerned to connect leisure forms and practice with cultural and social theory. My purpose is not only to apply social and cultural theory to illuminate leisure forms and practice. I am also concerned to delve into leisure forms and practice, especially the notions of freedom, choice and self-determination, in order to clarify certain features of social and cultural theory that I take, and have found among my students, to be opaque or oblique. In this latter regard, the study of leisure forms and practices is especially pertinent.

This is because it is in leisure that we are considered, and culturally represented, to exist in a state of voluntarism. By voluntarism is meant the realm of free choice and action determined by, and commensurate with, private conscience. One of the attractions of studying leisure is that it addresses people's free-time behaviour. Or to alter the payload of the term in a manner that is more apposite for the central arguments in this book, it explores what people plan and do when they *believe* themselves to be free. Those who wish to seriously study leisure must begin with a proviso from which they should never abstain in all that they do: the analysis of free time practice always poses the subsidiary questions, freedom from what? And freedom from whom?

In the ideology of Western, and especially American culture, freedom is judged to have reached an absolute pinnacle. It is what distinguishes life in the West from conditions in every comparative social system, present and past. Any attempt to submit that freedom is factually conditional seems, by comparison, to be mealy-mouthed and ungrateful. This is moot for students of leisure, because for over two centuries, leisure has become almost irretrievably fused with the concept of freedom. So much is this so that one may hardly dare speak of leisure in anything other than celebratory or triumphalist tones. To wit: leisure is the reward for work; it is the key component in what we now call the work-life balance; it is an asset for the community; it reduces crime; it broadens mutual understanding; it is the secret of a healthy mind and body; it is all of this and many other things that ordinary and most educated people automatically connect with the good life. It is even legitimate to speak of a sense of inherent privilege about those involved in the analysis of free time forms and practices. It is as if we who study leisure in the West occupy the mansion on the hill where the toil and trouble endured by previous generations of mankind has created an enriching space in which individual freedom, choice and life-satisfaction flourish as never before.

This is very understandable. As E.P. Thompson (1967) argued long ago, the rise of industrial society created the idea of leisure. It did so by sweeping away the complex, hidebound system of duties and rights supported by the *ancien regime*, and creating a new world of 'free labourers'. But there were tricky problems with this new world. As Thompson (1967) observes, it provided workers with mobility and leisure, but deprived them of traditional non-work rights and age-old systems of community support. It allowed people to spend their free time in whatever fashion they selected, so long as their non-work activities reinforce their competence as credible consumers and reliable workers. It encouraged workers to freely and fully develop their own capacities, subject to the caveat that these capacities tended to reinforce and extend competitive individualism and increase the profit margin.

This is a very strange idea of 'freedom' and comes with an even more peculiar idea of what 'leisure' means. In effect, 'free' choice and non-work activity is held to be inter-laced with principles of fitness to work and responsible citizenship. You can do whatever you like in your non-work time, providing that it affirms your competence as a trustworthy worker and a credible citizen. A whole complex network of controls was constructed to support this set of dispositions, this trajectory of so-called 'free choice'. It has burrowed so deeply into the Western cortex that it has colonized our world-view, supplying us with the whole vocabulary, *mentalité*, and set of discriminations which define leisure. It has made the concept of freedom so transparent and obvious that we only attend to it when our competence, relevance and credibility to act, and be accepted as free actors, is impaired.

Consider a fairly trivial example to substantiate the issues here: I am free to walk down the street with my shoe-laces undone. However, to do so will eventually prompt the disapproving attention of others. If I walk down the street with my shoe-laces undone every day, my neighbours will talk about me. Why do I go out like that? Why won't I listen to what people tell me? Is there something wrong with me? Should someone inform the authorities for my own protection and the safety of others?[1]

To repeat, this is a fairly trivial example. Nonetheless, it shows well enough that the meaning of freedom is conditional. What we call freedom depends upon being acknowledged as competent actors and credible citizens. But competence and credibility demand disciplined behaviour that is respected as proficient and judicious. Ordinarily, these qualities may be regarded as unexceptional and ubiquitous. In fact they are subject to quite precise pre-conditions. Competence requires *knowledge* of cultural and social mores; *monitoring* our feelings and actions to assess their impact upon others; and *discernment* to evaluate social situations accurately. Comprehension of the optimal management of the emotions, the facilitation of thought and the building blocks of credible 'people skills' is rooted in *emotional intelligence* (Goleman 1995). The regulation and presentation of competence involves *emotional labour* (Hochschild 1983). Building credibility and displaying competence in everyday life is learned behaviour and requires significant and continuous energy and effort. If this is true, what price leisure in a world in which emotional intelligence and emotional labour are ubiquitous?

Speaking to Others About Who We Are

Emotional intelligence and emotional labour are, I think, core concepts for the analysis of leisure forms and practice. This is because the display of credibility, relevance and competence in our 'voluntarily' chosen 'free' time activities *speaks* to others about who we are, what we hold to be valuable and how we can make a difference. This encompasses issues of what food and drink we should consume, how we should dispose of our waste products in the home, the right clothes to wear in given social settings, the amount of time that we ought to devote to exercise every day, the correct way of addressing people from different ethnic and racial groups, how we should relate to heritage and nature, our familiarity with sport, film, art and literature, our stance on sexual inequality and racial oppression and many other topics that are covered in the *work–life balance*. The field of leisure is the focal point in everyday life where these matters are addressed, exchanged and refined. Over and above the institutionalized and tightly organized regulations of the work-place, leisure is where we get the *people knowledge* and coaching skills that enable us to be recognized as competent, credible and relevant actors in the plethora of social, cultural and economic situations that we encounter. The field therefore comes with a variety of tacitly stated standards of discernment and *coaching* responsibilities. Modern men and women, who see themselves, and wish to be acknowledged as competent, relevant and credible citizens, take it for granted that the field of leisure is about accumulating emotional intelligence and using emotional labour to teach themselves and to coach others into more practically successful, ethically relevant ways of living. It is where we assimilate and develop the big picture about what is *au courant*, socially respected and cool. These are central resources in enhancing our competence, relevance and credibility among our peer group and wider social encounters.

At this juncture in the discussion I will use the terms emotional intelligence and emotional labour in fairly unqualified ways. My purpose here is to propose for the sake of argument that the unrelenting nature of these undertakings presents serious challenges to orthodox concepts of leisure. I will come to them presently. Before doing so, it is necessary to comment upon another dimension of the topic.

The emerging trends in the world in which we in the West are located accentuates the significance of emotional intelligence and emotional labour. To be regarded by others as competent, relevant and credible is the pre-requisite for, among many other things, achieving success in limiting the interests of the police and the law in what we say and do; developing and maintaining strategically profitable friendship networks; being greeted in other countries as a welcome guest; and finding and keeping a mate. These issues also possess a powerful and increasing *economic* significance. The commercial value of surface acting and spray-on sincerity has been extensively documented in the sociology of service work (Hochschschild 1983; Bryson et al. 2004). Over the last forty years one of the signal trends in the economically advanced industrial countries of the West is for the manufacturing sector to shrink and the service sector to expand. In the UK, the service sector now produces over 70% of Gross National Product (Office of National Statistics 2000). In 1961, four out of ten workers based in the industrially advanced countries were employed in the service sector; in 1971 the figure increased to five out of ten; and currently the figure is seven out of ten. By 2005, in the UK more than seven times as many people (22 million) were employed in the service sector than the manufacturing centre (3 million) (Blyton and Jenkins 2007: 69–70).

At the heart of this switch from extractive, factory and office employment to work in the knowledge-information and communication sector is the economic importance of *people knowledge* and *people skills*. Being comfortable in your own skin, knowing how to handle people, sensing when to break the ice, demonstrating sincerity and smiling relations, have considerable economic value in the labour market. The core resources involved in this are emotional intelligence and emotional labour. People knowledge and people skills are pivotal in having a good life with your neighbours, enjoying high status and gaining a good job.

Yet if all this is allowed, it casts a troubling shadow over the orthodox meaning of leisure. Traditionally, leisure is twinned with voluntarism.

Freedom, choice and self-determination are regularly presented as primary characteristics of leisure (Parker 1981; Csikszentmihalyi 1990; Neulinger 1981a, 1981b). But what does it mean to have 'time off' or 'freedom' if the pre-conditions of emotional competence and credibility as an actor are holding relevant resources of emotional intelligence and being adept in practising emotional labour? Since emotional life is an unrelenting feature of being human, it seems reasonable to propose that the accumulation of emotional intelligence and the practice and refine-ment of emotional labour can occur at any time and in any place (Katz 1999). If this is so, the question is, where do freedom or time off reside? Everything we do and every place that we inhabit has emotional learn-ing potential. Monitoring, discernment, internalizing and coaching, all require unpaid emotional labour. If we are engaging in labour, even if it is unpaid and pleasurable, we are doing something contrary to leisure as it is conventionally understood.

Given the colonization of all aspects of life by emotional intelligence and emotional labour, I see little point in trying to rescue orthodox asso-ciations between leisure and freedom, choice and self-determination. Indeed, it would be no bad thing to discard the notions of freedom and voluntarism from the field of Leisure Studies/Science on the grounds that they get the whole business of thinking about leisure off on the wrong foot.

Philosophically speaking, voluntarism means a realm of behaviour in which a field of zero or, at any rate, minimal constraints over subjective choice apply. However, this is nothing but a deluded state of mind since it is evident that every real life is played out in conditions of emotional labour, economic inequality, cultural difference and social context that condition choice, experience, our sense of imaginative possibility and much else besides. So when we say that we are 'free' or develop in a 'full' sense in our leisure, we are referring to something other than volun-tarism. However, such is the force of the neo-liberal insistence upon personal freedom and choice as the hallmarks of Western democracy, that it is all too easy to slide into the taken-for-granted assumption that they are universally *realized* conditions of everyday life.

For students of leisure, therein lies the rub. You might have free time at your disposal at the end of the working day. But you are not at liberty to dispose of it just as you please. Leaving aside the questions of moni-toring, reconnaissance, discernment, internalizing and coaching that relate to competence in emotional intelligence and credibility in emo-tional labour, there are the matters of inequality and scarcity to consider. At a basic level, time disposal relies upon income. Your capacity to dis-pose of non-work time is economically conditioned and culturally coded. It reflects distinctions of class, gender, ethnicity, education and bodily health. Of course, you are free to make choices. But the choices you make are contextualized by how you are situated in relation to scarcity. By scarcity is meant, the unequal distribution of economic, cultural, social and political resources and your position in relation to them.

It follows that if it is right to maintain that leisure forms and practices are economically conditioned and culturally coded, and also, that emotional intelligence and emotional labour have colonized life, how can leisure practice be reconciled with the concept of freedom? This is a recurrent problem in every critical approach to the study of leisure. In a nutshell, how can we be said to be free and not free at one and the same time?

Intentionality

I hold that the most satisfactory way of dealing with this apparent conundrum is to focus upon the topic of intentionality. To wit: adult, human subjects depend upon competence in emotional intelligence and credibility in emotional labour to successfully present themselves as relevant actors and they are situated variously in relation to scarcity; but they are also usually intentional actors, who have the capacity to be cognizant about the consequences of their actions. If it is my intention to spend Friday night at the pub drinking with my friends, this is a self-selected leisure choice. To elaborate: it may be the case that the aetiology of my choice is a combination of my class background, gender, age and occupation. Perhaps one might submit that these mechanisms *position* me to be more likely to want to spend Friday night in the pub. However, the decisive issue is the choice that I make to spend my time on Friday night thus, rather than attending, for example, a night-school course on the architecture of Frank Geary, or watering my house-plants. I might have a number of reasons to make this choice. It might be that I want to bring the week to satisfactory closure in the company of congenial colleagues by signing off with work colleagues in a leisurely social setting, or I might want to let off steam after the rigours of the week. What is crucial is that what I do is the result of *my* choice, and that I acknowledge it as such, rather than, for example, rationalizing it as a by-product of my background over which I have no influence. Since this is a choice that ultimately I make, with respect to the disposal of my non-work time, it must be right to describe the concrete process of choice as the intentional exercise of a leisure option.

Several provisos need to be entered here. It is one thing to propose that choosing to spend Friday night in the pub is *my* choice. But what if I act on the basis of subconscious or unconscious considerations? Such as, being in the pub on Friday night is what I have internalized as a desirable outcome, from the manufacturers of the liquor that I favour having presented this in their advertising campaigns as the appropriate time-use of a male consumer of my age, race, occupation and background. Or, being in the pub could be a way of *avoiding* family responsibilities that I find to be arduous and burdensome? Or, because my mother or father are unremitting teetotallers, who avidly disapprove of pub culture, perhaps I may have reacted against my childhood experience by favouring alcoholic sustenance in leisure as a way of demonstrating my independence from the parental rod?

An important methodological principle in Leisure Studies follows. It is that *the locus of leisure forms and practices is subjective intentionality.* By insisting on this, we have a defence against those who wish to submit that leisure is determined by our relationships to class inequality, racial difference or gender division. Leisure forms and practices are coded, and our potential to engage in them is influenced by many triggers that can be ultimately traced back to structural divisions. However, to insist upon the ultimate relevance of subjective intentionality, we nail our colours to the mast of the proposition that what individuals intentionally decide to do in non-work time is fundamental. We may be positioned in relation to unequal resources. Aspects of our behaviour may be constructed by this or that influence. But if we do not live on the principle that we have a mind of our own, in what sense can we be said to 'live' at all?

The focus on intentionality shows something of the complexity involved in something as apparently simple as deciding how to spend my leisure on a Friday night. But it is not enough. There are related issues of emotional intelligence having to do with the consequences of my actions that must be brought into play. Consider: my choice of going to the pub on Friday night may involve a calculation of the relation between drinking and health. Harmful drinking is a weekly intake of alcohol that leads to significant physical and mental impairment that harms the self and may cause substantial harm to others. In the UK, the standard of harmful drinking is 50+ units per week for men and 35+ units for women. Hazardous drinking means regular drinking above recognized levels at which alcohol is likely to damage health. For men this level is 22–50 units per week and for women it is 15–35 units. Ordinarily, awareness of the risks to my health and the wellbeing of others may limit the amount I drink on Friday nights. If this is the case, this awareness should be regarded as a constraint on my behaviour. If I recognize constraints to my behaviour in choosing to spend Friday night in the pub, in what sense can I be said to make choices freely? Rather, my freedom of choice is made in relation to the knowledge that I possess apropos of issues of how the pursuit of my pleasure bears upon others. This knowledge is conditioned by cultural and social factors. My exposure to it is a result of the position I occupy with regard to the distribution of knowledge. Knowledge is a scarce resource. Access to it differs according to various factors such as gender, education, age, income, race and occupation. So my decision about how to spend Friday nights and the length of time I should spend in the pub is directly related to social and economic factors which I may be aware of, but which I cannot control.

These factors *position* me and directly influence the intentions that I formulate and my trajectory of leisure behaviour.

Nor is this all. If I spend *every* Friday in the pub, it might be said to be evidence of compulsive behaviour. Friends might say that I choose to spend time in this way because I have an addictive personality. In that case, going to the pub on Friday is not a question of my freely seeking pleasure. Rather, it comes closer to what may be termed obsessive behaviour. If this is the case, my leisure choice turns out not to be about the exercise of freedom. Rather, it is about acting repetitively, without control over my trajectory of behaviour. As such, it may fall to my friends to ask me to reflect upon my choice of behaviour or seek help from a qualified person.

Classical liberal thought analyses leisure practice as the outcome and responsibility of the intentional choice of actors. Put simply, if I choose to smoke in my leisure time despite being aware of the medical risks that derive from so doing, it is my affair. Over the last fifty years the limitations in this position have been exposed. However, as a result of medical education and state/media proselytizing we have gradually become aware that many of the activities that we participate in for pleasure carry health risks for ourselves and others. In many areas, leisure forms have been colonized by a psychology of risk culture that focuses on the self-harm or harm to others that follow some form of voluntary behaviour.

Many of the leisure practices that were developed in the nineteenth and twentieth centuries as good for you or harmless are today castigated or demonized (Hughes 2003). The leisure industries associated with them have been forced to readjust. Tobacco, alcohol and food companies have introduced the concept of 'responsible practice' with respect to tobacco use, alcohol consumption and dietary intake. Responsibility is not simply defined as a matter for the individual self, it is also a question of the consequences of one's behaviour for others. Thus, secondary smoking threatens non-smokers with cancer; excessive consumption of alcohol increases the risk of causing an accident which might involve innocent parties; and obesity is not only a threat to individual mortality, it confronts the tax-payer with higher bills of medical provision. We have moved from an extreme liberal position in which it is an individual's right to do what they damn well please in their leisure and recreation, into something more circumspect.

You might argue that it was ever thus in Christian societies. For did not Jesus preach that you should 'love thy neighbour as you love yourself'? However, in practice, until quite recently, observance of this doctrine was discretionary. Only with the arrival of the modern welfare state in the early twentieth century, might it be said that elements of this doctrine were formalized and incorporated into the suite of civil rights and obligations. Even here, as principles of popular governance and resource distribution, they were quite limited. Namely, they were chiefly concentrated in relation to workplace practice, education entitlements, behaviour in public space, and care for children, the disabled and the elderly. What has happened in the last twenty-five years is that Western states have become more sensitive to the question of how leisure forms and practice imperil the wellbeing of Others.

A subtle shift in the meaning of intentionality in leisure forms and practice has occurred. It is no longer a question of considering the validity of leisure practice from the liberal perspective of the intentions of the self or his/her dependents and friendship networks. The issue has moved on to encompass this dimension and also address the consequences of intentional action in leisure forms and practice for others. Hence, legislation banning smoking in public places throughout North America and much of the EU was prompted by health fears surrounding the effects of secondary smoking. The campaign against dangerous alcohol consumption exploited and amplified public fears about alcohol-related teenage homicide and traffic deaths. Similarly, the recent gun massacres at Virginia Tech (2007), Tuusula High School (2007), Omaha Mall (2007) and the University of Northern Illinois (2008) elicited pleas to tighten laws on the sale of hand-arms, rifles and ammunition for hunters and sportsmen. Arguably, currently the biggest numerical front of resistance in leisure practice is against the environmental pollution and threat to climate change posed by the carbon footprint left by air travellers, Sports Utility Vehicles and other auto polluters. The attempt of states to manage this risk by imposing environmental taxes on air travel or car engines that contribute dangerous levels of pollution is a *cause célèbre* for those who insist upon the centrality of freedom of choice in leisure practice. But it is clear that the tide has remorselessly turned against them.

The two genies that have driven our understanding of the responsibilities of intentional conduct are emotional intelligence and emotional labour. It is the knowledge that some types of practice are harmful for us and others that has precipitated changes in social standards, qualities of discernment and legal imperatives. Telling others that we are comfortable with these changes and support them requires emotional labour. It is not enough to know that some types of practice are wrong for us and others. We must also sound a series of bells and whistles that signal social ease, sincerity and openness. We have all been touched by deep social forces that accentuate the importance of surface acting and spray-on sincerity in the labour market and the conduct of personal life. However, in this respect we are far from being equal.

Situated Action and Leisure

Given the current ascent of neo-liberalism, which holds that we are all ultimately *masters of our own destiny*, potential commanders of a 'can do' approach that will fix every misfortune, it behoves us to remind ourselves of an old, unfashionable countervailing proposition: namely, we must think of ourselves in leisure and recreation activity as *positioned* actors. To clarify, each of us is made by history and each has unequal access to scarce resources. History and scarcity condition our ability to act upon the world. The relation that we have to scarcity is heavily conditioned by the wealth of our families of origin. Our freedoms and the rationales that we invoke to justify them, are *positioned*.

It is natural to think of equality and inequality in terms of the family, since this is the immediate emotional context in which we are nurtured into, what some neo-liberals call, autonomous personhood. However, just as personhood can only be satisfactorily explained in relation to the family, an adequate account of the family must locate it in the context of the allocative mechanisms that regulate scarcity. Every society develops allocative mechanisms to handle the distribution of scarce resources. In Leisure Studies allocative mechanisms have been investigated in a number of ways. There have been interesting studies of how class distributes economic resources unequally, how scripts of behaviour in leisure are conditioned by class positioning and how the state interacts with class inequality to manage legitimation (Clarke and Critcher 1985; Blackshaw 2003). They have been joined by studies on gender and leisure which reveal the economic inequalities between men and women, the construction of personal identity in leisure practice through gender difference and the uses of gender representation to legitimate scarcity (Wearing 1998; Henderson et al. 1996; Aitchison 2003). There are fewer studies of leisure that reveal the work of the hands of colour and race in managing scarcity. However, studies in the sociology of sport have provided many pointers for students of Leisure Studies to follow. They have clarified how the allocative mechanism of race bestows advantages in respect of success in the labour market and political influence.

Allocative mechanisms are social devices to distribute scarce resources and legitimate the system. Legitimation is crucial. For the problem of scarcity raises questions of justice with respect to who gets what. Think of it in terms of a game model. In one team, one player commands more resources than the other players. This may reflect his/her superior skills, the authority he/she conveys, or mere precedent.

The distribution of power in society works on similar principles. One class has superior access to scarce resources in comparison with others . This superiority is justified by a variety of instruments. It might be that one class claims more resources because it claims to monopolize leadership skills over others. Or it might be that one class rules because it presents the case that it has always ruled and to break tradition would hazard the good of all.

The brute fact of inequality, and the consequences for emotional intelligence, emotional labour, personal confidence and social mobility that follow from it, is obscured by the neo-liberal emphasis upon individual freedom and personal responsibility for our actions. A neo-liberal might react to the proposition that inequality is universal by submitting that each of us has to deal with it in our own way. If fate has dealt us a bad hand it is up to us to use our brainpower and emotional intelligence to overcome adversity. However, there are problems with this sanguine view of things.

Personal drive and good fortune can go a long way in combating a difficult start in life. But the real issue is changing the playing field in which life chances are so heavily influenced by unequal access to scarce resources. It is not just a question of having this or that much money. It is a question of *habitus*. This raises difficult policy questions about the distribution of wealth and the role of restraint on personal freedom.

> Habitus is a term used in the sociology of Pierre Bourdieu. It means the collective frame of mind and patterns of behaviour into which one is born and which one embodies as a condition of family and community.

Leisure, Health and Mortality

An inkling of what is involved here may be provided by considering the issue of leisure, health and mortality. Few would disagree that almost nothing influences personal choice in leisure more than health and longevity.

Increasing longevity is sadly not a global universal fact. The *World Health Organization Atlas* of life expectancy for 2005 showed that the life expectancy in Australia, Canada, Spain, France and Italy was over 80; in the USA, North Western Europe and Japan, 75–80; Mexico, North West Latin America, North Africa, the Middle East, Central Europe and Argentina, 70–75; Brazil, and most of the former USSR, 65–70; India, Pakistan, 60–65; Central, West and Eastern Africa, 55–60 (www. worldpolicy.org 2005). The figures at the lower end of life expectancy are very different. The *CIA World Fact Book* reports estimated life expectancy for 2006 of 32.62 in Swaziland; 33.74 in Botswana; 38.62 in Angola; 42.73 in South Africa; 43.34 in Afghanistan; and below 50 in most of West, East and Central Africa.

Health, mortality and leisure participation are directly influenced by the position of individuals and groups in relation to economic scarcity. The differences between social classes in this respect are profound.

In the USA, the richest 1 per cent of households own 38 per cent of all wealth. The top 5 per cent own over 50 per cent of all wealth. The top 20 per cent own over 80 per cent of all wealth. From the late 1920s to the mid 70s there was a more or less continuous downward trend. Since the mid 70s the trend has reversed. The level of wealth inequality in 2003 was almost double what it was in the mid 70s (*Multinational Monitor* and Edward Wolff 2003).

In countries with a more 'Welfarist' approach to resource distribution, such as Australia and the UK, wealth inequalities are still striking. In 2004, the top 10 per cent of Australians owned nearly 50 per cent of national wealth. The bottom 10 per cent have nothing but debt (Headey et al. 2004). In the UK, 2004 official statistics show that the top 1 per cent owned 23 per cent of national wealth, an increase of 3 per cent since 1997 when the first New Labour government was elected. The top 10 per cent own more than 50 per cent of national wealth, and the wealthiest 50 per cent own 94 per cent of national wealth. Over the same period the wealth of the poorest 50 per cent of the population contracted from 10 per cent in 1986 to 5 per cent in 2002. As with the US figures, the data suggests that the trend of decreasing wealth inequality is being reversed. In 1911 it is estimated that the share of the top 1 per cent of the population was 70 per cent of national wealth. By 1936–8 it had fallen to 56 per cent; by 1960 is stood at 42 per cent; and in 1991 it had more than halved to 17 per cent. However, since the mid 1990s the richest 1 per cent have gained a further 6 per cent of national wealth, despite New Labour's commitment to distributive justice (www.statistics.gov.uk). The UK government defines poverty as an income that is 60 per cent of the median. On this basis, it is estimated that 21 per cent of children and pensioners and 14 per cent of all adults live below the poverty line. At the other end of the wealth ladder, it is estimated that the average annual income of a UK Chief Executive in the Finance, Business and Industry sectors of the economy was £600,000 (www.esrc.ac.uk).

Divisions of economic inequality extend much further than the question of what you can and cannot buy. Wealth brings access to social prestige and is positively associated with personal confidence, stability and security. Leaving aside the significant question of physical risk, which has partly been dealt with above, the absence of wealth is connected with higher levels of anxiety, stress and low personal esteem. Although Welfarist regimes have gone some way to correcting these divisions through policies of redistributive justice, Western societies still condone huge levels of economic inequality and major divisions in access and mobility. If we bear in mind the separate question of the wealth gap between the economically advanced and developing nations, it is clear that the subject of inequality is absolutely pivotal to understanding leisure forms and practice.

   The implications for leisure and quality of life are profound. Within the economically advanced core countries, the over-60 population is growing rapidly as a proportion of the total population. There is already a significant greying of the leisure/sport market. More people are likely to be in work for longer periods in order to build up pension funds. Similarly, the onset of ill-health and physical decline is being postponed by a combination of medicine, public health policies and the adoption of responsible diet and exercise. People are enjoying longer spans of freedom from chronic illness and greater access to paid employment. As a result, their participation in outdoor and cash-intensive leisure forms and practice is extended. If the retirement age is abolished and current health patterns are maintained, the over-65 group will have more surplus income in old age because their mortgage burden is likely to be repaid. One effect of this will be to obstruct employment and home ownership opportunities for younger people.

   Coming now to the global dimension, the majority population in the economically weak emerging and developing nations has much lower life expectancies and much higher exposure to risk from famine and chronic illness. Western leisure multinationals have out-sourced a good deal of their manufacturing to low cost, under-unionized labour markets in the Southern hemisphere and Balkans (Klein 2001). These markets also supply the wealthy metropolitan centres of the West with illegal supplies of drugs, pirated DVDs and CDs, contraband cigarettes and sex workers. Their cities, ways of life and unspoiled reserves of nature provide Western tourists with exotic travel destinations. Although the economic redistribution of wealth between the economically advanced and developing world is not insignificant, it is typically concentrated in the hands of the ruling class and illegal gangs and crime cartels (Glenny 2008). The leisure-rich in the economically advanced countries, and the ruling classes and illegal criminal groups in the metropolitan centres of the developing world that support them, have broken away from the leisure-poor. They have perpetual access to free time entitlement, leisure commodities, participation in sport and travel experience that simply have no equivalent in most of the economically emerging and developing world. The majority of the world's population is effectively a leisure under-class.

The Leisure of Billionaires

Unequal access to resources has a direct influence on leisure practice in terms of capital and expenditure. Indirectly, it influences choice through factors such as education, health and household space. It requires us to think very critically about what is meant by the concepts of individual and group freedom in leisure. Western democracies have cultivated strong models of citizenship organized around freedom, entitlement and responsibility. But the acceptance of high levels of economic and social inequality means that the positioning of individuals and groups in relation to the perception and experience of freedom, responsibility and entitlement is subject to wide variation and contradiction. A recipient of significant inherited wealth or someone who creates a fortune, is likely develop a broader latitude with respect to the law, notions of civic duty and personal responsibility.

In 2008, *Forbes* business magazine listed 49 billionaires resident in the UK, the richest of whom is the steel magnate, Lakshmi Mittal ($ 45bn). By contrast, in October 2008 the minimum wage for adults was raised to £5.73 an hour (www.esrc.ac.uk). Two thirds of minimum wage earners in the UK are women. Key characteristics of leisure have been defined as choice, flexibility, spontaneity and self-determination (Parker 1981). However, the discrepancy in wealth between Mittal and a worker on a minimum hourly wage is so colossal that to compare the two in relation to these characteristics is an affront to common sense. Mittal lives in a different world to most of the rest of us. He enjoys vastly wider lifestyle options, travel opportunities and access to social networks that carry high levels of social prestige.

In 2004 he bought a neo-Palladian mansion in Kensington Palace Gardens, London for £57 million. The property includes a ballroom, an underground car park and a floodlit swimming pool inlaid with jewels. In the same year he spent £30 million on six days of celebration for his daughter, Vanisha's wedding to the London-based investment banker, Amit Bhatia. Mittal's resources for mobility, security and cultural networks mean that his on-location experience of leisure operates in a qualitatively remote context from that of low-income or median wealth experience.

If one looks at the *Forbes* (2008) rich list the gulf between rich and poor, and the inequality of resources for leisure and recreation, is truly staggering. The number of billionaires in the world in 2008 was reported as 1,125, compared with 946 in 2007. By comparison with the *Forbes* rich list, the Annual Survey of Hours and Earnings (ASHE 2007) reported that the median pay for full-time workers in the UK in 2006 was £23,764 (£457 per week). The median for full-time male workers was £25,896 (£498 per week); for full-time female workers the median was £20,488 (£394 per week). Turning to the USA, statistics from Social Security Online report that the median annual wage in 2006 was $38,651 ($743 per week). At the time of writing the exchange rate is $1.89 to £1, so in sterling the median US annual income is £20,450 (£393 per week). In Australia, the Bureau of Statistics reported that the median annual wage is A$53,200 (A$1,023 per week). For males the median average income is A$55,800 (A$ 1,115 per week); and for women it is A$47,600 (A$915

			$(bn)
1	Warren Buffett	Investments	62.0
2	Carlos Slim Helu	Telecoms	60.0
3	Bill Gates	Software	58.0
4	Lakshmi Mittal	Steel	45.0
5	Mukesh Ambani	Petrochemicals	43.0
6	Anil Ambani	Diverse sources	42.0
7	Ingvar Kamprad	IKEA stores	31.0
8	KP Singh	Property	30.0
9	Oleg Deripaska	Aluminium	28.0
10	Karl Albrecht	Aldi Stores	27.0
11	Li Ka-Shing	Diverse sources	26.5
12	Sheldon Adelson	Casinos/hotels	26.0
13	Bernard Arnault	Luxury goods	25.5
14	Lawrence Ellison	Software	25.0
15	Roman Ambramovich	Oil	23.5
16	Theo Albrecht	Aldi stores	23.0
17	Liliane Bettencourt	L'Oreal	22.9
18	Alex Mordashov	Manufacturing	21.2
19	Alaweed bin Talal	Investments	21.0
20	Mikhail Fridman	Oil/banking	20.8

Figure 1   20 Richest people in the world (2008)

Source: *Forbes* Business Magazine

per week). Currently the exchange rate is A$2.25 to the pound, which means that the median wage in Australia expressed in sterling is £24,181. For men, the sterling annual wage is £25,363; and for women it is £21,636.

For the ultra-rich, the present tax system relies on charitable donations as the primary mechanism of redistribution. In 2006 Warren Buffett pledged $31 billion to the *Gates Foundation* to help address global healthcare issues. Similarly, in 2004 Lakshmi Mittal set up the Mittal Champion's Trust with a donation of $9 million to support 10 Indian athletes with world-beating potential; and in 2007 he matched the money raised on the BBC Comic Relief edition of the programme *The Apprentice* (£1 million).

These high profile donations are generous and welcome acts of philanthropy. But they hardly amount to a co-ordinated programme of global redistributive justice. There is a strong moral case for allowing the rich to dispose of their money as they see fit. But it is counterposed by the plight of the poor, and especially the world's hungry. In addition, the presence of a billionaire class in society who subsist with a broader sense of latitude in respect of questions of law, civic duty and personal responsibility is subject to the same objection made by Veblen (1899) in relation to the conspicuous consumption of the leisure class. Namely, it is socially corrosive to condone excessive latitude with respect to leisure conduct, since it will be subject to the laws of imitation. The trickle-down effect of a loose attitude to rules of leisure conduct will eventually weaken the fabric of society. What is to be done?

One solution favoured by the traditional Left is to impose punitive levels of taxation upon the wealthy, to generate resources for the state to redress the inequality gap. This is subject to many objections. To begin with, it is a disincentive to labour or investment, since the fruits of labour and investment that traditionally accrue to the individual are partly expropriated by the state. Similarly, positing a state response to inequality and a climate of latitude in leisure culture, absolves individuals and groups from taking responsibility over their own lives and forms of practice. Developing emotional intelligence and the emotional labour to function as a competent, relevant and credible actor is the prerequisite of citizenship. By invoking the state to act as a regulator in this sector, a diminished view of citizenship is enjoined, which in turn will deplete the stock of social capital and social energy in society.

In any case, a separate set of questions is raised if one moves away from the subject of economic and social inequality to that of the place of distinction among individuals and between groups (Bourdieu 1984).

It will quickly be seen that competition for distinction and prestige does not end with the birth of egalitarianism. It is worth going into this issue for a moment, since many approaches in Leisure Studies appear to argue the contrary case; that is, that egalitarianism will engender solidarity and combat injustice (Andrew 1981; Clarke and Critcher 1995).

Positional Goods and Leisure

The neo-liberal argument about managing scarcity is based on the proposition that too much government is bad for society. Individuals should be free to invest and engage in leisure practice providing it does not interfere with the liberty of others. The egalitarian argument is in favour of interventionist government to establish a level playing field to enable individual competition and enterprise to flourish. Private investment, labour and leisure must be subject to the greater authority of the common good. Upon this argument egalitarians claim a rational basis for fiscal intervention and central restraint of practice in respect of private investment, labour and leisure.

You can stand on this side or that side of the divide and find plenty of evidence to confirm either case. What seems incontrovertible is that no matter what system of managing scarcity is adopted individuals and groups will search for distinction and use leisure choice to signify honour, privilege and rank. In other words, there is a perpetual market for what the economist Fred Hirsch (1976) refers to as 'positional goods'.

These are goods that someone can enjoy only by depriving someone else of them. Their value is a function of scarcity. Because there are not enough of these goods to go around they command high status and economic value. If I have the best room in the Savoy Hotel and send my children to the best fee-paying schools, I am depriving someone else of access to the best hospitality experience and someone else's children of the benefit of the highest achieving educational environment. However egalitarian a society becomes there will always be a ranking of positional goods that conveys high prestige to those who are able to enjoy them.

Hirsch (1976) argues that the positional goods economy creates a permanent condition of relative deprivation. This law is true even in conditions of increasing affluence where more and more people become better off. As wealth in society rises, and my room in the Savoy Hotel falls within the income bracket of individuals and groups with lower social status, my propensity to book a more expensive room at the Hotel Pierre in New York will increase. Thus, the productive resources in society are progressively squandered in achieving ends of status that accumulate no general economic value.

Consider the issue in terms of the A&B analysis perspective[2] : If the incomes of A and B grow, but A's grows twice as fast as B's, the capacity of A to accumulate positional goods increases. If A consumes a greater proportion of positional goods his social status is magnified. If B witnesses the gap in positional goods consumption with A growing, his propensity to spend more of his disposable income in catching up will increase. Frank (2003) argues that the race to consume positional goods is to the detriment of collective wellbeing. One reason is that the race of the lower orders to match the consumption of the top quintile multiplies waste in society. If A spends his disposable income on the most powerful Sports Utility Vehicle (SUV), he creates the incentive for B to desire the same purchase so as to keep up with the Joneses's. If B's propensity to consume an SUV depends upon borrowing more he increases his level of indebtedness. If enough Bs emulate this pattern of behaviour, the indebtedness of the entire economy grows with corresponding risks to economic stability and growth. The argument updates Veblen's (1899) classic case against conspicuous consumption. Namely, that as societies become more wealthy the most well-off have a tendency to spend more on goods that have no economic productive worth, but high cultural cachet. The reason for this is that the consumption of waste automatically conveys to others liberty from the necessity to work. In societies where the work ethic is paramount, liberation from this necessity is coveted. Hirsch (1976) and Frank (2003) concur with Veblen's (1899) conclusion that conspicuous consumption imperils economic stability by allocating a dangerous volume of productive resources to ends that have no economic benefit for society in general.

Relative deprivation is a term coined by Stouffer et al. (1949) in their study, *The American Soldier*. It means the perception by an individual or group of being adversely positioned with respect to scarcity than comparable individuals and groups. The concept was developed in the context of the affluent society by Runciman (1966) to explain why some individuals and groups continue to feel disadvantaged despite experiencing rising levels of prosperity.

The burden of the argument is that relative deprivation, like the poor, will always be with us. Undoubtedly, we must be realistic about what social engineering and the spread of affluence can achieve. This is not to be inferred as a covert anti-egalitarian argument. Neo-liberalism is very reassuring for anyone who believes in the doctrine of free enterprise as the key to wealth creation. But it is also a confidence trick. To begin with, it turns a blind eye to the negative social and economic consequences of wealth creation that have to do with conspicuous consumption and re-gearing the engine of positional goods. The affluent society may make some people better off and generally increase the resources devoted to leisure, but it does not necessarily produce contentment. The law of relative deprivation means that the 'have's' will always position themselves economically in a manner that guarantees distinction from the 'have not's'. This law holds good irrespective of the level of economic growth achieved and the dedication of egalitarian policy.

This preferential positioning in relation to scarcity is not the reward for enterprise and industry, it is the expression of power. Warren Buffett and Lakshmi Mittal are not billions of times better than the workers on minimum wage. Their wealth is disproportionate to their talents and achievements and is only sustained by a system of unequal resource distribution that identifies scarcity as the spur to personal motivation. It is *power* that governs the allocation of resources and therefore the condition of scarcity. One could have a system in which personal want or protection of the environment was the key criterion of resource distribution. That this has not happened on a society-wide basis is testament to the might of the wealthy whose privileged position enables them to defend and enhance their privileged status in relation to scarcity.

The Dialectics of Positioning

Outwardly, the study of leisure is the study of how individuals exercise voluntarism; that is, the study of how individuals and groups make choices, exercise freedom and succeed or fail to achieve life satisfaction in leisure. But voluntarism is neither absolute nor unique. To subsist as a competent, relevant and credible actor, individuals and groups must accumulate, monitor and refine considerable emotional intelligence and expend significant emotional labour. This compromises orthodox notions of freedom, choice and self-determination that have been traditionally attributed to leisure forms and practice.

By this I mean: a) there are real differences between individuals and groups in respect of the choice, freedom and life satisfaction that might be exercised in leisure practice; and b) choice, freedom and life satisfaction must be considered as qualities of citizenship that are enmeshed with complex codes and representations that render them as attractive and desired characteristics in the conduct of life. Leisure is not just a matter of form and practice. It is a question of how form and practice is *represented* in relation to power. Individuals, groups and the leisure choices they make are located in a context of power. The defining feature of this context is unequal divisions between individuals and groups in relation to scarcity. This is somewhat disguised in everyday life, because leisure cultures typically focus upon *surplus*; that is, leisure forms and practice are organized around surplus time, surplus wealth and conspicuous consumption. However, surplus is a relative concept. No matter how abundant their access to surplus time and wealth, every individual and group is located in a context of scarcity.

The study of leisure addresses the dialectics between scarcity and surplus. By the term dialectics is meant the changing balance of power relationship between access to scarcity and the distribution of surplus. This requires the student of leisure to examine: how emotional intelligence and emotional labour are applied in leisure settings; the relationship between material and symbolic inequality and trajectories of leisure behaviour; and the role of institutional allocative mechanisms, principally the state, the corporation, religion and the media, in distributing resources and legitimating or 'normalizing' the historically and socially specific distribution of power. Further, since social, cultural and economic processes have now been fully revealed to be global and to work outside the law as well as within it, students of leisure need to operate with a conceptual canvas that incorporates globalization and illicit leisure, not as side issues, but as matters of central concern.

The next chapter is offered as a contribution to understanding the limitations of the old paradigm in leisure studies and making explicit the canvas that must be addressed if leisure and recreation are to be studied in relevant ways today. Before moving on to this, the high water mark of the old paradigm needs to be addressed: namely, the leisure society thesis. This thesis was the magic carpet that made the study of leisure so appealing to students in the late 1960s and 70s. It perpetrated a vision of leisure forms and practice that stressed social harmony, exaggerated the progressive effects of technological determinism, misconstrued the role of the corporation in forcing leisure behaviour to adopt the form of mere consumption activity, ignored the effects of globalization (particularly with respect to the development gap), neglected the question of illicit leisure and blandly reproduced the traditional connections between leisure, freedom and choice. From the perspective of an approach which understands the significance of emotional intelligence, emotional labour and material scarcity as the context in which leisure forms and practice are situated, the consequences of the leisure society thesis have been severe and on the whole negative. The leisure society thesis put the study of leisure on the map, but it committed it to studying a landscape that was ideal rather than real, wished-for rather than evidence-based.

2
THE LEISURE SOCIETY
THESIS AND ITS
CONSEQUENCES

Between the mid 1960s and mid 1970s, the leisure society thesis was a boon in the important matter of forcing people to take leisure seriously. After the restructuring of the global economy following the OPEC oil crisis of 1973, it became a blight. Globalization and the deregulation, delayering and out-sourcing of labour markets in the West obliged renewed thinking on leisure and work.[1] The 1970s witnessed the massive casualization of labour in the West (Schor 1992). Part-time and fixed-term labour contracts became commonplace, with the result that traditional rights to occupational welfare and holiday entitlements were reformulated. In addition, globalization transferred large chunks of manufacturing industry to the emerging world. Nowadays the leisure industry out-sources much of its business to suppliers where Western industrial relations legislation has weak torque or simply no purchase.

Globalization has also out-sourced the provision of many illegal leisure activities. Western gang cultures provide opportunist supply and distribution chains for demand in the market for illegal leisure forms and practices. However, underground Western criminal cartels control more sophisticated supply chains, with production centred in Africa, Latin America, South East Asia and the Balkans, while distribution, rigging of prices, extortion and market protection are organized at point of sale in the cash-rich metropolitan markets of the USA, Western Europe and Australia (Lim 1998; Mares 2005; Glenny 2008).

Deregulation, globalization and out-sourcing have combined to disrupt the leisure society thesis, making it seem shallow and irrelevant to today's conditions. The idea that progressive science, technology and ethical government will result in leisure-for-all now looks like a pipedream. This is not just a matter of the transformation in the traditional postwar attitude to work after the so-called Thatcher–Reagan revolution of the 1980s. The emotional organization and presentation of the self has undergone fundamental revision. I referred to the axial importance of emotional intelligence and emotional labour in achieving personal competence and credibility in the last chapter. Before examining the leisure society thesis at greater length, let me expand upon the challenges that these new conditions provide to the study of leisure and lifestyle.

Emotional Intelligence, Emotional Labour and Lifestyle

Lifestyle formation and effective interaction now requires the mobilization and application of significant emotional intelligence and emotional labour about issues of culture, medicine, environmental matters, recycling, trust, psychological and physical wellbeing, respect issues, personal presentation skills and time management. Hochschild (1983) was one of the first to comment upon this requirement. Her concept of *emotional labour* was developed to refer to the emotional competence and 'people skills' necessary for an economy in which the service sector (as opposed to agricultural and manufacturing labour) dominates the economy. The concept of emotional labour logically implies the refinement and continuous testing of emotional intelligence. The possession of people skills is a vital resource in creating the climates of trust and mutual respect that are conducive to healthy private life and profitable work relationships. Thus, the development and practice of emotional intelligence is a precondition of being recognized as an attractive, effective member of civil society and a credible member of the labour force. The skills that put a client at ease in the workplace are part of the same repertoire of emotional accomplishments and performance competencies that make one an acceptable member of social settings or an attractive mate.

Emotional labour refers to the preparation and application of emotional attitudes and competencies that are commensurate with the requirements of organizations and civic culture. Integral to the concept is the notion of labour performance; that is, the display of positive emotions, the repression of negative emotions, spray-on sincerity and 'can do' face-work, even when the individual is feeling the opposite. The acquisition of emotional labour competence is separate from the skills acquisition for 'doing the job'. It is not a matter of being certificated to have achieved a measured level of knowledge or trained to do this or that technical or professional function. Rather it is a matter of consistently displaying positive personal identification and competence.

As such, they pertain to general considerations of character formation and inter-personal conduct that relate directly to leisure forms and practice. The conventional notions of 'time off' and 'free time' have been eroded by the psychological coaching, drilling and pepping-up of emotions in work and non-work time to enhance abilities and competence in social management, self-management, social awareness and relationship management (Goleman 1995). Achievement as a family member, student, worker and citizen is conditional upon emphasizing and practising the virtue of informality over the rigidities of the bureaucratic personality and respect for cultural and ethnic difference (Sennett 1999, 2004, 2006). Being at ease in social and work settings is the pre-condition for personal and group goal achievement. The acquisition and practice of these accomplishments requires considerable *reconnaissance* and *monitoring* in a variety of settings.

Reconnaissance refers to the psychological checking of effective and innovative people skills in order to enhance the formation of character as a more attractive resource in the economic market and lifestyle relations. *Monitoring* refers to the practice of testing how people skills work in social settings and adjusting performance. Both imply that non-work practices such as watching television, reading newspapers and magazines, listening to the radio, mingling with others at dinner parties, conferences and many other social occasions involve acquiring and applying significant levels of emotional intelligence. The line between leisure forms and practices that generate pure pleasure and intelligence about the emotions that is necessary for the formation of attractive work and non-work character features is fuzzy. The concepts of reconnaissance and monitoring suggest that the application and refinement of emotional intelligence is inherent in leisure settings. This prejudices orthodox notions of 'free time' and 'time off' because it posits emotional labour as a general feature of character formation. The tone and pitch of emotional labour may differ in the workplace and leisure setting, but the practice is common to both.

Now one might quibble with Hochschild (1983) and Goleman (1995) who present emotional intelligence and emotional labour as defining features of modern life. There are plenty of historical studies that seize upon the same psychological mechanisms, types of awareness and social presentation skills in traditional society (Bailyn 1974; Elias 1983). These historical studies refer to what we would now call emotional intelligence and emotional labour but they examine them among the higher circles in society. For Hochschild (1983) and Goleman (1995) emotional intelligence and emotional labour are *generalized* features of contemporary citizenship. Knowledge about these matters and their practice is not

	Hours and minutes per day males/females	
Sleep	8.04	8.18
Resting	0.43	0.48
Personal care	0.40	0.48
Eating/drinking	1.25	1.19
Watching TV/DVD; listening to radio/music	2.50	2.25
Social life, entertainment/culture	1.22	1.32
Hobbies & games	0.37	0.23
Sport	0.13	0.07
Reading	0.23	0.26
All leisure	5.25	4.53
Employment and study	3.45	2.26
Housework	1.41	3.00
Childcare	0.15	0.32
Voluntary work	0.15	0.20
Travel	1.32	1.22
Other	0.13	0.15

Figure 2   UK time-use survey, people aged 16 and over (2005)

Source: UK National Statistics Office; www.statistics.gov.uk

confined or concentrated in elite circles. This has significant implications for how we think of 'time off' and practise 'free' choice.

Emotional Intelligence and Time Use

Traditionally, work has been conceptualized as disciplined time and leisure as free time (Haworth and Veal 2004). Some of the tensions in this simple bipolar model of time allocation were considered in the debates around time-use surveys. UK time-use data indicates that, with the exception of sleep, more time per day is spent in leisure than *any other* non-work activity, such as body maintenance, housework and voluntary care. The US data is organized differently by the *Bureau of Labor Statistics* (see Figures 2 and 3). Notwithstanding this, the pattern of leisure and other non-work activities in the UK and the US is remarkably similar.

The three main activities carried out by adults in the UK are paid employment, sleep and watching TV and videos/DVDs, surfing the internet or listening to music. The average hours spent in paid employment per day are just under 7; in sleep about 8 and in leisure about 5. The distribution of activities varies during the week. At the weekend both men and

	Hours and minutes per day males/females	
Sleep	8.54	8.7
Household activities	1.35	2.27
Eating and drinking	1.30	1.19
Shopping	0.94	1.46
Educational activities	0.47	0.43
Watching TV/DVD/ listening to radio and music	2.58	2.80
Caring for household members	0.34	0.72
Social life and entertaining	0.75	0.71
Telephone calls/email	0.12	0.23
Sport	0.39	0.20
Volunteering	0.14	0.15
Organizational, civic and religious activities	0.27	0.35
All Leisure	5.7	5.0

Figure 3   US time-use, people aged 15 and over (2005)

Source: US Bureau of labor statistics; www.bls.gov/tus

women spend more time sleeping and participating in leisure. On average men have 30 minutes more free time than women, although this is partly compensated for by the extra 20 minutes on average that women spend sleeping. Men are more likely to watch TV or listen to the radio and to take part in sport, entertainment, hobbies and using the computer. Women are more likely to spend time reading and socializing. Twelve per cent of household income was spent on leisure and recreation in 2006 compared with 9% in 1971. A further 12% was spent on leisure-recreation related activities (restaurants and hotels), compared with 10% in 1971.

The American Time Use Budget (2005) shows a similar picture (http://www.bls.gov/tus/) (see Figure 2). Employed persons work 7.5 hours per day on weekdays (men typically work 7.9 hours compared with 7.1 for women). Watching TV is the leisure activity that occupies most time (2.6 hours) although this is being challenged, and may already be over-taken by internet surfing. This is why global TV networks telecast news and some programmes on the internet. The destiny of the computer and the mobile phone is to be the main information/entertainment nexus for the population. The wide distribution of the internet, television and DVD and CD use in leisure points to the central importance of technology in the most popular Western leisure forms. The next most common leisure activity is socializing which accounts for 0.7 hours per day.

Men spend more time in leisure activities (5.7 hours per day) than women (5.0 hours). Leisure and sports typically account for 5.50 hours per day for men and 4.80 for women. Men spend approximately 8.54 hours sleeping and women 8.70. Students of time-use analysis have found the distinction between leisure and cognate non-work activities, like eating, drinking, grooming and watching TV to be rather fuzzy. If I spend part of the evening watching a television show with half an eye on finding new material for my lecture tomorrow on Reality TV, does it qualify as leisure or work? Similarly, if I come home and prepare a low calorie, high fibre evening meal should it be regarded as an expression of free choice or as observance of how well I have been coached in the relationship between prolonged life, diet and the work-life balance? Students of time-use have found it tricky to apply categoric imperatives of work and leisure to cognate activities of this type.

Perhaps the solution is not to apply categories of work and leisure and tick trajectories of observed behaviour against them. After all, this or that research classification scheme designed to encapsulate time budget use is of limited value in revealing the meanings, motivations and feelings of actors. Jonathan Gershuny (2000) is a leading figure in the field of time budget studies. According to him, there is a progressive trend in the allocation of leisure time. As wealth increases people have a greater propensity to engage in what Bob Stebbins (1992, 2002) calls 'serious leisure'; that is, free time activities that involve choices requiring the development of a skill and a career. The corollary of this is that greater wealth reduces the incentive for paid employment and increases the propensity to spend surplus income on leisure goods. For Gershuny this, in turn, increases economic and social wealth because it increases the demand for labour in the leisure industries.

But this model of time allocation has little of the psychological insight that a writer like Veblen (1899) brought to the question of leisure a century before Gershuny's theory was committed to print. Veblen eschews rational models of the relationship between wealth and time allocation. His perspective of leisure concentrates upon the emotional significance of free time behaviour and the intentionality of the actor. Veblen's theory of conspicuous consumption proposes that greater wealth is not simply an incentive to developing superior skills in non-work activities and husbanding a leisure career. Crucially, it proposes in addition, that the acquistion of skill is driven by social display. Again, this stresses the import of questions of coding and representation in leisure forms and practice. The display of the commitment to voluntary abnegation from paid employment conveys superior social standing. Emotional intelligence is a useful bridging concept between Veblen's approach to leisure activity as caught up in social positioning and the ambivalence in the time-use literature about the motivation and meaning of non-work time distribution. Grooming, body maintenance, exercise, cooking, reading newspapers and magazines, watching television and listening to the radio can all be read as husbanding emotional intelligence in order to increase competence. These non-work activities involve reconnaissance and monitoring work that enhance personal confidence and presentational skills. The display of competence is not simply required for work settings, it also applies to relations with parents, children, friends and leisure networks.

If pure leisure is the cultivation of a state of mind, as Pieper (1952) and De Grazia (1962) maintain, the resources required come from competence in emotional intelligence and emotional labour. To practise leisure as a state of mind you need to know and monitor data on social mores, totems and taboos. Reconnaissance and monitoring of some forms of knowledge may be more compatible with leisure settings since it is here that people let down their guard and engage in gossip and careless talk. The accumulation and sharpening of emotional intelligence and the management of emotional labour therefore does not stop when one leaves the workplace. It is a round-the-clock undertaking. By placing competence as the means and end of activity, the question of the centrality of emotional intelligence in building personal credibility arises. With it, old distinctions between work and leisure, disciplined time and time off, become untenable. Leisure and emotional intelligence go hand in hand, which acutely compromises traditional connotations of 'free time' and 'time off' in the literature on leisure forms and practice.

Why a Different Paradigm is Needed

Today, students of leisure need to reposition the debate about leisure forms and practice in relation to globalization, deregulation, emotional intelligence and emotional labour. This means taking on board a variety of issues pertaining to labour markets in the emerging and developing world, questions of global industrial pollution, the consequences of mass casualized labour for leisure participation and the role of international cartels and gangs in the provision of illegal leisure goods and services, the management of the emotions and personal presentation skills, that were scarcely considered at the height of the leisure society thesis. Twin corollaries of this are the construction of a more nuanced, multi-layered understanding of the context of location behaviour in leisure and the application of a wider canvas of agents participating in leisure forms and practice.

Forty years ago, during the era of the leisure society thesis, the field students of Leisure Studies/Leisure Sciences were disarmingly straightforward, not to say naïve, about questions of supply and demand in the leisure industry. The assumption that work was being displaced by leisure was widespread. The psychologist John Neulinger (1981b: 69) wrote:

> Something is changing in our society and potentially all over the world …
> The need for toil is on its way out. More specifically, the need for toil *for*
> *the average person* is on its way out. A select few had always managed
> to circumvent toil, labour without satisfaction, the endless routine of
> drudgery. But now for the first time in history, the possibility looms ahead
> that such may be the case for the majority of people, if not for all.

Neulinger (1981a; 1981b) presented this as the cornerstone of his case
for boosting public and private resources for leisure counselling. The latter
was portrayed as a professional service directed to providing individuals
with guidance, either with respect to how to use their free time in more
fulfilling ways or to provide positive responses to the chronic absence or
relative infrequency of leisure experience.

Re-examined with the hindsight of emotional intelligence, emotional
labour, globalization, deregulation, de-layering, the transfer of manufacturing jobs from the most advanced industrial economies to the emerging industrial world, and the literature on timeuse, a number of things are
clear about this position. To begin with, it addressed conditions in the
metropolitan centres of the economically most advanced nations, and
treated relations in the emerging and developing world as secondary.
This was a very ethnocentric model of leisure, and it was largely confined
to the professional class involved in the knowledge, communication and
information sectors as opposed to blue-collar and office workers.

In addition, this approach to leisure carries with it the assumption of
spontaneous adjustments to the demand for more free time. For example,
Neulinger's belief that leisure is replacing work will result in more public
funds allocated to train leisure counsellors to help those liberated from the
work ethic to cope with the challenges of the leisure-rich society. There
is no realistic assessment of the roles of resistance and struggle in resource
re-allocation. Instead, as day follows night, more leisure time and more
resources for leisure forms and practice are assumed to follow from technological and managerial innovations in reducing the working week.

Similar linear, causal relationships are presumed in the rewards of
leisure. In Neulinger's (1981a) leisure paradigm, intrinsic motivation and
perceived freedom are submitted to produce life satisfaction in leisure.
Csikszentmihalyi's (1990) discussion of flow also presents challenging
activity that achieves goal attainment as engrossing, pleasurable and
self-actualizing. Although Neulinger (1981b) allows that leisure counsellors are a requirement of the leisure age, he does not go into the forms
of addictive, obsessional or harmful behaviour that come in the wake of
more leisure; nor does he raise the difficult question of the corporate
and state interests that benefit from appreciable sections of the leisure
community subjecting themselves to forms of behaviour that are addictive, obsessional and harmful. The social psychological approach of

Neulinger and Csikszentmihalyi arbitrarily abstracts some leisure relationships from the life-world and boosts them with general significance. Power, division and the role of coding and representation in formulating perceptions and experience of leisure do not figure in these contributions. As a result, the question of the context in which work, leisure and personal goal attainment are positioned is massively underdeveloped. Instead, it is taken for granted that fulfilling leisure is the product of modernization, democracy and what might be referred to as the emergence of 'the good society'.

Typically, the issues of how industrialization and democracy are configured in relation to capitalist distributions of authority between elites and classes, no less than the topics of ideology, and the variations of the meaning of work and leisure between capitalist countries, are left fallow (Clayre 1974). The overriding presumption is that the absolute amount of free time in society is growing as a result of automation and that its distribution is becoming more equitable because of ethical management. The growth of leisure is interpreted as an unequivocal mark of social progress. Of course, the persistence of inequality and social conflict is acknowledged. But it is assumed that they will be subject to laws of 'natural' decline as technology, professionalization and ethical management form an unbeatable triple alliance to overcome and defeat the age-old problem of scarcity. In order to expose the limitations of this paradigm more explicitly and build the case for a new way of examining leisure forms and practice, it is necessary to go more systematically into the claims made by the leisure society thesis.

The Leisure Society Thesis

Max Kaplan (1960), surveying the 'recreation explosion in the USA' during the 1950s, was a pioneering advocate of this line of thought. An enthusiastic proponent of the hypothesis that leisure is the expression of voluntarism, he nevertheless listed associated variables of family, social class, subculture, community and religion and acknowledged their influence in providing variations in the perception and experience of leisure forms and practice. However, his treatment of these factors is uncritical and descriptive. His work is typical of the day in Leisure Studies, in omitting to integrate leisure forms and practice into a theory of the organization of scarcity and resource distribution. There is no engagement with the proposition that class, gender, race and status position individuals differently in relation to scarce resources; just as there is no discussion of how the requirement of personal competence and credibility condition what it means to be free and self-determining. The

idea that emotional *positioning* and *coaching* structures leisure choice
and the form and content of leisure is not seriously broached. 'Structure'
would have been regarded as much too questionable a term to employ
in relation to the question of positioning since voluntarism requires privilege to be assigned to the individual on a priori grounds.

Furthermore, Kaplan's (1960) work was glib about the relationships
between the American leisure industry, the global division of labour and
the shape of consumer culture. Instead, the progressive, creative aspects
of leisure choice for individuals are forcefully stressed. Kaplan (1960: 22)
lists seven essential characteristics of leisure; it

- is the antithesis to the economic function of work
- carries pleasant anticipation and recollection
- involves a minimum of involuntary social role obligations
- is associated with freedom and choice
- is closely related to the values of culture
- generally involves a play element
- stretches from activities of inconsequence to activities of significance.

Kaplan's (1960) study played an important part in raising the profile of
leisure among academics. He writes with the gusto of a person who
believes that society is inevitably steaming into a new age produced by
technological progress and ethical management: the leisure age, in
which the ugly features of industrialization and urbanization will be cor-
rected. This is typical of the majority of academic writers on leisure in
this period. There is strong, unquestioning approval of science and technology in Leisure Studies thinking at this time. Science and technology
are held to lead to an unprecedented progressive transformation of the
world. The leisure society thesis, and the catalyst behind the development of Leisure Studies as a significant field of enquiry are bound up
with an apocalyptic view of positive industrial transformation. Modern
academic interest in leisure is inseparable from the proposition that
scientific and technological development and the affluent society multiplies the range of choices and improves the quality of individual choice
and freedom. The links between leisure and pollution, exploitation,
repression crime, and social control belong to a subsequent, more
querulous generation.

Joffre Dumazedier (1967, 1974) provided an influential European
parallel to American studies of leisure. Leisure, he contends, involves
the suspension of institutional obligations (to family, work and society)
and forms of activity and experience that are associated with self-
fulfilment. He hypothesizes that leisure is emerging as the main institution in society. By this he means that leisure forms and practices
influence the jobs that people choose, the areas of the country in

which they live and the types of marital relationships into which they enter.[2] Although he does not draw the comparison directly, it is clear that he regards society to be on the brink of exchanging the work ethic for the leisure ethic.

Kaplan and Dumazedier were in fact proposing early versions of the leisure society thesis. Yet fittingly for a field of study that had for so long played the role of Cinderella to the more powerful disciplines of Philosophy, Business and Social Science, the buds of the leisure society thesis sprouted from elsewhere. They emerged from writers interested in modern social and economic development, especially the capitalist form of industrial development.

One of the most cogent expressions of this position is to be found in the 'logic of industrialization' thesis developed by Kerr et al. (1962). According to this logic, the process of the maturation of industrialization inevitably increases the resource allocation to education, welfare and leisure. Kerr (1962) and his associates were chiefly interested in the subject of the consequences of industrial maturity for management–labour relations. In part their concept of a 'logic to industrialization' is polemical, since the inference is that the Soviet-style command systems of the day would be forced to modify their ideology once industrialization in their territories reached an appropriate level of maturity. With the benefit of hindsight we can now see that this was the right answer to the wrong question. The Soviet-style economies were indeed obliged to deregulate labour markets and liberalize welfare, education and leisure arrangements. But they did so primarily because of ideological contradictions in the system and the inability of the economic substructure to support the communist empire in Eastern Europe, rather than as a result of obedience to the so-called logic of industrialization. Despite addressing the question of leisure *en passant*, Kerr et al. (1962) made bold predictions for it that were of foundational significance in the evolution of the leisure society thesis. Thus, they maintained that the future of leisure involved the radical diminution of work time, increasing pluralism, the efflorescence of creativity among the masses and the growth of tolerance for 'new bohemian' values.

Echoes of this rousing overture about the future of leisure can be found in the 'post-industrial society' thesis which succeeded the logic of the industrialism thesis (Touraine 1971; Bell 1974; Dumazedier 1974; Toffler 1980). This thesis repeated the emphasis on technology and ethical management as forces of liberation. Automation and the growth of the communication, knowledge and service industries were held to diminish the requirement for paid manual labour. Bell (1974) submitted that the centrality of knowledge is the 'axial principle' of the new society. In institutional terms, the University and the research lab are replacing the factory and the office as the hub of wealth-creation. If this is the case, extensive redefinition of the meaning of power, work and leisure is required.

Traditional analysis of management–labour relations assumed antagonism between the two interests. The motivation of management is to control costs and increase profits. As to labour, the goal is to increase wages and control prices. By proposing changes in the class structure relating to the decline of manual labour and the rise of a new professional-technical-managerial class, exponents of the post-industrial society thesis maintained that the rules of the game are changing. The new class is in the same position as the traditional working class in lacking ownership over the means of production. But their experience of university education and central role in innovation and research gives them much greater influence in the management of society. By the same token, their leisure choices are moving away from collective systems emphasizing solidarity and stability to more plural, dynamic forms and practices. The post-industrial society thesis explicitly twinned the growth of leisure with social progress. In a formula that raises many eyebrows today, it equated the expansion of leisure with the age-old dream of human emancipation.

The significance of the leisure society thesis in raising the social profile and cultural relevance of Leisure Studies cannot be underestimated. Traditional debates about change and development in industrial society presupposed that leisure is residual to work. Anxieties about the expansion of leisure were tinged with Christian convictions about the significance of the work ethic and the poverty of idleness. Leisure could never be the focus of the masses, since work was the means of wherewithal. Leisure was regarded to be a matter of personal choice; work was the stuff of individual and social survival (Clayre 1974; Cross 1993; Hunnicutt 1988; Hill 2003).

The leisure society thesis changed all of this. Now, under the influence of the logic of industrialism thesis and post-industrial society theory, it was no longer scandalous, à la Dumazedier (1967, 1974), to nominate leisure as the pivotal emerging institution in society. What people did in their free time set the agenda for life choices relating to education, work, marriage and politics. Leisure, which for decades was dismissed as the poor relation in academic research, suddenly became the touchstone to the future.

Even sociologists who were sceptical abut the full-blown versions of the logic of industrialism thesis and post-industrial society theory acknowledged that leisure must be taken more seriously. In Britain, the redoubtable Ken Roberts (1970: 9) characteristically commenced a major, influential career-long interest in the sociology of leisure with a canard against 'the great deal of polemical writing about the quality of man's leisure produced' over recent years and a commitment to engage in 'value-free' research to 'describe and explain how people in particular social situations use their leisure'. Roberts advocated a pluralist approach to leisure that recognized distinctions of class, race, religion and gender but ultimately held fast to the notions of the priority of individual choice and voluntarism. Cognate approaches were pursued in the work of Stanley Parker (1981) and Tony Veal (1987).

On the whole, the British contribution to Leisure Studies in the 1960s and 70s was more parsimonious and qualified than that of the Americans. For example, Parker (1981: xi) took care to remark that not everyone is participating in 'the leisure boom'. Veal (1987: 68–9) is also circumspect in maintaining that changes to leisure attitudes are not equivalent, resources allocated to leisure forms and practices are still subject to the laws of scarcity and that talk of 'the leisure age' is premature. Nonetheless, the British contribution was clearly stimulated by the leisure society thesis and took the greater cultural profile of leisure forms and practices to be an important and transparent fact of post-war culture and society.

The Traditional Framework: State–Corporate– Consumer–Academic (SCCA)

Looking back, the framework of agents identified as central in the leisure society thesis is disconcertingly simple. The key agents in leisure forms and practice are scant and awareness of the frictions and tensions within them and between them is paltry. It is not really an exaggeration to propose that it is confined to a fourfold typology of agents operating in the context of industrial-democratic society:

• The State

The state is recognized to be an agent of intervention establishing 1) the legal context of leisure forms and practice through its control of licensing and policing; 2) the moral context by means of its articulation of good or desirable leisure forms, practices and values; and 3) the strategic context through its guidance and allocation of resources with respect to the work-life balance. The state is conceived of as a neutral agent which simply translates needs into resource allocation. While at this time, the bilateral and multilateral circumference of state activity was not excluded, the analysis of the interventionist state was

concentrated upon the formation and conduct of policies within territorial boundaries. Divisions and frictions within the state between the
legislature and executive and different individual and group interests
were underplayed. Of course, changes in the operation of the state
were recognized. The transition from a laissez-faire mode to an interventionist mode was at the heart of the post-industrial society theory
of the state. In Bell's (1974) study, the emergence of knowledge as the
new 'axial principle' in the economy combined with the ascendancy of
a new 'intellectual and professional technocracy' assumes state intervention as a broker between competing interests and the chief means
of protecting and advancing the public interest.

The analysis of the state in Leisure Studies at this time was curi-
ously indifferent to the debates on the nature of state power in capitalist society (Miliband 1969; Althusser 1971: Poulantzas 1973, 1978).
Yet these debates produced serious objections to the pluralist model
of the state by demonstrating the relationship between state power and
class interests. By neglecting to engage with these debates the traditional framework in Leisure Studies produced an inadequate reading
of power and the relationship between class interests and the state in
positioning leisure forms and practice.

The pluralist model of the state assumes that power is fragmented and dif-
fused. The system of representative government provides a means of expression for a multitude of groups. The electoral process insures that populations
are protected from being dominated by predominant classes or interests.

Critics challenge this view by revealing the connections between parlia-
mentary systems and class-race-gender power.

• The Corporation

The leisure society thesis assumed a partnership between the interventionist state, corporations and universities. During the 1950s,
mass society theory in the US argued that modern consumption
exerted a levelling effect over leisure forms and practices.
Commercialization and the organization of mass events in sport and
recreation were held to produce passive consumers. In the work of C.
Wright Mills (1956) the military-industrial-state complex controlled by
a power elite rules work, leisure and society. Marcuse (1964) presented a stark analysis of consumer docility with his account of the
'totally administered, one-dimensional society' in which there is no
effective working class opposition. The military-industrial-state complex

condemns the masses to a 'pacified existence'. In these historical circumstances, the best hope resides in maginalized groups such as
students, feminists, the exploited and outcasts. Later Marcuse (1978)
argued that aesthetics offered an additional front of resistance that
could galvanize opposition. Nonetheless, the dominant theme in his
analysis is the crushing power of predominant military, business and
state interests. For Marcuse free time is categorically distinct from
leisure time. 'The latter', he wrote (1964: 52), 'thrives in advanced
industrial society, but it is unfree to the extent to which it is administered by business and politics.'

The leisure society thesis and post-industrial society theory abandoned this terrain. They recognized that corporations condition leisure
forms and practice. The mechanisms by which this is achieved extend
well beyond designing and marketing leisure commodities and services. Advertising, sponsorship and lobbying state officials and political parties are all part of the commercial leisure panoply. While the
term 'globalization' is not used, the post-industrial society thesis
presupposes that the emergence of the knowledge economy and the
service sector widens the focal plane of the leisure industry from
national and regional to international chains of demand and supply.

Instead of lecturing about the strength of corporate power and consumer passivity, the leisure society thesis and post-industrial society
thesis pointed to the new freedom offered by technology and ethical
management. The corporate power of *Disney, Coca-Cola, General
Motors, British-American Tobacco, Sony* and other multinationals is
envisaged in terms of a harmonious partnership between the university, the state and consumers. The pivotal force behind partnership
is the new knowledge–communication class who exert influence by
dint of their mastery over data and ideas. This class is dispersed
throughout higher education, the state and business.

There is nothing in this work which points to the role of leisure in
resisting corporate and state power. Instead, leisure tends to be presented as expressing personal freedom and social integration. No
serious attempt is made to explain the dynamics of the business organization, especially the tendency of capitalist corporations to strive to
engineer a monopoly over supply in order to make demand capitulate
to aggressive price structuring. Nor is the regulatory role of the state
in aiming for fair competition and consumer protection examined.

• Consumers

The leisure society thesis tended to present consumers as already
possessing and executing full citizenship rights. Differences of class, race

status and gender were recognized. But they were treated descriptively. Nothing in the thesis suggests that elements in a class that has nothing might want everything; or that a race which is marginalized might want redress; or that a status group which is sidelined might wish to challenge and oppose the dominant power; or that gender might situate some people in relation to scarce resources in a way that makes their relation to the status quo insupportable. The subtext is very much along the lines that Cheek and Burch (1976), following the influential social systems sociologist, Talcott Parsons, articulated in the 1970s – namely, that there is fundamental agreement between individuals and groups about the core values in society. These core values are transmitted to the population via the central institutions of normative coercion: the family, education, the judiciary, the police, medicine, social work and leisure and recreation.

If core values are successfully transmitted to populations on an inter-generational basis, how can social change occur? This is one of two of the main objections raised against the social system approach. The second objection is that the social system approach finds no place for social conflict. It over-eggs the pudding with a stress on consensus and solidarity. The subjects of difference and antagonism do not receive adequate treatment. Nor is this all. Looking back, the post-industrial society thesis took a remarkably optimistic view of the economic dynamics of post-industrial society. The distribution of leisure for all was predicted to increase. A mixture of the unprecedented bounty of science and technology and ethical government was to combine to make access to and participation in leisure more equal. If this is the case, the question is what incentive do scientists, technical personnel and state officials possess to ensure the reproduction of economic growth and social stability.

• Academics

The leisure society thesis had a rosy view of the part that academics would play in the post-industrial future. Bell's (1974) nomination of the 'axial' importance of knowledge and the university, logically implied a central role for university research staff. It was not clear how this role would integrate with state power or multi-national imperatives. The inference was that academics would fulfil the traditional role of intellectuals; that is, they would devote themselves to the disinterested pursuit of knowledge for the benefit of mankind. To this extent, it is safe to say that post-industrial society theory and the leisure society thesis appear to have operated with a latter-day version of Jean Jacques Rousseau's humanism, which regards humanity as basically good, decent and virtuous. Traces of this are also evident in the work of those critics who take on some central aspects of the post-industrial society thesis, yet remain very assured that social conflict is endemic in capitalist society (Gorz 1978; Aronowitz and Di-Fazio 1994). It is also evident in the approach of sociologists of leisure such as Ken Roberts (1970, 1978) and Stanley Parker (1981) who purport to adopt a 'value-free' perspective on leisure.

Given Bell's (1974) emphasis on the centrality of knowledge for matters of wealth creation, influence and power in the post-industrial leisure age, the idea of value-freedom was always going to be a challenging position to defend. Marxist writers on leisure rejected the notion of value-freedom on the grounds that it failed to deal adequately with the problems of class struggle and ideology (Andrew 1981; Clarke and Critcher 1985). Similarly, feminist authors argued that value-freedom is an expression of patriarchy that masks intractable male domination and the systematic subordination of women's perspectives (Wimbush and Talbot 1988; Aitchison 2003).

The leisure society has not come to pass. Some commentators argue that society has become addicted to consumption rather than leisure. Collective bargaining has focused upon the defence of jobs and overtime rights and workers have engaged in multi-employment regimes as guarantees of full family participation in the consumer market (Hunnicutt 1988; Schor 1992). In parallel ways, the literature on emotional intelligence, emotional labour and the new capitalism maintains that individuals subject themselves to round-the-clock reconnaissance and monitoring to equip them with the necessary knowledge and skills to be competent in the management of personal relationships and the labour market (Hochschild 1983; Sennett 1999, 2004, 2006). Similarly, greater understanding of the relationship between the growth of leisure industries and consumption in the West and sweatshop labour and exploitation in the emerging and developing world has established the proposition that one person's play is based upon another person's pain (Roberts 2004; Rojek 2005). The leisure society thesis presupposed perennial economic growth and the allocation of resources to education, leisure and welfare. The neoliberal revolution of the 1980s emphasized the importance of personal and group solutions to questions of education, leisure and welfare and attacked the notion of the comprehensive welfare state. This shift in philosophy encouraged a focus upon special events rather than comprehensive management in leisure sponsorship and resource allocation.

These developments, combined with globalization, deregulation, outsourcing and delayering have changed the relationship between leisure and other areas of life. In the context of the debate around emotional labour it is difficult to argue convincingly that traditional notions of 'time off' and 'free time' with leisure remain unproblematic. A new, more complex framework of Leisure Studies is required. Before coming to the task of sketching out its details, it is worth noting the major of the limitations of the Leisure Society thesis and SCCA Framework.

Criticisms of the SCCA Framework

The period between the early 1980s and the turn of the century was one of slowly abandoning some sacred cows in Leisure Studies and beginning the revisionist analysis of what leisure means in the context of globalization, deregulation, the casualization of labour and the increased longevity of populations in the West, with all of the implications for the provision of pensions and third age politics, and of course, the social and psychological prominence assigned to emotional intelligence and emotional labour. The prize sacred cow that was discarded was the leisure society thesis. This was a painful separation. The thesis was responsible for the high public profile that questions of leisure enjoyed between the mid 60s and mid 70s. Nonetheless, by the early 1980s, with the de-industrialization of cities in North America and Western Europe, the expanding awareness of globalization and the relationship between leisure consumption in the developed world, the provision of leisure services and commodities from the emerging and developing nations and the unequal positioning of multicultural and multi-ethnic groups in relation to scarcity, the old idea of a leisure dividend for all became untenable.

Revisionism in Leisure Studies focused mainly on questions of class inequality and gender domination (Andrew 1981; Clarke and Critcher 1985; Deem 1986; Green et al. 1987). As an aside, it should be noted that there was less published on the influence of ethnicity, occupation and subculture upon access to leisure resources. Revisionism took the form of attacking the realism of the leisure society thesis and post-industrial society theory. The persistent nature of class and gender inequality was prominently stressed. For example, Clarke and Critcher (1985) demonstrated the profound influence of class distinctions in leisure experience. Among other things, class is a key factor in determining if you have private or public housing; whether you have private transport or rely on public bus and rail services; and if you have regular long-haul holiday experience or local holiday experience. Their study also showed the limitations of the interventionist state in correcting class inequality. For example, public investment in the arts and museums is presented as benefiting the middle class more than the working class since the former make use of these facilities with an incidence that is disproportionate to their numerical size. Post-industrial society changed the context in which these inequalities are played out, but it does not produce a classless society. On the contrary, class inequalities change in accordance with the transformations in the context in which leisure forms and practice are located. It is not a question of class inequalities remaining the same or that they are invulnerable to egalitarian state policy. Rather, it is a question of the stubborn character of class to persist as a key allocative mechanism of leisure resources in capitalist society.

Feminism was especially important in making the issue of embodiment pivotal in the study of leisure forms and practice. The treatment of the female body as a type of property in male-dominated society raised a series of critical questions. Some of these pertained to the nature of leisure industries, notably cosmetics, fashion and women's magazines, in perpetuating ideals of the female body and, by implication, degrading body types that do not comply with these ideals.

Feminism also opened up the subject of the emotions and particularly the question of the relationship between the emotions and rationality. The latter concept is associated with the Enlightenment. Rationality was then contrasted with magic and myth to contend that clear, unambivalent, precise ways of being and living in the world are possible. By following this or that rational order of things, life is shorn of ambiguity and stress. The feminist concentration upon the emotions in everyday life exposed the repression involved in insisting on assigning priority to rationality. Rational approaches were associated with masculine attempts to assert power and deny difference. The (unintended) result of rationality, therefore, is dehumanization, since it denies the central force of the emotions in existence and everyday life.

Poststructuralism and postmodernism supplied another turn in the revisionist moment. Perhaps the significance of this contribution was not fully apparent in the field until the start of the new century (Aitchison 2003; Blackshaw 2003). But its influence was felt much earlier as part of a reaction to both Marxist and Feminist critiques (Bramham 2002). Poststructuralism redefined the traditional politics of resistance by portraying power as discourse and disrupted traditional understandings of knowledge and representation.

Following the influence of Foucault (1975, 1980, 1981), leisure was reconceptualized as a field of discourse in which individuals and practices were positioned. By stressing the importance of discourse poststructuralism moved away from an approach to power that defined it as an external, constraining influence over individuals and groups to a standpoint that treated power as a condition of language and embodiment. For Foucault, power is not something that is imposed upon us by others, it is a constitutive part of practising and being recognized as a person. The focus of analysis therefore shifts from examining power as the expression of contending polarities to picturing it anew in terms of a shifting continuum between interconnected parties. In addition, the question of control is supplemented with the issue of self-control. What we choose to do in leisure and other areas of life is not just a matter of the influence of this or that group. It is an issue of the expectations and event horizons that we bring to making a decision to become attached to a particular leisure form or practice. By choosing not to engage in blood sports as a leisure pastime I am drawing upon various ethical and cultural arguments, but I am also exercising power. This view of power is an advance on those positions that it criticized because it conveyed the important distinction that power is always and already enabling as well as constraining. The theoretical intersection between discourse and embodiment revitalized awareness of the micro-politics and diversity of resistance. Challenging received forms and practices of leisure was reconceptualized as a condition of bodily competence as opposed, for example, to the action of this or that class, gender or race.

Postmodernism directed similar arguments against the leisure society thesis and post-industrial society theory. It took issue with the notion of unity and solidarity, preferring instead to emphasize diversity, fragmentation and change. It adapted the poststructuralist argument that discourse and representation shape meaning by submitting that there is *no* meaning outside discourse and representation. Extreme forms of postmodernism propose that reality has disappeared. For example, in the work of Jean Baudrillard (1981, 2004) the mass media is treated as if it is a genie that has escaped from its bottle and fatally dissolves the shadow line between illusion and reality.

Postmodernism was successful in clearing away some ossified propositions in Leisure Studies. For example, after it, the proposition that leisure is freedom, or that class struggle is the key to understanding leisure forms and practice, do not hold water. It opened up a terrain for exploring questions of identity and meaning in leisure that assumed that neither of these things is fixed or uniform. Through postmodernism it becomes much easier to think in terms of the diversity of identity, the multiplicity of meaning, recognition and tolerance of difference. The *context* for thinking about leisure forms and practice was transformed.

With postmodernism came an emphasis in social and cultural analysis upon multiculturalism, multi-ethnicity, the politics of difference and globalization. It was less successful in generating questions of leisure policy. It is one thing to build leisure policies around multi-culturalism, multi-ethnicity and globalization. It is much more difficult to tackle international state power and multi-national influence to create ethically sound policies to combat pollution, consumer manipulation and mephitic leisure forms.[3] This is because postmodernism lacked a coherent concept of society. In stressing diversity, difference and multiplicity it was not clear what collective forms were left to enhance leisure experience and social wellbeing. Decentring meaning led to many important insights about manipulation and power. But perpetual decentring is a policy-maker's nightmare since it provides no clear way forward. Postmodernism and poststructuralism therefore each produced an impasse that has not yet been overcome. The probability is that it will be eventually filled by some version of a politics of will in which one vision of leisure and society is presented over others as the best way forward. However, we are not at a stage of thought and practice where a tenable vision of this type has emerged.

Does this mean that Leisure Studies *après* the postmodern turn has run into a blind alley from which it cannot escape? The evidence for this is weak. Leisure Studies is currently in a condition in which many of the old 'certainties' generated by the leisure society/post-industrial society moment have been discarded. New approaches to the question of leisure have been devised and implemented. These have not produced a new governing paradigm in Leisure Studies in which the majority agree on the meaning and agenda for leisure. However, they have redefined the key agents in the field and produced a much wider canvas for the investigation of leisure forms and practice.

A Framework for Leisure Studies Today (SCCASMIL)

Leisure Studies today retains a basic concern with the parts played by the state, the corporation, consumers and academics. Unlike the situation at the height of the leisure/post-industrial society thesis, these agents are no longer defined in essentialist terms. The influence of poststructuralism and postmodernism has left its mark. It is now normal to think of the state, the corporation, consumers, and academics in terms of frictions, divisions, process and multiple meanings. We are far more attuned to questions of differentiation, resistance, challenge, opposition and the market in illegal leisure activities. The central players of the SCCA framework remain but their composition, status and terms of operation have been reformulated in important ways. This reflects the prominence now assigned to globalization in conceptualizing the context of leisure forms and practice. Let us work through this framework in more detail:

• The State

The state must still be analysed in Leisure Studies as a central regulatory body. It controls the judicial parameters of leisure forms and practice, governs policing, allocates public resources, articulates a public ethical agenda and represents public leisure interests abroad. Unlike the period of the leisure society/post-industrial society thesis, the state must now be considered in a significantly reformulated way. The old pluralist notion of a neutral agent, pursuing a publicly accountable 'honest broker' agenda of intervention which dominated post-war thinking is now untenable. *Internally*, the traditional divisions between the legislature, the executive and the judiciary remain pertinent. But the *pluralist* model of the state in which the three main sections of activity are held to be the mere tools of elected parties is now widely regarded as unduly simplistic. The state is recognized as performing an *ideological* function in massaging public opinion to take this or that view of issues of collective concern. This function answers to power *interests* that are not confined to questions of party, but extend to struggles between classes, races and public sphere elites. In short, the legislature, executive and judiciary are acknowledged to be not simply the servants of the people, but the instruments of social interests whose end is to present the activities of the state as being neutral or above sectional interest. Social interests leave their mark on the state and create the conditions of future resource exploitation and development. They do so through a complex interaction of bargaining, manipulation and alliance. Social interests are parts of the state, but the state is more than the sum of its parts. This is one reason why social interests struggle so keenly to acquire hegemony. The old leisure society model of the state as a sort of representative keyboard that translates popular will into public policy has been replaced by something more complex and realistic. The same applies to the other wing of state operations.

Externally, the state is held to retain geopolitical spheres of interest. For example, US policy on human trafficking and the international drugs trade is particularly vigilant in investigating supply chains from Central and Latin America. Similarly, European Union policy with respect to the regulation of the labour market and the provision of leisure commodities and services is alert to the significant internal supply market of cheap Eastern European labour which contravenes legislation on the minimum wage, rights in the workplace and therefore challenges traditional divisions between work and leisure. In a wired-up world in which the 24-hour marketplace obtains, the conventional notion of spheres of interest is too restrictive. Globalization presents a series of common risks to leisure practice in the shape of biochemical hazards, global warming, digital piracy and international cartels supplying illegal leisure resources. It follows that there is no assured territorial integrity for the state and that legislation and policing must now openly embrace a global dimension.

These issues are not confined to the fields of international relations, diplomacy and comparative sociology. Leisure Studies must pay heed to them. For leisure forms and practice between territorially defined boundaries is affected by them.

For example, one of the most contentious and urgent topics on the global agenda is climate change. The Kyoto Protocol (1997) committed signatories to implement a significant reduction in greenhouse gas emissions by 2012. The agreement is thwarted by the decisions of the US and Australia to withdraw from the provisions of the United Nations Framework Convention on Climate Change (UNFCCC). The non-participation of the US is particularly significant. According to UNFCCC, the US population, which consists of 4.6% of the world's population was responsible for 36.1% of carbon dioxide emissions in 1990. The European Union, with 6.3% of the world's population, was responsible for 24.2% of emissions in the same year. Australia, with a population of 20 million, has the highest emissions per capita in the developed word and is the 17th largest greenhouse polluter. The US and Australian governments base their non-participation on the argument that the Protocol is unfair to the industrialized countries and damages jobs in the domestic economy. The leisure sector in the US and Australian economies has been successful in lobbying government and public opinion that cutting carbon dioxide emissions in the automobile and travel industry carries unacceptable costs to lifestyle. Yet this self-interested isolationism has produced unintended consequences. For one thing American exceptionalism on the questions of global warming and tolerance for energy-inefficient transport as a leisure resource and lifestyle option is widely condemned as arrogant and deluded. The plea for America to put its house in order is echoed domestically with the revitalization of eco-friendly groups such as Greenpeace America and KyotoUSA who have raised public awareness of carbon footprints and unregulated automated transport as a leisure resource. The traditional notion that the state possesses supreme legislative, executive and judicial powers over a geopolitically defined territorial unit still holds water. But the idea that states go it alone and freely determine their policies on work, leisure and much more besides demands considerable caution. With respect to environmental issues and leading forms of illegal leisure activities, such as the trade in narcotics and sex trafficking, nation-states face common risks which require multilateral strategies, partnered legislation and co-operative policing. At both the internal and external levels then, the analysis of statecraft in the management of leisure forms and practice needs to be over-hauled and redefined.

• The Corporation

At the height of the leisure society thesis there were few in-depth studies of the leisure corporation. This is nothing short of astonishing given the emphasis in critical accounts of the manipulative influence of capitalism (Andrew 1981; Clarke and Critcher 1985). What were the critics of capitalism doing by attributing this or that effect to capitalism, without testing their attributions in the real-life setting of flesh and blood capitalist entrepreneurs and the corporations that followed their rule? Too often, the result was a shallow view of corporate capitalism in general. With respect to leisure, the role of the leisure corporation in governing an international division of labour and managing wage rates and conditions of work to ensure price competitiveness in the biggest, most lucrative markets of North America and the European Union was significantly under-researched. This resulted in considerable ambivalence over the question of what leisure corporations actually do to connect demand with supply.

The roots of the corporate involvement in leisure are still debated by historians (Cross 1993; Kammen 1999; Hill 2003). Some give primary emphasis to the commercialization of folk and amateur leisure forms. This was achieved through the commercial co-option of leisure supply and demand chains that traditionally involved no cash nexus. Gradually, pay became presented and accepted as the prerequisite for play. This pattern has been traced in forms of dance, theatre, music, sport and style (Russell 1997; Dunning and Sheard 2005). Others give more weight to the argument that commercial leisure entrepreneurs seize upon technological and cultural innovations to package new forms to entice the masses to consume (Kasson 1978; Gartman 1994). However, scarcely any dissent from Roberts's (2004: 21) proposition that over the last one hundred years commercial leisure has become overwhelmingly, the main leisure provider.

What does it mean to provide leisure commercially? At the simplest level, it means the exchange of money for leisure commodities and services. The commercialization of leisure involves product research and development functions to either identify or implant leisure demands in the population. An accessory of this is the development of marketing and advertising to communicate data about leisure products to potential consumers and to finesse product image so that the desire to consume becomes compelling. In democratic societies commercialization also implies the development of statutory, advisory and monitoring bodies to protect the consumer from unscrupulous, false claims about products and services. The development of the counter-culture in the 1960s was extremely important in challenging irresponsible capitalism. The force of counter-culture arguments to take the interests of marginalized groups like ethnic minorities, the disabled and children seriously was designed to *replace* capitalism with a version of 'business for, and by, the people'. It is a matter of conjecture to say how much of this was connected with a grass-roots sentiment to transform society in favour of the collective ownership and control of the means of production, and how much reflected the desire of radicals to steer society in this direction.

Most observers now agree that the unintended consequence of the counter-culture was the *reform* of capitalism (Frank 1997; McGuigan 2006). By pointing to consumers that were excluded from the advertising, marketing and product development pitch of corporations, the counter-culture provided the incentive for these businesses to become more concerned with questions of 'relevance' and 'ethical responsibility' (Frank 1997). Admirable though these measures may have been, notably in taking social inclusion more seriously, their cumulative effect was to augment the appeal of capitalist corporations by making them seem 'realistic' about consumer needs. By comparison the state and traditional capitalist corporations were often presented as cumbersome, unwieldy and out of touch. This process of reform had the effect of increasing the monopolistic market share to which capitalist organizations aspire while at the same time appearing to take account of consumers who, hitherto, had been invisible or referred to with a muffled voice.

For students of leisure, the result is that we must pay attention to the skill of successful leisure corporations (and other branches of corporate capitalism) in maximizing profit margins while claiming to respect consumer rights. Why this is quite a trick is that capitalism functions on the principle of producing goods and services in the cheapest market and selling them in the most expensive market. To put it differently, consumers must always pay more with respect to the price of a commodity or service than the cost incurred by the capitalist of market supply. This difference represents the margin of profit to the capitalist.

What writers like Frank (1997) and Sennett (2006) persuasively argue is that the 'new' capitalism has learned from the counter-culture. At its best it has adopted a socially significant critical edge to questions of social exclusion, injustice and intolerance while continuing to extract surplus value. I (2007: 115–34) refer to new capitalism as *neat capitalism*. By this term I mean a knowing, deliberate attempt by entrepreneurs to offer *smart* solutions to social, cultural and economic questions. The use of the term *neat* is intended to convey the self-approving manner in which neat capitalism is theorized and practised. Neat capitalism regards itself as presenting relevant, savvy *stateless solutions* to the problems of society and the world. As such, it draws on the sentiments of the common man. Of course, it is expressed in the mouths of men and women who have much greater influence than ordinary men and women. I am thinking of business leaders like Richard Branson, Charles Saatchi, Steve Jobs and the late Anita Roddick. These are no-nonsense capitalists who regard most aspects of the state as unimaginative, pettifogging and inefficient. The new Right term, *the nanny state* could have been invented for these figures. Traditional capitalists, such as Andrew Carnegie, Joseph Rowntree or J.P. Morgan, generally favoured patronage as the mechanism of social progress. They offered personal solutions, usually informed by Christian belief systems, to public questions that the state sector could not answer, such as poverty, homelessness, overcrowding and crime. Neat capitalists side with both 'the silent majority' and the voiceless and the victims of calamity. They act as moral entrepreneurs highlighting what is held to be ignored or fouled-up by the state machine. As such they are unelected political agents who offer stateless solutions to urgent social, economic and political issues on behalf of the silent majority. They do all of this and they still make vast amounts of money by extracting surplus value from labourers and charging the margin to consumers.

The example to which I often refer is Richard Branson's response to the tsunami in South East Asia in 2004. The tsunami was an ecological catastrophe in which thousands died and thousands more were made homeless. Branson caught the public mood of objection to the dilatory response of Asian and Western states to the tragedy. He offered a spontaneous practical solution in offering some of his Virgin Air Fleet to provide relief. This was applauded as a stateless solution to an urgent social problem. It also operated as free global advertising for Branson's Virgin group of companies. TV viewers were presented with the message that Virgin seeks relevant solutions that are more swift and flexible than the efforts of the state. The step between seeing Virgin as more relevant and regarding the Virgin brand as inherently good is a small one. Branson's practical solution to the tsunami had an authentic philanthropic function of doing good. Yet it would be foolish to ignore or deny the business output which was to identify Virgin as a problem-solver *par excellence*.

• Consumers

Frank (1997) offers a convincing view of the model of consumer culture that animated advertising executives in Madison Avenue, and the satellite of industrial corporations and business concerns that they represented in the 1960s and 70s. It is a culture of married, heterosexual couples, in which the husband is the bread-winner and the wife is the home-maker. This culture is unemployment-proof. Crime is a constant threat, but it is confined to a murky, marginal cast of under-socialized, anti-social individuals. The judiciary is incorruptible. Policing is even-handed and fair. The culture is presented as a world in which there is substantial agreement about central values and social responsibilities. This is the social system depicted by Cheek and Burch (1976) in their account of the functions of leisure forms and practice.

From the vantage point of multicultural and multi-ethnic groups, today this view from Madison Avenue seems fanciful and out-of-touch. The concept of consumers with which we now operate is of people living with, and through, difference. By this is meant a perspective that embraces multi-ethnicity and multiculturalism. Difference is not understood only in terms of categorical distinctions but also the entire system of social ordering in which these distinctions are positioned and relate to each other. For example, in societies dominated by white history it is a matter of how non-whites are located historically and contemporaneously in relation to scarcity, status and other distinctions.

In addition, it is necessary to use the concept of disembedding in relation to consumers in contemporary society. The mass media, the internet and other branches of modern communications provide opportunities for consumers to contrast local and national conditions with international and global circumstances. This may contribute to the restraint of global capitalism. For example, in 2008 the Apple iTunes store was forced to reduce the price of track downloading in the UK market from 79 pence to 74 pence. This was partly achieved by the pressure of consumer groups to standardize the UK price of legal downloading with that charged by Apple to other members of the European Union.

More generally, mass communications enables consumer disembedding that contributes to the dissemination of issues relevant to enhancing Care for the Self and widening Care for the Other. It provides consumers with a resource for the understanding of international market conditions and labour relations systems in the leisure sector. Of course, this does not mean that consumers possess perfect market knowledge. Nonetheless, even in the state of imperfect knowledge they have access to more cross-cultural data than previous generations.

• Academics

The leisure society thesis brought the question of leisure to the lips of academics, many of whom were hitherto indifferent or patronizing about the academic study of leisure.

In the 1970s and 80s it was the main catalyst for the growth of academic departments of Leisure Studies. These departments responded to growing medical evidence of the relationship between the work– leisure balance and health, and increasing public awareness of the value to communities of well-resourced leisure, recreation and heritage provision. After the 1990s, with deregulation, privatization and globalization, Leisure Studies began to be overtaken by the sub-disciplines of Sport Science and Tourist Studies.

Leisure Studies was disadvantaged by a traditional preoccupation with wider quality of life issues relating to the work-life balance and the restructuring of industrial society. These issues suggested an abstract quality to the field, that was not compensated for by the practical agenda of leisure, recreation and health management. In comparison, the links between sport and good health and tourism and widening personal and collective horizons seemed much easier for most people to grasp and apply. Leisure Studies was forced into a defensive role as newer, more 'relevant' fields of study began to increase student rolls.

In addition, Leisure Studies was closely tied to public sector employment and its critical wing was attached to a public agenda of social progress. The activist side of the discipline identified with developing leisure policy in relation to welfare issues and social engineering.

Students with degrees in Sports Science, Event Management and Tourist Studies were more attractive to private sector entrepreneurs intent on managing the expansion of gym culture, health clubs, package tours and post-tourist travel á la the *Lonely Planet* and *Rough Guide* franchises.

Academics in Leisure Studies cannot convincingly point to the leisure society as the future. The notion of a social transition to a qualitatively different type of society in which leisure values dominate has been replaced by an interest in the structural constraints on freedom, having to do with class, race, gender and status; and also, the question of the ideological connotations of leisure. The strong emphasis upon the value of emotional intelligence in lifestyle and work relations queries the relevance of traditional notions of choice, self-determination and time off. At its most interesting, academic Leisure Studies grapples with the issue of how social interests exploit and develop the ideology of leisure in societies founded upon organized inequality and the necessity to engage in paid employment.

• Social Movements

A variety of social, cultural and technological factors have combined to devalue the power of the state to act as a political agent. The

social democratic parties that emerged in the nineteenth and twentieth century had clear ideological differences between a market and
a state solution to social, economic and political questions. It is
now widely argued that there is an ideological crisis among both
Left and Right (Beck 1992; Giddens 1998, 2000; Linklater 1998).
Left- and Right-wing solutions are no longer seen as viable. A mixture
of ideological policy and strategy is now advocated, with partnerships with voluntary organizations, corporations and special single
issue interest groups (such as Greenpeace, Oxfam, Make
Poverty History).

The literature refers to the emergence and interaction of specialist
single issue interest groups as *sub-politics*. The term was coined by
Ulrich Beck (1992). Within the field of Leisure Studies over the last
twenty years the impact of these groups is demonstrated most forcefully in the emergence of the events industry. Special events like Live
Aid (1985), Live 8 (2007) and Live Earth (2007) raised public awareness of specific issues and generated income for third world relief
and sustainable ecology. They belong to the category of neat capitalism which offers stateless solutions to specific social, economic and
environmental issues. These solutions may be designed to expose
the shortfalls of state policy or to provide immediate funding for
urgent global issues. They are external to party politics although economic sponsorship and cultural partnerships with governments may
be sought in pursuit of their objectives.

• Illegal Leisure

Leisure Studies has never really come to terms with the fact that millions of people devote huge parts of their leisure to illegal activities.
A report from the United Nations Office on Drugs and Crime (2007)
estimates that 200 million people worldwide engage regularly in the
consumption of illegal narcotics. Demand in the world's biggest single market, North America, is thought to have stabilized. In contrast, the market in South East Asia and Australasia has grown
rapidly, fuelled by a flood of amphetamine-based stimulants supplied from sources in China. Mares (2006: 58) submits that nearly
50% of the adult population in the US have participated in illegal
drug use. The most popular drugs are marijuana, cocaine, heroin,
and psychoactive drugs such as amphetamine (meth), LSD, GHB
(Gamma Hydroxybutryrate – the so-called 'date-rape' drug) and
Ecstasy. Contrary to popular opinion, official statistics in North
America, Europe, Australia and Japan indicate the illicit drug use is
found across every category of class, ethnicity, national origin, gender,
profession and occupational status.

None of these features are compatible with efficient policing. Global entertainment piracy has damaged the profitability of many multi-nationals in the leisure sector. The fourth annual Digital Music Survey by Entertainment Media Research (2007) found that 43% of their poll of 1,700 people illegally downloaded music between 2006–7, rising from 36% in 2005–6. Only 33% cited the risk of being prosecuted as a deterrent against unauthorized downloading, compared with 42% in 2006 (http:// www.entertainmentmediaresearch.com).

The International Federation of Phonographic Industries estimates that one in three CDs exchanged in the world is an illegal copy (IFPI 2006). What does copyright piracy mean? It refers to the unauthorized reproduction and exchange of copyrighted intellectual property in the form of sound recordings, motion pictures, software, photographs, video games, books and articles. Illegal exchange occurs over two main highways. Duplication and sale of copyright material is part of black-market metropolitan culture. Siwek (2007) calculates that each year piracy costs the US economy $580billion in total output, costs American workers 373,575 jobs and $16.3 billion in lost tax revenue.

Digital piracy raises many serious issues for students of leisure. Two should be mentioned here. The first is the simple question of the theft of digital entertainment property via illegal downloading and the reproduction of software. As we have already seen, estimates differ about the size of this problem. For obvious reasons, the offence is private and has a high chance of avoiding detection. Criminologists argue that crime is influenced by the agent's judgement of morality. For example, it may be that a colonized citizen believes that the property laws are immoral since they are founded upon the appropriation of domestic property by the colonizing force. This is a defence often used by terrorists and political prisoners to justify their acts. With respect to illegal downloading the question of morality is opaque since the offence against the copyright holder is invisible and indirect. The separation of the offence from the copyright holder means that the offender often downloads in the belief that he or she is engaging in victimless crime (Wolfe et al. 2007).

Moral problems with respect to this issue are compounded if one examines the question of digital piracy from the perspective of an offender in the emerging and developing world. Not only is it the case that much digital entertainment software is beyond the average *per capita* income, but also multi-national corporations and the leading industrial nations are widely seen as imposing a cap on development by keeping wages low and extracting wealth. The *Sao Paulo Declaration* (1998), issued by the World Leisure and Recreation

Association and the *Charter for Leisure* (2000) approved by the World Leisure Board, are both committed to the global proselytizing of leisure and recreation values and the expansion of participation.

Article 3 of the *Sao Paulo Declaration* states:

> All governments and institutions should preserve and create barrier free environments e.g. cultural, technological, natural and built, where people have time, space, facilities and opportunity to express, share and celebrate leisure.

The internet represents one of the most cost-effective, ubiquitous technologies to achieve these ends that has ever been invented. Illegal downloading may be interpreted as an act that exploits the full potential of the system. Leisure professionals focus on conditions in the emerging and developing world with some interesting moral questions.

Another aspect of digital crime that has not been sufficiently widely examined by students of leisure is the proliferation of computer viruses. Harmer et al. (2002) estimate that over 55,000 separate computer viruses have been identified. A virus is a piece of malicious software that is created and exchanged with the intention of system disablement. They are aimed at disrupting business operations, banking transactions, military organization and airline schedules. In August 2003, the *SoBig* virus was estimated to have caused $30 billion in damage across the world (Balthorp et al. 2004). System disablement may be the aim of a hacker who holds a grudge against business, the military or society. But it is also a leisure pursuit for those who regard hacking as a challenge to their faculties and a means of outwitting the system.

Katz (1988) wrote convincingly of the pleasure and honour gained from beating the system and traced many acts of crime back to this source. Hacking belongs to the same category and is worthy of much greater consideration by students of leisure.

The aim of the revised framework of Leisure Studies is to alert students and researchers to the full range of breadth and dynamics of the field of force in which leisure practice is positioned and develops. The purpose is not to deny the proposition that individuals have choice. The prominence given to intentionality in leisure acts in Chapter 1 of the book is designed to situate subjective decisions in the dialectics of leisure forms and practice. The parallel emphasis assigned to emotional intelligence, emotional labour, social and economic positioning, and the categorization of leisure forms and practice as types of engagement with the problem of scarcity, are ways of relating individual practice to questions of inequality and power. *Atomized* views of leisure present the subjective intentions of the actor as the focal point of leisure practice. *Deterministic* views erase subjective intentionality by making practice the reflection of allocative mechanisms of class, gender, race, status and other structural agents. The revised SCCASMIL framework sketched out here seeks to focus thinking and research on the dialectics of the interface between subjective intentionality and structural influence.

3
ROADBLOCKS TO FREE TIME

Just as individuals are positioned by history in relation to scarce resources, so too are fields of study. For most of the twentieth century the Academy regarded Leisure Studies to be a peripheral field of study. The resources allocated to students in the field were scant. Originally, those who aspired to dedicate themselves to the investigation of leisure as a vocation were typically labelled as mavericks, oddballs or more commonly, simply insignificant academics (Tomlinson 2006). They battled against the widespread condescension that leisure is insignificant and the lofty liberal principle that what takes place in leisure is a matter for private conscience providing it does not interfere with the liberty of others. The students they attracted tended to have a nebulous interest in the use of free time and a generally heartfelt, but somewhat vague notion of social improvement through physical exercise, the cultivation of the mind, recreation or sport. It might have been that they devoted themselves to these activities in their spare time and were pitting their free time passions against guided study. Or it might have been that they regarded leisure and recreation as beacons of Western civilization that ought to be cherished and respected. Scarcely any entertained the prospect of a career in leisure, sport or recreation. There were good reasons for this.

Since the nineteenth century the history of organizing leisure forms and practice had been dominated by the philosophy of volunteering. After the 1880s, 'civilizing a rough' was a prominent motif in the rational recreation movement (Borzello 1987). Passing on the values of respectable society and improving the physical stock of labour as a reserve army for mobilization at times of war were regarded as the duty of the activist middle class. The organization of walks, scientific instruction, health and fitness, amateur sport, reading and art classes were praised as suitable for the volunteer spirit.

By the end of the nineteenth century in most Western nations, the state understood the relationship between leisure provision and improving the urban quality of life and crime control. But it stopped short at devising and implementing a holistic policy of leisure provision. There were many reasons for this. In the first place, rapid urban and industrial growth introduced new problems of overcrowding, disease and unrest in metropolitan centres. In developing progressive policies to remedy them, education, health, housing and welfare were judged to have precedence over the public purse.

Another major barrier to state intervention in leisure was the laissez-faire approach of the nineteenth-century state. Under the influence of liberal philosophers such as J.S. Mill and T.H. Green, the state was charged with the task of formulating and applying the law and maintaining social stability. With respect to leisure forms and practice, conduct was conditioned by the liberal principle that individuals may do what they like in their free time providing it does not interfere with the freedom of others. This principle was itself interpreted liberally by the state. Campaigns of rational recreation to root out alcohol dependence and vice, and to improve what we would call the work–life balance were tacitly supported by the state.

It wasn't until the late 1960s that leisure was recognized by the state to be a citizenship right (Coalter 2006a, 2006b). More funds were diverted into parks, recreation and leisure centres at this time. Leisure and recreation provision were advocated as instruments for the state to build the good citizen and the good society. As a result, the public sector in these areas expanded, with more jobs for leisure and recreation graduates and eventually, more demand for university-level training in these fields.

However, as we shall see in more detail later (pp. 133–59) in the 1980s the expansion in the public sector leisure market which followed was blocked by neo-liberal policies of individual and group responsibility for free time practice and competitive tendering which sought to out-source leisure provision from the state sector.

The work/life balance refers to cognition of multiple life demands on time and energy and the acceptance by employers that workers need to juggle responsibilities at home and the workplace. It involves the recognition of workers as parents and carers and a commitment to the designing work/life ratio to enhance citizenship. Employment strategies which are typically used to enhance the work/life balance are job sharing, working from home, sabbaticals, placements, maternity/paternity leave, employee assistance programmes, workplace facilities such as crèches and medical centres, regular appraisals, health screening, on-site exercise facilities or subsidised access to gyms. Underlying this is the proposition that better citizens are more productive workers (Clutterbuck 2003).

It is worth commenting on the singularity of the prolonged laissez-faire approach to the public provision of leisure, which extended well into the twentieth century. The 1880s are often referred to as the origins of the *interventionist state* (Hall et al. 1978); that is, a public orientation in which the state came to assume greater responsibility for regulating standards of public health, the educational curriculum, issues of family conflict, standards in the workplace and the regulation of the environment. Between the 1880s and the 1980s, Western European states expanded powers into many areas of private life, notably health, family relations and training for the employment market. Leisure and religion were perceived as the last redoubts of private conscience. It would not be correct to regard them as no-go areas for the state, for the use of leisure events to promote civil disobedience was met with force by the state (Donnelly 1986). But this was a residual capacity that was only exercised when leisure practice threatened or produced social friction. In other respects, the state might tell you what your children must learn at school; it might force you to seek counselling if you have trouble with your family; it might assume powers to remove and incarcerate members of the family and the community who are regarded as a danger to others; it might outlaw the cultivation of this or that crop in your garden, or issue a permit to indicate where you may and may not walk; but it drew the line at interfering in your free time (providing that it did not impede the freedom of others), or demanding what God you ought to follow. Public thought on leisure acknowledged private conscience as the cardinal principle governing the distribution of free time.

Cautionary Tales: Prohibition and Illegal Downloading

Wherever this cautious principle has been abandoned it is generally agreed to have ended in disaster. The most famous example is Prohibition. Between 1920 and 1933 US temperance groups were successful in introducing and applying Prohibition. This outlawed the sale, manufacture and transport of alcohol in the US. Most historians of leisure now see it as a blatant attempt by the state to colonize and direct private conscience and regulate leisure. It failed for two reasons.

Firstly, banning alcohol simply created a black market exploited by organized crime. Most historians of crime in America regard Prohibition to have been a God-send to the enlargement of Mafia power and wealth. The vast profits made during this period underwrote the Mafia's entry into legitimate business, such as legalized gambling, in the 1930s and 40s.

Secondly, the public rapidly dismissed Prohibition as an unacceptable intrusion into private conduct. The popular view of leisure practice in

America mirrored the cardinal principle of liberal thought; namely, that it is the right of individuals to act as they please so long as their actions do not interfere with the pleasure of others. If people choose to drink for pleasure despite the acknowledged health risks they should be free to do so, providing it does not result in behaviour that intrudes upon the freedom of others.

Sensitivity to state interference into matters of private conscience continues to be evident in the question of the distribution of leisure practice. Consider the current debate over the illegal downloading of copyrighted music, film, software and other types of intellectual property. Currently the recording industry in the US and the UK is involved in a crusade to banish illegal downloading of intellectual property. The Recording Industry Association of America (RIAA) reports that illegal downloading and piracy costs the global music industry $12.5 billion every year. The UK record industry trade body, the British Phonographic Industry (BPI) estimates that unauthorized downloading between 2004 and 2007 has cost the British recording industry £1.1 billion. Both organizations pursue a high profile, rolling programme of legal prosecution against unauthorized downloaders.

Yet there are widespread public concerns that the trade's legitimate concern to protect copyright produces unacceptable restraints upon the exchange of culture. The rights of copyright holders and the state to interfere with the private use of copyrighted material are implacably challenged by consumers.

The state has moved from a strategy of inflexible and punitive fines on illegal downloading to a half-way house which is more conciliatory to questions of private conscience. For example, a discussion document produced by the Department of Culture, Media and Sport (DCMS) and the Department for Business, Enterprise and Regulatory Reform (DBERR) issued in February 2008, contained proposals for extending policing powers to curtail unauthorized downloading. Under the lobbying proposals the BPI will gather evidence about people suspected of illegal downloading and present it to the relevant Internet Service Provider (ISP). The ISP will be required to send a warning notice to the person suspected of illegal downloading. Three warnings will result in account termination. The proposals transfer the responsibility for enforcing policing from the BPI to the service provider. Managers of ISP systems have always insisted that they are simply providing portals of information exchange and have resisted pleas to control content. The Internet Service Provider Association (ISPA) is the UK's trade association for the industry.

The ISPA has raised many legal difficulties in enforcing the proposals. What if the illegal downloader is freebasing on someone else's unsecured Wi-Fi connection? What if someone uses shared space such as an internet café or a university terminal? Or what if file sharers develop encryption and 'tunnelling' devices to avoid detection? More generally, do consumers want organizations like the BPI or the state to be given extended legal powers of surveillance to investigate line-use and issue allegations against users? Viewed from this perspective the proposals smack of the Big Brother state in which private life is routinely monitored for material that offends the powerful.

In the US the defence against file sharing has applied a different set of arguments having to do with defending the American way of life. In particular, file-sharing companies have sought support from the First Amendment; that is, 'Congress shall make no law respecting an establishment of religion, or prohibiting the free exercise thereof; or abridging the freedom of speech; or of the press; or the right of the people to assemble, and to petition the government for a redress of grievances.' Freedom of thought and free speech run very deep in the American psyche. Restricting the exchange of information and ideas is a form of censorship. Of course, the RIAA and BPI are not against the exchange of information or ideas. They are in favour of the sovereignty of copyright that provides for the authorized exchange of intellectual property to involve a monetary relationship. Yet for many downloaders it is by no means clear that the RIAA and BPI are entitled to claim jurisdiction of copyright after the point of sale. If I buy a CD I might be said to hold the warranty over how I choose to use the recording. I might copy it onto my iPod; or burn it onto a blank disc and give it to my daughter; or load it onto my website. These actions infringe copyright, but there is also a sense of common justice that proposes that when an item is purchased consumers have the right to use the material as they see fit. This line of argument identifies self-regulation as the preferred means of dealing with the problem of illicit downloading. This is tantamount to repeating the principle that private conscience is the best means of regulating free time behaviour.

In support of it, organizations like the ISPA point to the success of the Internet Watch Foundation (IWF) in the UK. This self-regulatory body, funded by the EU and the wider online industry, works in partnership with the Home Office, the Ministry of Justice and the DBERR to regulate the availability of potentially illegal internet content relating to images of child sexual abuse hosted in the UK and anywhere in the world; and the incitement of racial hatred content. The organization claims that less than 1% of potentially illegal content has been hosted in the UK since 2003, down from 19% in 1997 (http://www.iwf.org,uk/public). The main weapons of the IWF are not 'name and shame' campaigns or legal action. On the contrary, they seek to widen industry and popular awareness of responsible internet use to build trust between ISPs and end-users.

Leisure and Private Conscience

The sovereignty of private conscience is a seasoned principle in the European tradition of social and political thought reaching back to the

Ancient Greeks, and mediated through Christianity (Dumont 1986: 23). Modern society defines the community as a collection of free individuals. Each individual is viewed as the bearer of the common values that theoretically represent the greater whole. As such, free individuals recognize moral restraints on their behaviour that derive from their voluntary membership of the community. If I play my iPod too loudly on a bus or train I accept that you have the right to tell me that I am interfering with your public space. If you become rowdy in a bar or pub, I expect you to acknowledge my complaint that this behaviour is unacceptable because it conflicts with my privacy. In other words, the recognition that belonging to a community carries certain duties and responsibilities is a condition of feeling part of, and being recognized by, the group. So individual liberty is built upon the notion of reciprocal constraints on behaviour that we observe as a voluntary condition of being free men and women (Mcfarlane 1978, 1993).

In the late nineteenth and twentieth centuries the interventionist state emerged as the secular guarantor of these restraints. The state regulated private life through a combination of three devices. *Licensing*, which imposes financial requirements and time limits upon participation in leisure forms that are judged to be against the public interest if taken to excess. *Policing*, that applies the law made by representative bodies to keep the peace and guarantee the sovereignty of private conscience providing it does not infringe the liberty of others. *Persuasion*, that applies argument and example to tip the leisure choices of individuals and groups into approved directions.

From the standpoint of the SCCA framework, the regulation of leisure involves a simple causal relationship in which the state enjoins private conscience to conform to public priorities by a combination of the law, licensing, policing and persuasion. For example, the legislation on Prohibition in the US defined the consumption of alcohol as inciting and expanding vice. A straightforward and direct relationship is assumed between what the provisions of the law and personal practice. As we saw above, Prohibition involved some pretty ropey assumptions about personal psychology and group adaptation. Many individuals held the law to constitute an unacceptable incursion into the realm of private conscience. In any case, informal drinking cultures and gang supply chains became so adept that they effectively neutralized the enforcement of the law. The SCCA framework operates with a limited understanding of the centrality of emotional intelligence and emotional labour in conveying competence and credibility.

The SCASSMIL approach to leisure forms and practice is far more inclusive in its terms of reference. At the psychological and social level, it makes provision for illicit behaviour to get around legal regulations by proposing that subjective choice is always and already positioned in relation to scarcity. This positioning is a precondition of choice in that it allocates knowledge and power to individuals and therefore allows for intentional leisure behaviour to occur. This behaviour may reproduce the distribution of scarcity or it may resist it. But it is always a precondition of intentional action. In the case of Prohibition, emotional intelligence and emotional labour adapted to the new regulations over leisure forms and practice by redefining the state as an unacceptable burden on scarcity. The wants of consumers of alcohol confronted a universal law that made abundant provision for eradicating the practice from every corner of society. However, because the provisions of the law were widely regarded to be contrary to the credible wants of competent citizens, practice and leisure forms were redefined to occur in subterranean settings. In effect the law was seen to be an ass, so that ways around the law were widely regarded as valid.

From the perspective of the SCASSMIL approach the relationship between state regulation and private conscience is far more nuanced and many-sided than is allowed for in the SCCA framework. If a given leisure form or practice is perceived by individuals and groups to possess validity, they will find ways of protecting and expanding it over and beyond the restrictions of the state. In such circumstances, leisure ceases to be a matter of play. Crucially, it becomes *representative*. Slowly, individuals grow conscious of what leisure means as a statement of character in the sight of others and how it positions them in relation to access to scarce resources in general. In this way leisure can have a political significance in 'speaking' for moral codes and lifestyle values that the state wishes to suppress.

If one turns to another historical example – leisure in puritan society – one can see more clearly how emotional intelligence and emotional labour are used to defend and expand leisure forms that are stigmatized by the community. Historical analysis of leisure forms and activities in puritan society demonstrates that the allocation of resources to practices that did not enlarge God's presence was regularly dismissed, belittled and oppressed. Daniels' (1995: 16–17) discussion of leisure and recreation in colonial New England recounts influential tracts of the day that praised 'sober mirth' and inveighed against the activities of the 'frolic colt'. Benjamin Colman's (1707) work *The Government and Improvement of Mirth, According to the Laws of Christianity, in Three Sermons* elaborated a list of what colonial New Englanders judged to be valid and invalid forms of leisure and recreation. Daniels (1995: 17–18) quotes him at length: 'Sober mirth' is charming and graceful so long as it is 'innocent'. Leisure and recreation should 'do no injury to God or our neighbour' or 'transgress society, holiness or charity'. Colman warned against the social dangers of 'carnal mirth' and 'licentious mirth'. This has no truck with 'innocence', 'neighbourly love' or 'sobriety'. It is the part played by the 'merry drunkard' the 'ill timed' mirth-maker, the 'idler'. These perturb the stability of society because, as Colman puts it, 'sensuous lusts love company; men can't game and drink and be lewd and laugh alone' (quoted in Daniels 1995: 19).

Clearly then, in puritan society leisure was subject to the judgement of the community, generally embodied in the figures of the temporal and spiritual leaders who governed religious, economic, social and political life. Just as clearly, puritan leisure was the basis for turning banned and stigmatized forms and practices into *causes célèbres*. The fact that a good deal of leisure takes the shape of a play form means that free time practice carries the capacity to go beyond legal regulations by dramatizing their arbitrary or absurd nature.

The anthropologist Victor Turner (1982) argues that there is a duality of freedom in leisure forms and practices that makes a good deal of leisure practice inherently political since it carries ludic or experimental qualities with respect to the concept of normative order. In Turner's (1982: 37) words, leisure is:

> 1) *freedom to enter*, even to generate new symbolic worlds of entertainment, sports, games, diversions of all kinds. It is furthermore, 2) *freedom to* transcend social structural limitations, freedom to play ... with ideas, with fantasies, with words, with social relationships [emphasis in original].

Leisure is therefore inherently paradoxical. It is the primary normative institution in society popularly associated with freedom and choice. In leisure we develop the common practices that exploit and develop the structural conditions of our community, race, ethnicity and nation. However, in being a normative institution which is intrinsically organized around freedom it permits individuals and groups to enter into and generate relationships that resist, challenge and transcend normative structure.

Elsewhere, Turner (1974) uses the term *anti-structure* to refer to the dissolution of normative social structure, with its role-sets, statuses, jural rights and duties etc. In the Prohibition era, s*peakeasies* were informal leisure institutions that overturned the rules of the Prohibition lobby by subjecting them to ludic discipline. Leisure is particularly effective in this regard because it uses the vernacular of play to compromise the absurd and arbitrary nature of structural rules. The anti-war demonstrators who marched on the Pentagon in 1967 did not attack the troopers who opposed them, they put flowers in their guns. Similarly, the G8 anti-capitalist and Reclaim the Streets protests mainly used ludic forms to expose the authorities, such as organizing a game of cricket in Parliament Square, throwing flour or fruit at politicians or dressing up in outfits of clowns, pranksters or tricksters.

The Cultural Turn, Postmodernism and Leisure

With hindsight, Turner's ideas about anti-structures and ludic discipline were harbingers of a much wider shift in politics, theory and culture that has come to be known as the cultural turn. This is a movement in ideas and lifestyle that began in the late 1970s and became fully fledged in the mid 1980s. At its heart is the proposition that structural rules are culturally conditioned. By the mid twentieth century structuralism had successfully posited the arbitrary relationship between the signifier and the sign.[1] In doing so, it undermined old nineteenth-century and early twentieth-century notions of transcendental or privileged meaning. These ideas led to the crackpot realism of Hitler, the atom bomb and the arms race.[2] Poststructuralism took over this vein of thought by arguing that all meaning is multiple so that to prioritize one meaning over another is an act of violence, since it denies difference and pre-empts empathy. The cultural turn involved analysing everything as culturally coded and meaning as something that is represented rather than real.

This had important implications for politics and lifestyle. In the nineteenth and twentieth centuries Marxism argued that the paramount vocabulary of social reality reflected the ideology of the ruling class. In every epoch the ruling ideas are the ideas of the ruling class. The first wave feminists followed a similar line of reasoning in their attack on patriarchy. Women lived in a world dominated by the ideas and emotional preferences of men. In common with other forms of nineteenth- and twentieth-century thought, Marxism and feminism criticized ruling power structures in order to replace them with transcendental systems of liberation, equality and justice.

Under the ludic discipline of the cultural turn, every transcendental system was understood to eventually impose limits. The necessity to be liberated was in its own way a form of authoritarianism, since by definition, it negated other ways of being. Structure always begets anti-structure. There is no zero point to discovering difference or Otherness, because embodiment, emplacement, nation, race and locality are all understood to be culturally coded, representations of reality. Although it was unusually receptive to movement and change, postmodernism provided the anchor for many of these arguments. It rejected the notion of grand narratives in history such as progress, nation and even science. Identity was portrayed as a violent method of denying difference and the deferral of meaning. This was often portrayed as the return of Nietzschean nihilism. In fact postmodernists recognized a new solidarity around the acknowledgement that the central categories of modernist thought are deeply authoritarian, the multiplicity of meaning and respect for difference. In aesthetics and lifestyle this translated into a new interest in forms of architecture, fashion and bodily adornment that seized upon, and expressed, hybridity and difference. So middle-class Westerners who adorned their bodies with clothes, jewellery and piercings that made reference to the emerging and developing world and/or the unemployed and poor became a sort of living tableaux of the postmodern *mentalité*.

The interest in leisure benefited enormously from the cultural turn and postmodernism. If everything is culturally coded and meaning is arbitrary, why work? Leisure and play became the new means of culturally savvy self-expression. It was no longer necessary to insist on strong divisions between the worlds of work and leisure. The meaning of each merged into the other, so that work could be a kind of play and leisure a kind of work. This was very different from the 1970s when the leisure society thesis argued that leisure would replace work as the central life value. The cultural turn and postmodernism abolished transcendental meaning, so the idea of a central life value possessed no purchase. Expression became focused on tangible, measurable criteria. In terms of lifestyle values, because there is no falling back on collectivity, what you see is what you get. So embodiment and consumerism become radicalized. Cash-rich Westerners registered difference through piercing, decorative gender bending, and wearing *Benetton* or *FCUK*. Benetton were the pioneers in so-called shock advertising, which used images of taboo subjects like AIDS patients, a duck covered in oil, a soldier holding a human bone and dying people to make a point about the stigmatization of illness, global pollution, international violence and the sanitization of everyday life. Shock advertising is used by what I call 'neat' capitalist corporations to build the brand by associating branding with wider social movements of racial awareness, gender inequality, anti-violence and responsible environmentalism. In Chapter 8 I discuss how neat capitalist corporations have colonized many forms of leisure.

However, there are big problems with subjecting everything to ludic discipline. To hold that the views on Creation of Sayyid Qutb, one of the chief intellectual architects of the revival of Islamic fundamentalism, are superior to Darwin's theory of evolution is more than a matter of cultural relativism.[3] It raises enormous issues about objectivity and truth. The cultural turn and postmodernism imply that all of these issues can be ultimately reduced to questions of cultural coding and representation. Regardless of whether you are an Islamic fundamentalist, a dyed-in-the-wool Darwinian or a ludic postmodernist, the earth really does go round the sun and smoking really does correlate with cancer. The cultural turn and postmodernism filled a space that had been vacated when a certain kind of politics based upon the polarization between Left and Right was no longer tenable, and when globalization sliced through age-old assumptions about a variety of autonomies relating to individual choice, political theory and the nation. In addition, if one approaches them from the perspective of emotional intelligence and emotional labour, postmodernism and the cultural turn may be plausibly analysed as ways of expressing competence and credibility in an era when many of the certainties associated with the Enlightenment and modernity seemed up for grabs. Leisure forms and practice were caught up in this by becoming marked with the insignia of difference and hybridity. Through embodiment, consumerism and related areas of leisure choice, individuals and groups could say something about their relationship to truth, authority and power.

However, even at its height, the influence of the cultural turn and postmodernism did not dissolve the question of private conscience. People who could accept that meanings are multiple, that difference and deferring are everywhere, would still go to Church on Sunday or offer *Salat* at the mosque. One could accept the omnipresence of cultural coding and still be emotionally attached to the idea of individual freedom. These examples of private belief were not stray tufts resisting the onslaught of first science and then the cultural turn and postmodernism. They were ramparts of traditional thought bringing together hundreds of millions of people, who opposed the proposition that all forms of structure are subject to ludic discipline. Religious conscience is such an important buttress for many forms of private conscience, and such a major influence over leisure practice, that it merits consideration in its own right.

Leisure and Religious Conscience

The academic study of leisure, which institutionally speaking, is a product of the second half of the twentieth century, is outwardly about the free decisions of men and women who are themselves civilly distinguished from all preceding societies by reason of the achievement of secular reason and universal freedom (de Grazia 1962). However, one can object to these notions of secular reason and universal freedom and leisure on the grounds that they neglect to engage with one of the most obvious features of contemporary society, which is the persistence of religious belief. In respect of the West, it is frequently stated in the literature that we live in secular societies in which organized religion is on the wane. Yet data from the 2001 Census in the UK gave reason to propose that it would be precipitate to discount religious belief as a significant factor in leisure choice and participation.

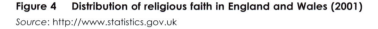

		%
Christian	36,000,000	77.7
No Religion	7,733,032	16.1
Muslim	918,000	3.2
Hindu	467,000	1.2
Sikh	301,000	0.7
Jews	252,000	0.5
Buddhist	144,093 0.3	

Figure 4   Distribution of religious faith in England and Wales (2001)
Source: http://www.statistics.gov.uk

The figures indicate that 7 out of 10 people describe themselves as 'Christians'.

Of course, it is one thing to describe yourself as Christian and another to consistently comply with the edicts of Christianity. I may register myself as belonging to the Church of England, yet I might not practise Sunday observance and omit to follow the teachings of the Church on divorce, family life, codes of address, and much else besides. Yet the Church has a direct influence upon me through its relationship with the history of the country, the code of manners and English law. It is not a matter of me following the article of religious ordinance or respecting the relationship between the history of this ordinance and the letter of the law. It is a question of being positioned and enwrapped in a culture in which the traces of Christian religious ordinance permeate the laws and conventions of the day. Nor does this end the matter. For it implies that the influence of organized religion is apparent only in the secular revisions and formulations of law and respectable society. This ignores the condition of large sections of the population in Western society for whom traditional organized religion remains a coherent, vital entity in the construction of lifestyle, work relations and leisure practice.

For devout believers in religious faith observance carries special behavioural demands and requirements of character that directly influence leisure choice and participation. As an example, consider Sharia. This is the body of Islamic religious law that 3.2% of the population of England and Wales follow and 0.5% of the population in the US. Based upon the *Qu'ran* (the religious text of Islam), *hadith* (the sayings and doings of Mohammed) and *ijma* (consensus), it is more than a system of criminal justice. It is respected as 'the way' or 'the path' governing work, family, leisure and recreation by its followers. It offers external guidance to aspects of everyday life dealing with economics, politics, banking, contract law, the use of stimulants, sexuality and social issues. With respect to leisure forms and practice, the influence of Sharia law divides into four main categories of behaviour:

1) Dietary

   Sharia prohibits the consumption of swine and intoxicants. It bans the slaughtering of an animal in any other way than the prescribed manner of *tazkiyah* (cleansing), by invoking Allah's name and cutting the throat of the animal to drain its blood.

2) Dress Codes

   Women are required to cover all of their bodies except their face and hands. Men have a more relaxed dress code. They are required to cover their body from knee to waist. Sharia law recommends that women wear the *Hijab* (headscarf) so as to preserve modesty and avoid unnecessary attention from people who wish to flatter, display envy, exhibit attraction or make sexual overtures.

3) Marriage and Divorce

   The *Qu'ran* mentions two types of marriage: *nikah* and *nikah mu'tah*. The first aims to be lifelong. Under its provision the couple inherits from each other. Men can marry up to four wives, but only if they are treated equally. *Nikah mu'tah* is *haraam* (forbidden) by Sunni Muslims. It means 'marriage for pleasure', meaning a union with a predetermined point of termination. Traditionally the couple do not inherit from each other and the male is not responsible for the economic welfare of the woman. A woman who marries under *Nikah mu'tah* is not considered as one of the four wives recognized under *Nikah*.

4) Penalties

   Penalities are known as *Hadd* offences. They are not universally adopted in Islamic countries. Some nations, such as Saudi Arabia, claim to live under pure sharia law and implement *Hadd* offences in a consistent, comprehensive fashion. In other nations, such as Pakistan, the penalties are not enforced. Most Middle Eastern countries, including Jordan, Egypt, Lebanon and Syria have not adopted *Hadd*. The *Qu'ran, hadith* and *ijma* lay down a series of prohibitions and punishments in respect of unlawful sexual intercourse (outside marriage); false accusations of sexual intercourse; the drinking of alcohol; theft and highway robbery. For example, theft is punished by imprisonment or amputation of hands and feet depending upon the rate of repeated crime. The punishment only applies to those declared adult and sane. It is not imposed if the thief repents.

   The *hadith* prescribes stoning to death as the penalty for married men and women who commit adultery. For unmarried men and women the punishment set down in the *Qu'ran* and *hadith* is 100 lashes.

Muslims comply with Sharia according to their personal conscience. Over 50 countries are members of the Organization of the Islamic Conference and their inhabitants observe some form of compliance with the law.

		%
Christian	159,030,000	76.5
Non Religious	13,116,000	13.2
Judaism	2,831,000	1.3
Muslim	1,104,000	0.5
Buddhism	1,082,000	0.5
Hinduism	766,000	0.4
Unitarian	629,000	0.3
Wiccan/Pagan	307,000	0.1
Spiritualist	116,000	0.05
Native American	103,000	0.05

Figure 5   Distribution of religious faith in the US (2001)

Source: American Religious Identity Survey (ARIS) http://www.gc.cuny.edu/faculty/ research

In 2008, Rowan Williams, the Archbishop of Canterbury, incurred heated media attention for arguing that the adoption of some aspects of Sharia law in the UK is 'unavoidable'. The Archbishop was castigated for being over-permissive and insensitive to followers of deeply rooted national traditions of belief, who felt beleaguered by Sharia doctrines.

There is no doubt that Sharia law is a bone of contention not only between Muslim and Christian communities but within differentiated layers of Muslim life. Fundamentalists regard it as the sanctified way of life laid down by the Prophet. They point to the prevalence of rape, teenage pregnancy, gang violence, alcoholism and drug addiction in the West as evidence of the moral laxity and nihilism engendered by permissive values. If this is what more leisure brings, most fundamentalists respond with scorn. In contrast, Western liberals denounce Sharia as a reactionary philosophy that fails to respect difference and tolerate non-conformity. With the reaction against puritan values in the West, matters of diet, grooming, dress, marriage, divorce and free time behaviour are held to belong to the sphere of private conscience. As we have already seen, there is a strong taboo against religion or the state interfering with the distribution of free time. Resistance against Sharia law is also evident among Muslims. Many find it too severe, too judgemental, with respect to the ambivalence and contradictions of modern life. At the same time they balk at siding with the blanket condemnation made by many Western liberals.

Be that as it may, the example demonstrates that religious belief continues to be a force in secular society. If I had more space I might go into the detail of how Catholic, Methodist, Unitarian and other types of religious belief system set down boundaries for the allocation of resources in free time activity and forms of practice. These have to do with questions of freedom of expression, rights of assembly and freedom of action. In the Catholic faith something as simple and straightforward as a divorced woman having sexual relations with a single man is an object of surveillance and censure by the religious community. A woman in this position cannot just act as she pleases. Formally, she must seek counsel from the parish priest or respected elders in the community. To non-believers this seems self-righteous and antiquated. Just as being lectured to about what to wear, what to drink and what to say in public, especially when in the company of people from another faith, is frequently viewed to be both intimidating and intrusive. However, it is unwise to think that this is universally the case. After all, in both the UK and the US non-believers are, by some distance, in the minority. The close-knit moral communities of Benjamin Colman's day may have receded and been forced into retrenchment by the rise of secular permissive values, but they are far from being extinct. Among minority ethnic communities and in rural areas, their influence is transparent. The student of leisure would do well to be cognizant of them so as to avoid heedless generalization about the universality of achieved freedom in the West.

Regulation, Positioning and Leisure

The case of religion provides a clear example of a causal relationship between a belief system and the constitution of private conscience. It is only one, particularly transparent, kind of regulation that derives from the world of ideas rather than the material level of economic inequality. Others might take the form of racial prejudice, subcultural intolerance, sexual exclusion or nationalist superiority. All of these examples position knowledge and power in relation to scarcity and influence the propensity for this or that type of intentional behaviour. When we state that, in Western society, the field for the academic study of leisure comprises what free men and women do in their free time we must add the caveat that the Western idea of freedom is partly rhetorical. Its limits may be tested in courts and debated in philosophy. But it has limits.

The academic study of leisure has recognized the existence of limits. Studies of class and leisure have forcefully demonstrated that choice and practice in free time are conditioned by inequality (Clarke and Critcher 1985). Feminist approaches have elucidated the topic of gender, embodiment and leisure by demonstrating the position of women as property in leisure forms and practice (Henderson et al. 1996; Wearing 1998). The contribution of figurational sociology has identified the role of 'thresholds of embarrassment' and standards of 'repugnance' which are formulated in the course of the civilizing process and which regulate personal conduct (Elias and Dunning 1986). Poststructuralist approaches have drawn on the work of Michel Foucault to highlight the significance of power, knowledge and discourse in conditioning leisure forms and practice (Aitchison 2003). These writings have contributed to the development of a perspective on leisure which acknowledges that freedom carries with it constraint and that constraint implies social and economic forces which position individual and group behaviour. I can pursue leisure activities that fulfil the dictate of my private conscience. But my private conscience is a thing that is closely tied-up with the values of my family, community, education and work-group. It reflects the power divisions and interests thereof. My private conscience may reinforce the values of the community, in which case my leisure practice is that of a model citizen. Conversely, I may dissent from the values of my community and adhere to the values of some subculture or counter-culture located as an anti-structure of dissent and resistance. Acts of resistance in leisure do not necessarily sever the ties between private conscience and the values of the community. On the contrary, they make private conscience an issue in that I have to justify why I choose non-conformity or resistance in my free time in settings where there is a disposition to tolerate and confirm my leisure trajectory of illicit behaviour.

This brings us to the nub of the matter with respect to leisure and private conscience. Every man and woman conforms to what Durkheim (1893) described as the *homo duplex* model of humankind. In the words of Durkheim (1893: 129–30):

> There are in each of us, as we have said, two consciences: one which, consequently, is not oneself, but society living and acting within us; the other, on the contrary, represents that in us which is personal and distinct, that which makes us an individual … We cannot, at one and the same time, develop ourselves in two opposite senses. If we have a lively desire to think for ourselves, we cannot be strongly inclined to think and act as others do. If our ideal is to present a singular and personal appearance, we do not want to resemble everybody else. Moreover, at the moment when this solidarity exercises its force, our personality vanishes, as our definition permits us to say, for we are no longer ourselves, but the collective life.

Leisure is generally regarded to be voluntary behaviour. In the work of de Grazia (1962) it is portrayed as freely chosen activity, independent from the constraints that govern the other areas of everyday life. But what is legitimate voluntary behaviour with respect to my private conscience may conflict with the normative voluntary behaviour that is labelled as legitimate by the state. The state is not a neutral body. Historically and operationally it reflects the influence of social and political interests. The clash and contradiction of these interests precedes the formation of the state and influences the boundaries of normative voluntary conduct. By the term *normative voluntary behaviour* I mean the activities and forms that are sanctioned by society as producing personal and social benefits. The mechanisms through which sanctioning occurs are called *institutions of normative* coercion. Examples include the family, schools, voluntary associations and the various branches of the state apparatus such as the judiciary, the police, social work and so on. The term coercion is used because the range of activities and forms in which individuals engage is potentially infinite. They are no more immutable than the appetite for pleasure and life satisfaction in humans is immutable. Normative institutions impose boundaries on voluntary action and choice by privileging some types of activity and forms of voluntary behaviour as beneficial. If we follow the *homo duplex* model consistently, every choice of voluntary behaviour that I make pits my private conscience against the boundaries delineated by the normative institutions of coercion. I may elect to follow a leisure activity that reproduces these boundaries. Or I may dismiss them as arbitrary or intolerable. These boundaries regulate leisure behaviour, but they are fuzzy.

For example, consider one of the basic human drives: sex. So ubiquitous, so insistent, it is no wonder that a good deal of resources in leisure are devoted to sex. Blue movies, pornographic DVDs, gentlemen's clubs, brothels, massage parlours, adult magazines, adult reality TV shows, all belong to this category. Society and the state are in favour of consensual sex providing that it involves partners who are not bound by the moral constraints of marriage. A single man might chose to devote his leisure time to having as much sex as possible. If he elects to devote himself to this path of activity, he is very likely to incur the wrath of some feminists, who will regard his choice as irresponsible and exploitative. He may respond to this by only having sex with prostitutes since, outwardly at least, there is consent from the prostitute to be exploited. In the UK, it is not illegal to pay for sex, or to receive money for it. However, many of the activities associated with it such as soliciting, kerb-crawling, pimping and keeping a brothel are against the law. So long as he does not engage in kerb crawling he will not run foul of the law in electing to spend his leisure in the company of prostitutes.

Of course, there are many moral arguments that can be directed against his leisure choice. In treating women as property he is consolidating patriarchy that positions women as objects of male power. He is supporting a section of the black economy in which sex workers possess no employment rights and are at risk. His choice raises the difficult question of whether it is acceptable to consider prostitution as leisure. From the perspective of some males it is clearly a free time option and a significant one at that. There are no reliable official statistics. However, based on EUROPAP regional reports, it is estimated that currently 80,000 people work as sex workers in the UK (out of a population of 60 million); in Germany (population 80 million) there are 300,000 sex workers; and in Italy (population 58 million) there are 60,000 (http://www.people.ex.ac.uk). Brewer et al. (2000) estimate that 23 out of every 100,000 people in the US are sex workers. These workers are overwhelmingly female and their clients are male. There is an argument that prostitution is not about choice but about social pathology. The argument is strengthened by the well-documented preponderance of narcotic and alcohol dependence among sex workers and the organized violence used by pimps and brothel keepers to force some women into sex work. To describe sex work as a social pathology is moralistic. To the extent that it portrays sex workers simplistically as victims and male clients as aggressive agents it misses some of the key features of the industry, such as the voluntary choice of some women to engage in sex work in preference to other occupations and the friendship networks that build up between sex workers and clients. Research by Phoenix and Oerton (2005) and Campbell and O'Neill (2006) addresses the connection between performance and prostitution. This is a complicated issue. A judicious approach to the subject of the experience of sex workers and their clients must seek to avoid making either sweeping moralistic or permissive generalizations. The research cited suggests that while civil justice may be offended by the practice of prostitution, sex work is often compatible with social inclusion and female empowerment.

The *homo duplex* model helps us to think of this in more accurate ways. However, Durkheim's reference to 'two consciences' is misleading since it implies that our conscience and that of society are stable and uniform. By picturing our sense of self as a product of self-organizing mutuality and reciprocity a different take on identity emerges. By being positioned in relation to scarcity through historical circumstance we achieve a sense of personal direction and worth. But this is not the result of an act of *seigneurial* self-determination. It is a flexible, mobile phenomenon, which changes in relation to different social settings. In leisure practice we encounter settings that are generally more relaxed than work. In functioning in them we use different resources and facets which are not so much drawn out of the reserves in our personality, but which arise from positioning and being positioned in social settings in which a different regime of tolerance to mutuality and reciprocity applies.

The question of *homo duplex* in leisure practice helps us to pinpoint the various layers that are relevant in the academic study of leisure. To begin with, the study of leisure is simply about the trajectory of external behaviour in a given location. This might be called *location practice*. A good deal of the resources devoted to the academic study of leisure focus on location practice. Experimental psychologists and sociologists of empirical leisure may tell us how many people go to the local gym more than three times a week, and the physiological and social functions that gym-work produces. They may tell us what correlations exist between white water rafting and income, education and age. The academic journals of leisure are overwhelmingly dominated by questions of quantitative analysis and they are of particular interest to state funding organizations seeking hard data to support leisure policy. They are not enough.

The *Methodenstreit* Debate and Leisure

Quantitative analysis has its place in the academic study of leisure. But it cannot enter the minds of people engaged in leisure practice or see the world through their eyes. In German sociology there was a long and famous debate between those who believed that the methods of the natural sciences (*Naturwissenschaften*) are sufficient to understand the human life-world (*Lebenswelt*), and those who argue that these methods cannot take us beyond an understanding of external causality in behaviour and argue for the development of human methods (*Geisteswissenschaften*) that are directed to elucidating the experience, motivation and context of behaviour. This became known as the so-called *Methodenstreit* debate involving philosophers such as Wilhelm Windelband, Wilhelm Dilthey and Heinrich Rickert. It divided between those who believed that natural science is 'nomotheitic' because it is concerned with the analysis of external causal relations that supports the development of law-like statements, and social science is 'ideographic' because it is concerned with the unique, non-repeatable aspects of behaviour. The nomotheitic method is generalizing because it involves the steady accretion of facts to build up a coherent world-view. In contrast, the ideographic method is anti-generalizing, since it reveals the diversity and variety of world-views and assumes that views are contingent and subject to change. Schutz (1962) later made the distinction that the objects of the social sciences are different from the objects of the natural sciences in that the former deal with sentient beings who attribute meaning to the physical and social context in which they are located.

In turn, this raises the issue of the place of values and facts in the analysis of human relations. If we use the nomotheitic perspective to examine how people use their free time we will focus on the common, external, causally based trajectories of leisure behaviour. From the standpoint of those wedded to ideographic method, the nomotheitic perspective is objectionable on two counts.

Firstly, it confuses what is most common with the dominant perspective in a human group. I might associate leisure with mobility, but this is because I belong to the group that has sufficient disposable income to exercise meaningful choice in my free time behaviour. Because I have a car, take regular trips by aeroplane, surf the net daily and have a mobile phone, it does not mean that my leisure lifestyle is applicable globally. The World Bank defines poverty as living on an income of below $2 per day. In 2001 it was estimated that 1.1 billion people lived below $1 per day and 2.7 lived below $2 per day (http://web.worldbank.og). The population of the world is estimated to currently be about 6.5 billion (https://www.cia.gov/library/publications). For the population who live in poverty, the leisure lifestyle that we take as either normal or achievable in the affluent West literally belongs to another world.

Secondly, in taking what is external as its object of enquiry, nomotheitic method glosses over the subterranean, the hidden, the various leisure practices that are disguised either because they are illegal or because they are situated on the edge between licit and illicit behaviour (Lyng 2004). Externally, you may appear to be a well-adjusted individual, who enjoys healthy, outdoor leisure activities that reproduce what most people take to be the central values of society. But this might hide an inner world or a world that is lived behind closed doors in which the central values of society are resisted or opposed. Private conscience may apply to this world, but it is aware of its location on the edge of boundaries and social rules. Therefore, it adopts a strategic attitude to disclosure. It employs mutuality and reciprocity but it does so with discernment and judgement. In leisure we enter a different regime of mutuality and reciprocity, but it is still a regime organized around boundaries and limits. The old idea that leisure is freely chosen time or time used without the constraints of everyday life, which was made by Pieper (1952), de Grazia (1962) and others was a ladder that enabled us to look at leisure seriously in a social context in which work was deemed to be the central life interest. But it is a ladder that we must now kick away because it produces a false view of leisure as pure voluntarism. This is an enticing cul-de-sac in which many commentators of leisure have been trapped for decades. In leisure we are not *free*. It is more accurate to propose that in leisure we are differently *positioned*.

The Recreational Use of Drugs

Consider the case of the recreational use of illegal drugs. I may choose to spend part of my free time taking cocaine or heroin. We know that significant numbers of people make this choice every day. In a society as complex as ours, in which there are many veils of appearance and layers of privacy, we can never be really certain of the numbers who regularly take cocaine and heroin for recreational purposes. Notwithstanding this, the specialist organizations that investigate the recreational use of illegal drugs maintain that they have a good hunch of the extent of the practice. In the UK the Centre for Drug Misuse Research (http://www.gla.ac.uk/druguse) estimates that there are 340,000 regular users of cocaine and heroin. To help visualize what this figure means, one might observe that this is roughly equivalent to the population of a town the size of Norwich in East Anglia. Between 2004–6 the figure increased by 30%. In the US, the National Survey of Drug Use and Health (NSDUH 2004) reported that 1.4% of the population has tried heroin and 14.4% cocaine.

Turning to the use of marijuana, it is estimated that over 50% of the US population between 18 and 58 has used the drug (NSDUH 2004). In the UK the British Crime Survey (HMSO 2008) reported that 1,357,000 of 16- to 24-year-olds used marijuana. This constitutes 21% of the age group, compared with a peak of 28% in 2000. The potent form of 'skunk' cannabis now accounts for 70% of the British market. This compares with 15% in 2002 and has been driven by the growth of 'cannabis factories' run by organized criminal gangs, many of whom are Vietnamese. Possession of small amounts of cannabis ceased to be an arrestable offence in the UK in 2001. However, it is still subject to confiscation. In the US it remains illegal to possess, buy, sell or cultivate marijuana, although 12 states have introduced a measure of decriminalization to permit the drug to be used for medical purposes. The case of the recreational use of illegal drugs demonstrates the problems involved in legislating for and policing private leisure activities.

The decision to use illegal drugs for recreation may appear to be solely a matter of private conscience. In fact it is heavily influenced by peer group pressures and has clear correlations with social and economic factors. Illicit drug use is associated with risk taking, neuroticism, having a higher educational qualification, being single, being unemployed, smoking, heavy alcohol consumption and living in a more affluent area (Wadsworth et al. 2004). There is considerable evidence to suggest that 'sensible' illicit drug use has been de-stigmatized in many social circles and is not an object of censure in some recreational groups (Parker et al. 2002). Williams and Parker (2001) argue that recreational drug use is compatible with otherwise conforming personalities. Their research questions the stereotype of the drug user as belonging to a non-conformist stratum with polarized or oppositional values. The drug user understands Durkheim's *homo duplex* distinction between two consciences. But the presentation of illicit behaviour is coded and represented to avoid incurring negative social reactions. Drug users adopt a *strategic* attitude to their consumption of illegal substances. It is a matter of reading recreational settings and anticipating social reactions to determine the tolerance to illicit practice. We think of addictive personalities as helplessly caught in the grip of this or that habit. In fact, the research of Parker et al. (2002) discovered considerable discretion and taste in drug use. Various shielding methods and blocking devices are employed to disguise illicit behaviour from detection and censure. Underlying them is a moral distinction between what is right for the individual and the performative culture that is required by society. Large numbers of illicit drug users present a public face of having leisure activities and interests that are 'normal'. Compatible with this is covert practice in the recreational use of illegal substances.

In order to understand the mental and moral elements at play in people's leisure here, we must turn briefly to the contribution of cultural criminology. This is a fairly new approach to the study of deviance that combines elements of Cultural Studies with Criminology (Ferrell and Sanders 1995; Presdee 2000). Cultural forms, including types of leisure, are studied as practices of resistance and opposition against dominant social interests. Through the development of leisure lifestyle, individuals and groups exchange and reproduce social values that are not encouraged or licensed by the institutions of normative coercion. The cornerstone of this perspective is that to understand criminal behaviour a distinction must be made between the act and the social reaction to the act. If I take skunk marijuana I am breaking the law. If I take skunk among habituees who use it as a regular leisure resource, I am living *outside the law*. Within my circle of habituees I am occupying space and engaging in practice that is *legitimate* in the eyes of the group.

The main lesson of cultural criminology is that everything turns on the context and social reaction to the act. Crime does not exist in the act itself. The attribution of crime is the result of social and cultural processes that invest the act with a criminal quality. Illicit leisure acts have no intrinsic meaning. The taking of skunk marijuana only becomes a crime when it is detected. It is only *detected* if those who observe the practice do so as investigators or citizens acting in the name of the law. If I locate my use of skunk marijuana in social circles in which nobody regards himself or herself to be an investigator or citizen acting in the name of the law, I am not subject to the risk of detection since the leisure practice in which I engage is recognized as a sign of belonging. Social life contains countless semi-visible and subterranean spaces in which leisure activities resist and oppose the normative order. Nor is it a question of 'them and us'. Individuals are perfectly able to hold down a good job, make a contribution to the community as well as regularly engage in forms of leisure practice that are classified as illegal.

The criminalization of leisure practice is a corollary of the expansion of the interventionist state. Play forms organized around the use of drugs, animal sports, graffiti, hoax emergency service calls, photocopying and downloading copyright material and public nudity have been criminalized in the name of respectable society (Ferrell and Sanders 1995; Hayward 2004). In some cases this involves the criminalization of entire subcultures that are labelled as crimogenic. Performers, producers, distributors and retailers of rap and 'gangsta rap' music have faced arrest and conviction on obscenity charges and confiscation of albums; and art photographers such as the late Robert Mapplethorpe and Jock Sturges were accused of 'pandering obscenity' and subject to legal censure (Ferrell 1999: 404–5). It is not just a matter of the relationship between private conscience and the laws of society. The media play a considerable role in the amplification of some leisure forms and aesthetic subcultures as a threat to society. Jenkins (1994) demonstrates how the media amplify moral panics in respect of drug use, youth violence and homicide scares.

Technology is also relevant. Some forms of technology make criminal activity a by-product of maximizing the potential of the system. If I buy a laptop I possess the potential means of downloading intellectual property anywhere in the world. I may download a piece of music or a film which is advertised as being free, but which is actually subject to copyright control. I may do this in good faith, with no criminal intent. I may just want to maximize the possibilities that my laptop affords. Yet from the standpoint of the copyright holder I am breaking the law. As such, as an unauthorized downloader of copyright protected material I am liable to criminal prosecution.

For students of leisure committed to global inclusion, empowerment and distributive justice the moral complexity of the issue is compounded if one turns to the use of technology in the emerging and developing world. The *Sao Paulo Declaration* (1998) and the *Charter for Leisure* (2000), published by the World Leisure and Recreation Association, commit leisure educators and activists to breaking down barriers to enable free and full participation in leisure. This commitment was conceived in terms of increasing aid for leisure forms and practices, from the economically most advanced countries to the developing and emerging world. One of the most effective technologies in breaking down barriers is the internet. It is far more efficient in increasing global access to the scarce global resource of intellectual property than government policy or NGO initiatives. The internet is low cost, flexible and potentially universal. Yet what should the attitude of leisure educators and activists be to illicit downloading of intellectual property for personal use in Africa, China, India, South East Asia, Latin America and the poorest economies of the old Soviet bloc? Is it morally justifiable to seek the prosecution of someone who earns less than $2 per day and uses a shared internet site to download the latest album by Amy Winehouse or the newest film by Spielberg? Should leisure educators and activists cognizant of the history of third world exploitation by the economically advanced nations favour a one-size-fits-all policy of internet monitoring and policing? Or should a less punitive policy be advocated in the emerging and developing world, with the focus of policing concentrated on outlawing ISP cartels and criminal gangs?

Coming back to the question of the recreational use of illegal drugs, plainly, the state is against the practice and has set aside a portion of public funds to pursue this end. Some of these funds are assigned to education and policing. The health risks of using drugs that are classified as illegal, and the censure that derives from being detected in the form of financial penalty or imprisonment, are matters of public knowledge. Despite this, it is transparent that state policy has not deterred people from using proscribed drugs for recreational purposes. Some types of drug use are increasing. Other types of drug, notably the consumption of cannabis, involve over 50% of the US population in the 18–58 age group. The attraction of illegal drug use is not confined to the physical, chemical effects of consumption. Cultural criminology has identified a range of social and cultural attractions that derive from the practice. Being on the edge of the conventions of straight society, bending rules and flaunting authority are part of the adrenalin rush that propels illicit leisure practice (Lyng 2004). Katz (1988: 312) refers to 'the delight in being deviant'. Presdee (2000) refers to the 'excitement' and 'pleasure' that accompanies transgression and make a distinction between the adrenalin rush that follows breaking the law and getting away with it and the voyeuristic thrill attached to observing illicit behaviour. The heavy content of Hollywood movies, television dramas, theatrical productions and popular music that is directed to criminal activity, having your illegal cake and eating it, reveals the scale of the voyeuristic fascination with rule bending, law breaking and triumphant forms of illicit leisure activity.

The SCASSMIL framework seeks to root leisure analysis in observable forms of location and practice in leisure behaviour and to explore the layers of complexity that constitute the context for trajectories of leisure behaviour. The aim is to produce an approach to analysis that is more inclusive and relevant than the old SCCA framework that underpinned the leisure society thesis approach. Let me give an example to make the difference concrete.

What Can You Learn from a Game of Cards?

Imagine you are engaged in the scientific study of card players. The point of commencement might be examining card players in casinos, gambling clubs or some other leisure setting in which card playing occurs. Naturally, location practice cannot occur unless players come to the location. The proper scientific study of this leisure form must establish correlations between card players and income, education, gender, ethnicity, race, employment status, addiction to intoxicants and other social and economic factors. A lot of interesting stuff can come out of this data. You might establish clear correlations between blue collar workers and frequenting a particular type of casino; or having a specific level of education and belonging to a gambling club.

Attempting to explain these correlations may take you down some interesting paths of sociological and leisure research. It may be that your sample of card players demonstrates a strong correlation with class background so that you might investigate how historical factors and the structural distribution of unequal resources have combined to produce a propensity in some to place their reliance upon gambling as a staple pastime in their diet of leisure activities. You might find that men outnumber women among gamblers, and this might lead to questions of embodiment and emplacement and their relation to access to leisure resources. Within these questions are latent issues having to do with the economic, political, social and cultural distribution of power. These might compel you to ask how identity is constructed in society, what forms of representation communicate leisure forms to us as attractive and how leisure choice is coded in this or that community.

The empirical approach to leisure tends to begin and end with topics relating to the external trajectory of leisure behaviour. The typical methodological practice is to measure this trajectory quantitatively and establish hypotheses between factors that support short- or medium-range hypotheses. To continue with the example of card players for a moment, empirical research might establish a correlation between regular gambling at the card table and an addictive personality. This might produce a research hypotheses that examines how particular types of addictive personality turn to gambling at the card table as a staple leisure activity, rather than reading literature or collecting postage stamps. It might correlate these personalities with specific traits of class background, gender, race and ethnicity. Alternatively, it might take the form of an examination of how gambling is related to risk culture (Beck 1992). If everyday life is experienced as a series of risks such as global warming, terrorism, mugging, economic meltdown and unemployment, it may encourage fatalistic attitude formation. The question of card playing may therefore take us to larger, philosophical issues having to do with ontological insecurity; that is, the psychological belief that our lives are, in a fundamental sense, neither safe – nor secure.

A belief that our future is written in the cards is often a product of a lack of education. But it may also reflect considered, educated reservations about the capacity of rationality and science to regulate subjective and group behaviour. A disposition to fatalism may also be connected to what Freud called *thanatos*, or the death drive. A throw of the dice or a shuffle of the pack of cards may be interpreted as symbolizing a sense of futility with the value of planning for anything in life. Who are we to say what will happen next in our lives, or whether we will be alive tomorrow, or next month? Despite our best-laid plans to protect ourselves and our families, the future is always out of our hands. In addition, gambling often takes the form of compulsive behaviour. Repetitively, it yields to indifferent forces. Life follows the same trajectory. No-one wants to grow old and die, but it is the fate of embodiment to do so.

In gambling then we experience the andrenalin rush of subjecting ourselves to the laws of chance. But we also experience the larger subject of yielding to mysterious forces that we cannot control and do not understand. Analysing a game of cards moves from the observable patterns of behaviour of players, to larger issues that involve much broader questions of knowledge and power relating to the allocation mechanisms of scarce resources, practices of legitimation and resistance.

As the expanded SCASSMIL framework is designed to demonstrate, this is also the condition of Leisure Studies. It does not inhabit some sort of supernatural realm in which the rules of everyday life and the social interests behind them cease to apply. The advertising departments of the digital industry and the sports impresarios behind global competitive sports portray leisure and sport as a break from the drudgery of everyday life. By owning a particular leisure commodity, whether it be the latest Jaguar automobile or Apple Mac laptop, or participating in a specific leisure or sports pastime as a spectator, such as the final of the superbowl or the latest *Star Wars* blockbuster from George Lucas, you are entering a world that is represented and coded as being more rich and meaningful, where the mundane rules of the 9–5 work-a-day world of paid employment and domestic labour don't apply.

But this is not the case. Elias and Dunning (1986) refer to 'the quest for excitement' in 'unexciting societies'. By this they mean societies in which aggressive and sexual drives have been heavily conditioned so that they are expressed only in specific social settings. Bureaucracy, rationalization and the regimentation of the working week are all part of this process of conditioning. For Elias and Dunning (1986) what drives it is the civilizing process that multiplies the chains of interdependence between people and brings new veils of privacy and personal restraint into the conduct of social life. In their account, some forms of leisure and particularly some types of sport, transfer the 'dampened down' instincts and transfer them into a different 'key' or 'register'. The illusion of participating in or watching these leisure and sport forms is that they are exciting for their own sake. In fact the excitement they generate is relational and assumes a level of regimentation and predictability in the rest of life. In the work of Elias and Dunning (1986) this question of life balance is primarily explored at the level of the unintended consequences of the civilizing process. If one adopts their perspective, analysing a game of cards leads you to the question of social development and how power, mutuality and reciprocity enwrap individuals in an unplanned and uncontrolled web of constraints which position them to pursue this or that course of action. Gambling at the card table conforms to the unplanned, uncontrolled thrust of the civilizing process because it elevates chance and fetishizes it as the principle of destiny.

Needless to say, the figurational approach associated with Elias and Dunning (1986) hardly exhausts the permutations of theoretical speculation that can be applied to analysing a game of cards. For example, examining the subject from the perspective of critical theory leads to a different path of analysis.

Leisure and Consumption

According to critical theory, the precondition of your subjective enjoyment in leisure and sport settings is an objective social system organized around the repression of instinct and servitude to the work ethic. Repression is not total. It is cantilevered so that, for example, in some settings we experience the thrill of being at the whim of chance, as we do when we play a game of cards, or more generally we experience a degree of freedom when we select leisure activities. Marcuse (1964) coined the term *repressive desublimation* to help us understand this cantilevered effect. This was partly designed to modify Freud's (1939) thesis that civilization is based upon the repression of the instincts. The affluent societies that gave birth to the leisure society thesis in the 1960s appeared to falsify Freud's thesis because they celebrated the positive value of free time and created new opportunities for the exercise of choice in leisure, sport and play. They appeared to be about overcoming repression with a permissive value system that challenged the old division between freedom and constraint. Marcuse's concept argued that the subjective release from repression that the new entertainment and leisure industries produce is conditional upon the objective repression that the system requires. By playing a game of cards, watching a movie or visiting an art gallery you have time off, and exercise subjective choice, but the system requires you to return to the treadmill of paid labour, subjecting real needs to the dictate of the employment contract and competitive consumption. That is why Marcuse describes desublimation – the temporary breaking free of the chain-mail of constraints – as ultimately *repressive*. In agreeing to accept a little freedom in leisure, we accept that we must submit to the organized repression of freedom in the rest of life. For Marcuse (1969: 22):

> Organized capitalism has sublimated and turned to socially productive use frustration and primary aggressiveness to an unprecedented scale – unprecedented not in terms of the quantity of violence but rather in terms of its capacity to produce long term contentment and satisfaction, to reproduce the voluntary servitude … The capitalist production relations

are responsible not only for the servitude and the toil but also for the greater happiness and funds available to the majority of the population.

Consumer culture elicits false consciousness in consumers. Possession becomes psychologically conflated with being and competition between individuals is practised as the God-given state of affairs. According to this form of consciousness, consumers see themselves as free when they play cards or engage in other self-determined leisure pursuits. However, this freedom is a delusion because it fails to address that the forces of capitalist production that permit repressed desublimation in some leisure and sport settings are working behind their backs to ensure that the idea of working in paid employment for a living remains a matter of 'choice'.

Marcuse regards the principle of repressive desublimation as objectionable. The main reason for this is his conviction that the forces of capitalist production have far outstripped the relations of capitalist production. He follows Marx (1858) in holding that the relations of production are a fetter upon the free and full development of the forces of production. What does it mean for the relations of production to become a fetter upon the forces of production? Think of land, labour and capital as forces liberated by human enterprise and invention. The world of industry, invention, technology and science herald a world in which untold wealth and the flowering of human capacities is possible. What inhibits them primarily is not the want of inspiration, enterprise or industry, but the submission of these principles of invention and growth to a system of allocative resource distribution that requires profit to be diverted to the capitalist class. The enormous gain in productivity achieved by science and technology is appropriated mainly by the capitalist class. The rest of society is left with a relative increase in wealth and some crumbs of freedom. The popularity of the entertainment and leisure industries verifies the blind readiness of the masses to devour these crumbs as proof of human progress. In doing so they simply fulfil the requirements of repressive desublimation inscribed by a system based upon organized class, gender and race inequality. As Marcuse (1969: 21) puts it:

> The entire realm of competitive performances and standardized fun, all of the symbols of status, prestige, power, of advertised virility and charm, of commercialized beauty – this entire realm kills in its citizens the very disposition, the organs, for the alternative: freedom without exploitation.

That we now see this argument as flawed rests partly upon the conceit involved in the concept of false consciousness. The concept maintains that the masses do not know their own minds. To live in consumer culture is to live in a state of semi-oblivion in which the handling and possession of commodities is misconstrued as freedom. Yet we know that most people are aware of inequality and exploitation. Many genres in leisure forms such as critical theatre, the literature of exploitation and the cinema of class, race and gender manipulation, latch on to the question of what Marcuse calls repressive desublimation and investigate it in powerful, enriching ways.

It is also true that Marcuse's argument now seems flawed because capitalism has triumphed over other models of organizing society, notably state socialism. The alternatives no longer seem untried or utopian. They seem to be not only *history*, but the *past*. Wherever the market establishes itself, it drives out effective resistance and meaningful opposition. It creates a population that may live on bad terms with many aspects of capitalist organization and capitalist logic, but who nonetheless measure out their lives as if there is no serious alternative. In such circumstances, the limited freedom at our disposal in leisure is presented as the best we can hope for. Technological innovation and progressive management styles increase the range of leisure commodities, widen the sphere of commodified leisure experience and make work patterns more flexible. However, the free and full development of mankind requires the deconstruction of the existing mechanisms of resource allocation in favour of an egalitarian global system capable of delivering equality and freedom. The social and political interests that are positioned preferentially in relation to the existing distribution of scarcity will not allow this to happen. So gambling at the card table may be interpreted as an act of resignation; that is, it dissipates energies at a precise nexus of leisure, rather than allowing a concentration at a higher level to change the system. In critical theory leisure is theorized as both manipulating the masses to believe that they live in the best of all possible economic and social systems and diverting their surplus energies into capital so that the system of organized exploitation and repression is enhanced.

Leisure analysis therefore proceeds from the local to the general, from simple causal relationships to more complex far-flung sets of relationships. The *Lebenswelt* of leisure is where direct location practice occurs. Through this practice individuals encounter and build sensuous, moral and political apprehensions of leisure. The context of location practice is not random. In it unique, unrepeatable events occur. Although every action we take in leisure practice is unique, it also follows a pattern. I may play my hand of cards in a way that is unique, but the dealing between hands and the outcome of the game is governed by rules. These rules refer to the context in which leisure practice is located. This context is subject to well-observed principles and, in some cases, laws that shape intentional conduct. This is the nomotheitic level in leisure studies. It has to do with the wider allocative mechanisms that regulate access to scarcity.

Leisure analysis therefore involves the interplay of the idiographic and nomotheitic levels. It should desist from grand theory which produces universal theories of leisure forms and practice because the level of scientific knowledge to substantiate work of this type is not sufficient. Equally it should avoid confining itself to positivist accounts of trajectories of leisure behaviour and associated variables. Examining what people actually do in their leisure is indispensable. But mere fact-finding is a sorry end in itself. The challenge is to build empirical findings upon what is scientifically known about leisure forms and practice and to carry them forward by informed speculation. As the sociologist Robert Merton (1969) maintained, the latter is an art rather than a science. It demands intuition and imagination rather than mere conversance with the fundamentals of empirical sociology and psychology. Merton was in favour of producing testable knowledge of what he termed 'the middle range'; that is, the range of analysis between fact finding/number crunching and grand theory. This is the position adopted here.

It is germane to our interests because the academic study of leisure is divided into two camps. The camp dominated by quantitative methods and positivist analysis is known as Leisure Sciences. The camp that follows qualitative methods and interpretive analysis is known as Leisure Studies. These camps are not simply distinguished by methodological and analytical distinctions of perspective. They correspond to different spatial formations with contrasting histories. Leisure Sciences predominate in the US; and Leisure Studies predominate in Western Europe and the settler societies of the Commonwealth. This raises the important question of the global division of labour in the academic study of leisure. It is a hugely neglected question. Yet despite globalization and the emergence of much wider channels of communication, the take you have on leisure is heavily coded by the country in which you are located and the academic conventions of the curriculum to which you are attached. Applying the SCCASMIL framework is not simply a matter of being cognizant of factors that are absent or obscured by the SCCA framework. It is also a matter of examining the balance of power relations within the field of Leisure Studies/Leisure Science. Some groups in the field apply a gatekeeper function that permits some perspectives and forms of knowledge to be fully and freely articulated and casts others out to the marshlands. Those who seek to apply the SCCASMIL framework in the analysis of leisure forms and practice must be aware that they face a struggle with exponents of the SCCA framework who occupy key academic and management positions in the field and who often control the key journals and conferences.

The balances of power involved here extend from questions of dominant paradigms – pre-eminent ways of thinking about leisure and recreation and doing Leisure Studies/Leisure Science – to issues relating to the balance of power in the global academic division of labour between the dominant producers of knowledge about leisure forms and practice and the rest.

The question of regulation in Leisure Studies/Science has two dimensions. Firstly, the organization of the field demarcates territory for investigation and sets an agenda for research. This in turn raises questions of professionalization, the exchange of ideas and the paradigm of knowledge that informs field activity. Secondly, because leisure forms and practice are *positioned*, the issue of how resources are allocated, the types of leisure forms and practices that receive prestige and the mix between public and private investment in leisure resourcing, are pivotal. The remainder of the book examines each of these dimensions. The next three chapters focus on the organization and exchange of knowledge in the field. They argue that some of the contradictions in the meaning of leisure derive directly from debates held during the formation of the field as to whether more leisure is a blessing or a curse. The professionalization of the field has been heavily influenced by this topic. It has produced competing validity claims about what counts as 'good' or 'serious' research which regulates resource distribution and output.

Chapters 7 and 8 of the book examine the roles of the public and private sectors in resourcing leisure forms and practice. I argue that within Leisure Studies/Science there has been a bias in research for finding state-centred solutions to resourcing. Against this, in what has come to be known as the era of 'new' or 'neat' capitalism, *stateless solutions*, generated by corporations which regard themselves to be socially responsible, have played a larger role in resourcing leisure forms and practice than is ordinarily realized. The chapters explore the meaning of stateless solutions and indicate their implications for the field.

The final chapter turns to the impact of sectoral specialization on the field. Over the last thirty years, the emergence of Sports Science, Tourism Studies and Special Event Management has stolen the thunder of Leisure Studies/Sciences. The collapse of the leisure society thesis has compounded this problem. It has made many query the relevance of leisure as an academic field. As one might expect in a book of this type, the final chapter takes issue with the question of irrelevance. It submits that the field raises issues of resourcing and ethical governance that Sports Science, Tourism Studies and Special Event Management cannot accomplish. Leisure Studies/Science is the encompassing field in which the newer specialisms in free time forms and practice should be located.

4

VISIONARIES
AND PRAGMATISTS

To maintain that the roots of the academic study of leisure are somewhat dense and tangled is an understatement. The modern question of leisure did not simply spring from the mouths of industrial nineteenth-century workers craving more freedom, or from utopian visionaries bent upon dreaming of a better world. It was posed practically by doctors of medicine troubled by the social and physical effects of urban over-crowding; it harried judges, the police and social workers who struggled with solutions to urban crime and the socialization of model citizens; it worried clergy who viewed secular forms of leisure as threatening the religious community and the work ethic; it vexed educators who struggled to construct a relevant curriculum for what we now call the work–life balance; it dogged town planners intent upon building peaceful social and interracial communities in the urban landscape; and it captured the imagination of the downtrodden who were able to see in leisure a vision of the world turned upon its head, a world of personal freedom, unadulterated creativity and collective wellbeing. The emergence of the central institutions of normative coercion not only codified the lines between acceptable and non-acceptable behaviour, normal and abnormal leisure, it also generated the training, coaching and policing mechanisms that regulated free time behaviour. These included the judiciary, the police, state educationalists, medical practitioners, psychiatrists, social workers and the media. The product of these various discourses, and the traditions associated with them, is the emergence of the self-policing individual with the 'second nature' of accumulating emotional intelligence and practising emotional labour to demonstrate competence and credibility.[1] What we now call emotional intelligence and emotional labour gradually becomes so critical and insistent on the performance of competent behaviour that it compromises the notions of 'time off', choice and freedom. Even the practice of 'chilling' today is a performance activity that requires an acceptable setting, codes of representation and the social paraphernalia of coding and representation that signifies the suspension of pecuniary enterprise and industry. Emotional intelligence and emotional labour is tied to the *homo duplex* model of human conduct that proposes that we always act *in the eyes of society* as well as *for ourselves*.

In his sociological work, Durkheim (1897) proved this by demonstrating that even the most private act of suicide has a transparent social dimension. He relates egoistic, altruistic, *anomic* and fatalistic suicide to social conditions, demonstrating, for example, the relationship between suicide and social integration, religious membership and the health of the economy. The same holds good for free time behaviour. It involves the internalization of various social conventions, tips and hints that draw a line between responsible and irresponsible, licit and illicit forms of practice. It is *relevant performance*, the requirement to demonstrate voluntary abnegation from paid employment, that is the instigation of conspicuous consumption and the various rituals of distinction, that Veblen (1899) writes about with such brilliance in *The Theory of the Leisure Class*. It is also relevant performance that is behind the 'front' and 'back' region management strategies of entertainment and leisure settings and the history of 'markers' in tourist settings that is elucidated with such insight in Dean MacCannell's (1976) book, *The Tourist*. Similarly, in Richard Sennett's (2004) study, *Respect*, which takes as its subject the formation of modern character, it is behaviour in the sight of others, the personal consequences of 'bad behaviour', that are – *without anyone directly telling you about them* – the compass of free time choice and action.

MacCannell (1976: 92) defines *front* regions as the setting in which hosts and guests or customers and service persons meet, and the *back* is where the hosts or service persons retire between performances to relax and to prepare. Examples of back regions include, the kitchens in restaurants, the dressing rooms in theatres or the changing rooms in sports stadia. The concepts are borrowed from Goffman (1959: 144–5), who distinguished between front and back spaces in which contrasting forms of physical design, social ordering and associated roles apply. For Goffman, back regions are generally closed to audiences and allow for the concealment of props and other activities that might conflict with the performance out front. Essential to this is the idea that back regions are bound up with mystification and the logistics of persuasive presentation.

The concept of 'marker' is developed from semiotics. MacCannell (1976: 110–111) applies it to refer to any information about a leisure or tourist setting. This encompasses textual, audio-visual and oral cultures of coding and representation. Markers are like signifiers in semiotics; that is, they are both information and the vehicle of information about the leisure or tourist setting. Because they represent the setting, they may involve exaggeration, hyperbole and allegory. Markers therefore both represent a setting and create a space in which the representation of the setting is inscribed and over-written. As such, the space of the marker is also the place in which manipulation and ideology operate most freely.

Even psychologistic studies of leisure, which focus on the individual experience of freedom and intrinsic satisfaction, operate with the notion of boundaries that stimulate personal enjoyment and life satisfaction. For example, Csikszentmihalyi's (1990) influential concept of 'flow' connects subjective enjoyment with the achievement of socially defined ends, such as doing challenging activity which requires the execution of skills, goal achievement and receiving feedback and merging action and awareness. In the psychological condition of flow the individual loses all sense of self and becomes engrossed in behaviour that is experienced as satisfying and enriching. The notion of performance, the matching of personal and social boundaries together, is the tacit criterion for examining the quality of flow experience. The significance of performance is even more obvious in Neulinger's (1981a) leisure paradigm that identifies perceived freedom and intrinsic motivation as the core of subjective satisfaction. Although he treats the concepts of perceived freedom and intrinsic motivation in a sociologically unparticularized manner, it is clear that their origin and meaning is social. What we perceive as freedom depends upon our location in relation to scarce resources and the conventions and traditions of coding and representing scarcity in which we are situated. For example, questions of scarcity will be defined differently by working class Muslim families compared with middle class white Christian families because they are located in contrasting positions of scarcity that define the horizon of their views of common practice and life expectations. Similarly, unless we subscribe to a model of biological determinism in which intrinsic motivation is presented as entirely genetically determined, or a version of religious determinism in which our intrinsic motivation is accounted for as the result of the will of a Supreme Being, the only remaining explanation is social factors. All of these approaches, then, carry some version of subjective performance that, in turn, presupposes the use of emotional intelligence and the application of emotional labour.

We are accustomed to associating the birth of modern thought about leisure with the general issue of progress. This is a one-sided, distorted perspective. The birth of leisure is also tightly bound up with the anxieties and neuroses surrounding urbanization, industrialization, the break-up of traditional society and the presentation of relevance, competence and credibility in the self. The growth of leisure created new spaces for diversity and resistance where before scarcely any obtained. It contrasted work-driven existence with personal contemplation and fellowship built around revitalized social values. It was the space in which sincerity, trust and reciprocity were forged and extended, and where impressions of competence, relevance and credibility could be passionately confirmed or ruthlessly liquidated. Leisure was a source of personal fulfilment and group satisfaction for some, and a cause of worry and fear for others. This history of pro's and con's, dangerous costs and stupendous benefits, continues to permeate the field, making it hard to think clearly about the meaning and potential of autonomous choice in leisure. Its contradictions ran through the first academic curricula of leisure and recreation studies and remain divisive to this day.

Modern Origins of the Study of Leisure

In order to understand the nature of these contradictions more fully it may be helpful to distinguish the modern power blocs and associated traditions of thought that positioned leisure as an appropriate subject for academic teaching and research. The roots of the public debate over, and provision for, leisure education and services are embedded in the rational recreation movement of the 1870s. This movement was a combination of progressive forces of muscular Christianity, eugenics and urban reform. Broadly speaking it focused leisure education and provision around four blocs of issues and associated research traditions:

1) Personal Growth and Enrichment
    Leisure provision was associated with increasing physical health and broadening personal horizons. A mentally alert, physically robust population was identified as a desirable social goal. One reason for this was the industrial requirement for strong, adaptable manpower. But the nineteenth and twentieth centuries were also a period of warfare between nation-states. The role of leisure in producing a fit reserve army of warriors that could be swiftly co-opted into military campaigns by the interventionist state was well understood by the rational recreation movement. The organization of sport and outdoor recreation skills cultivated by the Scouts and Boys' Brigade carried clear quasi-militaristic overtones and mixed them with Christian principles of fellowship and devotion (Mackenzie 1984: Mangan 1985; Samuel 1988). Rational leisure and recreation were associated with the outdoor world of Muscular Christianity and pious self-improvement. But there was a shadow-world to Muscular Christianity and pious self-improvement. It was the feral, infected world of prostitution, alcohol abuse, drug dependence, street violence, crime and the other types of vice and degradation that undisciplined leisure brought in its train. The contradiction between leisure as progress and leisure as the abyss, carried religious overtones of salvation and damnation through the exercise of free choice.

2) The Beautification of Life
    The 'City Beautiful Movement' in the US (1890s–1900s), which included the landscape architects behind New York's Central Park,

namely Frederick Law Olmstead and Calvert Vaux, twinned the public provision of leisure with the beautification of life. Drawing on strands from the Beaux Arts movement in France, and the Garden City movement in the UK, the 'City Beautiful' movement was dedicated to opposing slum development by creating a 'concrete grove' in the city in which a balance between Industry and Nature was preserved (Wilson 1994). The notions of urban 'garden districts' and 'green belts' were expressions of the Humanist desire to build a better world in which leisure and work reinforced one another in a spirit of harmony. The converse position stressed that urban and industrial blight is unavoidable. While beautifying life was regarded as an aim worth supporting, the work ethic was valued as the key to prosperity and progress. The reform of industrial society set great store by the argument that disciplined leisure reinforces the work ethic. Yet it also clipped fears about idleness and inactivity from their roots in Christianity and transplanted them in relation to over-crowding, under-education and the urban malaise. Anxieties about mephitic, invasive and wild forms of leisure crystallized in public policies of urban policing and moral regulation.

3) Moral Reform
The public provision of leisure services sought to achieve correspondence between leisure activities and moral reform. Historians identify the right to leisure as one of the expressions of the high-water mark of Victorian liberalism. But this right came with conditions.

In the British case, Beaven (2005) traces four phases of development in the relationship between leisure forms and citizenship. The first phase in the 1850s and 60s defined leisure as a citizenship right, but was founded on a segregated model of full citizenship. The principles of segregation were property and sex. The Electoral Reform Acts of 1832 and 1867 extended the right to vote for males, but limited it to property holders. It was not until 1884 that unskilled labourers were enfranchised. As for women, those aged over 30 gained the right to vote in 1918. It was not until the Equal Franchise Act of 1928 that women gained equal voting rights with men, i.e. that all men and women over the age of 21 were awarded the right to vote. The extension of the franchise came with a new perspective on the relationship between leisure and citizenship.

The second phase of development identified by Beaven, between the late 1860s and the first world war, envisaged a new moral relationship between the individual and the state, focused on national demands rather than civic duty.

The third phase, during the inter-war years, tied state-sponsored leisure forms to economic efficiency and the requirements of employers.

The fourth phase, during the second world war, related leisure forms to building morale and social cohesion. Throughout all four stages the state and the reforming middle class identified guided leisure with social improvement and the moral improvement of the population. Of course, several studies trace working-class reactions to moral programmes launched by the ascendant class to disseminate standards of good practice in the use of free time (Gray 1981; Borzello 1987).

These reactions were developed within a public context that identified youth as vulnerable to the temptations of idle time and cheap popular amusements. The rational recreation movement's identification of the responsibility to supervise and direct youth led to recreational forms entering school curricula, to scouting and Christian-based organized types of leisure and the publication of 'respectable' children's comics and literature. Rational recreationist's were also concerned to reform urban locations in which drink, prostitution and gambling were endemic. Their solution was to introduce organized sports, cultural events and educational facilities (Heeley 1987).

4) Health and Crime

Part of the power of 'City Beautiful' philosophy was that it posited a relationship between urban design, improving personal and public health and combating crime. The health benefits of clean air and exercise underwrote the nineteenth- and twentieth-century expansion of municipal parks, libraries, public halls, baths and museums. Being in touch with Nature and the appreciation of culture and physical cleanliness were regarded as a way of improving the mental hygiene of the nation.

After the first world war this ethos became influential in the prison reform movement. In the UK, Alexander Patterson developed the philosophy that the primary object of detention was not punishment, but to educate and improve the offender. He was at the helm of a movement to re-gear the Borstal system. As part of the criminal code of 1908, the Borstal sentence was built upon a military model of regimentation, discipline and authority. Patterson advocated the introduction of an alternative system based upon the values of the public schools, which sought to instil values of pride, loyalty and *esprit de corps* in pupils. Assistant governors were encouraged to think of themselves as 'house masters'. In 1924 the uniform for Borstal officers was abolished and officers were encouraged to become more involved in the activities of the boys, especially the leisure activities. Summer camps were introduced, and a move to an open prison system for some offenders was pioneered. The first open prison in England was established as Lowdham Grange, Nottinghamshire in 1930; followed by North Sea Camp, near Boston, Lincolnshire (1935); and Hollesley Bay, Suffolk (1938) (Ruck 1951).

Leisure Studies grew out of rational recreation and the relationship between them is complex. Rational recreation identified leisure with personal improvement, class example and responsibility, the progress of civilization, moral regulation, health control, the protection of heritage and Nature. What we now call 'emotional intelligence' was concerned with being informed and equipped with data about these issues and harnessing this in the organization of lifestyle.

There was another side to rational recreation. It associated leisure with idle hands, dangerous and potentially seditious thoughts, the development of narcotic dependencies and anti-social behaviour. Free time and free individuals carried with them the logical possibility that people could think for themselves and therefore do anything. On one side this pointed to the liberation of personal and group creativity. Against this, was the more disturbing prospect of individuals and groups questioning their position in relation to scarcity and the prerogative of the wealthy to have privileged access to scarce resources.

Leisure was therefore both coveted and feared. This formed the stock of values and lifestyle options out of which Leisure Studies emerged. As the forces of technology, industry and science advanced, the allocation of resources to leisure and recreation expanded. This raised the separate question of distributive justice. Portions of the resources amassed by the wealthy were reinvested in public works, like parks, swimming baths and recreation grounds. However, the gap between the rich and the poor dramatized the issue of leisure and inequality. This general issue produced three subsets of questions, broadly related to the socialist, liberal democractic and conservative traditions of thought.

Must the wealthy be deprived of their superior access to economic and cultural scarcity so that the distribution of leisure for all might be improved? This is the chief question that arises in socialist accounts of leisure and progress.

Should the wealth of the rich be subject to progressive taxation and the leisure culture of the rising industrial classes given new acknowledgement and respect? This is the question that emerges from the liberal democratic interrogation of the topic of leisure.

Can the superior values and wealth of the rich be preserved against the tide of claims for redistributive justice made by the representatives of popular culture – a culture that the elite tradition hold in low regard? This might be described as the nucleus of the modern conservative tradition on leisure.

What spins off from the progressive forces that create more leisure and recreation is a wide-ranging debate about the correct basis of organization for this new society. Surplus production alters the relationships of individuals and groups to scarcity and challenges the means of representation through which questions of access and scarcity are traditionally communicated. The birth of modern leisure is therefore indissoluble from the topic of the management of free citizens in civil society. Modernization brings with it an abundance of time and resources. But it also raises the questions of the purpose of abundance and free time. Many faced these questions with nothing akin to equanimity. John Maynard Keynes (1931: 328) expressed the matter powerfully in his essay on 'Economic Possibilities for our Grandchildren':

> There is no country and no people I think, who can look forward to the age of leisure and abundance without dread. For we have been trained too long to strive and not to enjoy. It is a fearful problem for the ordinary person with no special talents to occupy himself.

As we shall see presently, the same problem preoccupied the philosopher John Dewey (1916). How can self-determined occupation translate to the benefit of society? Dewey took a pragmatic line and regarded this as, above all, a matter of educating what Keynes called 'the ordinary person' in forms and practices of leisure that are appropriate to the industrial age. Those who held fast to the classical view regarded the pragmatic solution as the deformation of leisure. For it implied complying with the exigencies of time famine and technological innovation thrown up by modernization, rather than taking steps to transcend them in favour of a view that identified leisure with intrinsic worth.

None of these questions has gone away. Rather they have been continuously revised and repositioned. They are relevant to the question of the academic division of labour in the study of leisure because they are the immediate context for the movement to devote some scholarly resources to leisure. Broadly speaking, the scholarly study of leisure drew on two different power blocs of thought about leisure: those of the Visionaries and the Pragmatists.

Visionaries

Visionaries identified leisure as the central component of the good life. They were influenced by the Aristotlean ideal of leisure as a practice of intrinsic worth, distinct from play, rest and work. In *The Politics* (1962: 302) Aristotle writes:

> [W]hat are the proper activities of leisure? Obviously not play; for that would make play the object of living, our end in life, which is unthinkable. Play has its uses, but they belong rather to the sphere of work; for he who works hard needs rest and play is a way of resting, while work is insepa-rable from stress and strain. We must therefore for therapeutic reasons admit the necessity of games, while keeping them to their proper times

and proper uses; taking exercise in this way is both a relaxation of the mind and, just because we enjoy it a recreation. But the way of leisure that we are speaking of here is something positive, in itself a pleasant, happy existence which the life of work and business cannot be.

On this reckoning it is a sorry misuse of the term today to connect leisure with 'time off'. For the latter presupposes work-centred existence. It is precisely this form of existence that Aristotle holds to be incompatible with leisure. One can rest and play after work. But leisure means giving oneself over to an object of intrinsic worth. This is an exacting definition of leisure since it assumes that individuals possess the wherewithal to isolate themselves from the harum scarum of gaining a living and cultivating enriching personal relationships. Instead they would singularly devote themselves to the life of observation and contemplation. Aristotle appreciates that the freedom of the leisured elite is not like the mundane scope of choice and self-determination afforded to everyone else. It is exalted. It permits freedom without boundaries of time since the only recognized obligation is the inherent worth of the activity at hand. However, he omits to pursue to its endpoint the logic that the exalted freedom of a handful is based upon the menial labour of the legions. What logic operates here?

According to Aristotle, humans occupy the apex of animate existence. Although men and women partly share the nutritive, reproductive and motor constitution and functions of animals and plants, they are categorically distinguished by the faculty of Reason. It is only given to men and women to behold history as a network of causes and effects and, upon this basis, to make provision for the future. For Aristotle, the life of observation, meditation, cogitation and speculation for its own sake is the highest fulfilment of Reason. In this sense, leisure is the most noble object to which men and women can aspire and devote themselves. Yet if all give themselves over to meditation, cogitation and speculation, the necessities of life cannot be obtained. For life to continue and grow the expenditure of time and energy on menial labour is required. According to Aristotle, providence has happily found the solution to this problem. Only a fraction of mankind possess the capacity to develop the prerogative to Reason to the utmost. The majority are vegetative and do not possess the capacity or inclination to develop observation, cogitation and speculation to the highest levels. Providence ordains that nature and social convention produces a slave class to do the necessary work that society requires to survive and prosper. Upon this substructure exists a free, superior class that devote themselves to the leisurely life which concerns itself with things that are intrinsically worthwhile and culturally important to society.

This ideal of leisure as being connected to free time forms and practices that are of intrinsic worth resurfaces in the rational recreation movement and egalitarian planning in the nineteenth and twentieth centuries. It is a deeply troubled perspective on leisure that became more aggravating as successive generations struggled to democratize the distribution of free time and the allocation of scarce resource for licit enjoyment. This is because Aristotle identifies leisure quite narrowly as a state of mind given to a handful to cultivate. As a member of the elite you are at liberty to observe and contemplate to your heart's content. The inherent difficulty with this is that it is a model of leisure that is tacitly predicated on the exploitation and oppression of the majority. As the pressure for distributive justice, empowerment and social inclusion grows, the allocative mechanisms that underwrite gross inequality are subject to critical scrutiny. By the mid nineteenth century the context for this was that the creation of wealth unleashed by the productive forces of capitalism made mincemeat of the Ancient proposition that leisure is prime steak to be savoured by the few.

The rising industrial classes of the industrial age took over many aspects of the Ancient ideal and redefined them as the preserve of everyman. Visionaries were influenced by the City Beautiful movement that saw in industrial leisure a means of universally enlarging the horizon of contemplation, fellowship and civility in urban settings and improving what is called today 'the work-life balance'. Leisure was no longer seen as the entitlement of the few but an instrument of social engineering and civic reform that combated the worst excesses of industrialization, urbanization, inequality and consumption. This did not extend to redefining leisure as a means of resistance and opposition. The conflation between leisure and a state of mind was retained. To it was added the proposition that organized leisure carries a therapeutic dividend in enhancing the identification between the people, the nation, wellbeing and Christianity. The rational recreation movement used physical training and sport as a means to invigorate youth with the values of Christianity and Empire (Springhall 1977). In this period then, the Visionary perspective of leisure became more inclusive. Leisure ceased to be thought of as a characteristic of the elite and became transformed into a central value of industrial civilization.

In the academic study of leisure Visionary views are most powerfully expressed in the writings of Josef Pieper (1952) and Sebastian de Grazia (1962). These authors present leisure as a state of mind. Pieper's (1952) account is mediated through a number of anxieties having to do with the absence of religion in contemporary society. Divine worship is portrayed as the most complete articulation of the leisurely state. In this Pieper demonstrates his debt to Aristotle. For he defines leisure as pure contemplation. He writes (1952: 41):

> Leisure is a form of silence of that silence which is the prerequisite of reality: only the silent hear and those who do not remain silent do not hear. Silence, as it is used in this context, does not mean 'dumb ness' or 'noiselessness'; it means more nearly that the soul's power to 'answer' to the reality of the world is left undisturbed. For leisure is a receptive attitude of mind, a contemplative attitude, and it is not only the occasion but also the capacity for steeping oneself in the whole of creation.

There are strong overtones of religion here. The 'silence' of leisure is portrayed as carrying with it theological awakening. 'Noiselessness' is an *entrée* into the deeper questions of the creation and meaning of life. De Grazia (1962) does not equate leisure with divine worship. His (1962: 14) work identifies the same connection between leisure and free or pure contemplation, to which he also adds music (why not drama, painting or poetry?).

From each of these accounts it follows that those who can live a leisurely existence are still in the minority. For industrial society places the burden of paid labour upon the majority. In doing so it condemns the common man and woman to the distraction of earning a living. This state of distraction allows for free time but it does not supply the wherewithal for leisure. Free time is colonized by organized amusement and consumption. Most people do not have the time to devote themselves to a life of contemplation, reflection and fellowship. True leisure is therefore scant in industrial society. 'Leisure,' writes de Grazia (1962: 5) 'refers to a state of being, a condition of man, which few desire and fewer achieve.'

Pursuing a slightly different tack, Huizinga's (1944) work emphasizes the importance of a historical perspective in studying leisure forms. He takes issue with the conventional view that places leisure as less important than work. For Huizinga, play and leisure forms are the seat of creativity and invention. Leisure has provided revisionist opportunities to recast nature, culture and society. It has helped humans to rethink themselves and their relationship to the external world. Huizinga (1944: 197–201) disapproves of the commercialization, standardization and regimentation of industrial culture.

The conflation of leisure with contemplation in the writings of Pieper and de Grazia now seems rather lofty. We have become accustomed in industrial society to equating leisure with acting, doing and having, so that to think of it in terms of a lifetime of repose and meditation seems eccentric. When we have free time the last thing that most of us want to do is to observe or contemplate. We want to get on with consuming culture, buying commodities, gardening, exercising the body – all of the thousand and one things that paid labour, as the bane of life, postpones and procrastinates as the reward for itself and which emotional intelligence and emotional labour identify as conditions for competence and credibility. Contemplation for its own sake has been replaced by the narrower value of action. The importance of emotional labour in demonstrating competence, bestows a purposive gait upon free time activity. This has made some commentators query the relevance of the classical Greek view to contemporary society (Veal 1987: 23–5). Leisure needs to be formulated in relation to the exigencies of modern industrial society. As more abundance is created through industrialization, the subjects of distributive justice and educating the masses raise the question of redefining the meaning of leisure in the industrial age. Coming to terms with the industrial age and realistically assessing the leisure forms appropriate to it was the challenge that the Pragmatists set themselves.

Pragmatists

The Pragmatists do not dispense with the Ancient Greek notion of leisure. They adopt what they take to be a realist stance on the question, and conclude that in the industrial age, to confine leisure to contemplation and a liberal education is foolishly restrictive. Leisure is regarded as both a state of mind and a set of practical accomplishments relevant to 'the work-life balance' and civic order. Broadly speaking, Pragmatists are fellow travellers with Visionaries in stressing the benefits of leisure to mankind. Whereas Visionaries chose to develop this argument at the level of ideas, Pragmatists seek to apply them practically to society. They concentrate their efforts on the curriculum and urban planning. The strategy they adopt is to focus on the value that leisure contributes to evidence-based issues of health, crime control, urban renewal and civic virtue.

Among Pragmatists, John Dewey (1916) is a significant author. He takes over many of the features of the classical Greek perspective on leisure but pits them against the strengths, weaknesses, opportunities and threats presented by industrial, urban, democratic society. His object is to determine the principles of a 'worthy leisure for all'. Aristotle's discussion is obviously of limited value to this end because it was developed in a slave state. It is one thing to maintain that the majority of men and women should be assigned to a mechanical, vegetative labour by the normative institutions of coercion that applied in Ancient Greece. But this is neither here nor there in modern industrial democracies, since men and women are formally free.

According to Dewey this does not mean that Aristotle's thought on leisure must be discarded as a historical curiosity. On the contrary, he believes Aristotle to have been right about two fundamental things. Firstly, the mechanical, vegetative state is the antithesis of leisure. That which restricts free contemplation and the exercise of mind and body is the enemy of the free and full development of Reason.

Secondly, play and consumption are inferior to understanding, the development of appreciation and the free play of ideas. However, the notion that those who engage directly in the work of transforming nature into human use values should be condemned to subsist in an unfree state of existence while the free play of understanding, appreciation and intelligence is restricted to the elite is now indigestible in the body politic.

Aristotle's view of leisure distinguished between culture and utility. It confined culture to an elite with the means to pursue the intrinsic worth of activities and condemned the majority to a life of production and service.

Some aspects of this dualistic view of leisure and society carry over into the organization of education in democratic society. In Dewey's day a minority received a liberal education designed to equip individuals with appreciation and understanding, while the majority laboured in work and business. Yet industrial progress depends upon the practical application of geometry, arithmetic, communication and sound principles of management. Aristotle would have regarded these activities as belonging to the world of utility and, as such, he would have dismissed them as distractions from the world of contemplation and reflection that, he believed, was the proper preserve of leisure activity.

For Dewey, this distinction no longer applies in industrial society. The development of machine culture and automation has extended the volume of leisure and developed the requirement for educated, skilled, flexible workers. Those who devote themselves to acquiring industrial skills are not menial labourers. The education and training of those involved in technology and the sciences raises questions that are of the same order as for those who follow a liberal education. What is required is a revised education system that reconciles liberal principles with an acquaintance with the larger features of work. In a democracy thought must be the guide to free practice and leisure the reward for taking on the responsibility of service for all.

The pragmatic tradition in the academic study of leisure is associated with scholars like Charles Brightbill, Allen Sapora and Christopher Edington. It identifies leisure as a major element in life satisfaction. Optimal lifestyle is defined as 'the integration and balance of the physical, mental, emotional, intellectual, social and spiritual aspects of a person' (Edington et al. 2004: 18). Leisure and recreation are not portrayed as values of civilization that are independent from industry, technology and science. Rather they are presented as being interdependent with them. Leisure services contribute to optimal lifestyle management through several means. These include awareness building, transmission of cultural heritage, knowledge and skills acquisition, attitude and character formation, sensory stimulation, promotion of skills acquisition and providing structures and facilities for the enjoyment of leisure. Leisure education is tied to citizenship. It aims to make better citizens and more integrated communities. The social means through which this is accomplished is professionalization.

Leisure and Professionalization

Pragmatists have sought to define and apply universal standards of practice and institution-building. A significant development here was the emergence of the World Leisure Organization, founded in 1952 with a brief to discover how leisure might enhance human growth, and personal and group development.

Professionalization is the codification of training and practices into impersonal rules that can be used to independently assess the standing and conduct of those maintaining professional status. Typically, it involves the establishment of a curriculum and objective monitoring. Professionals monitor themselves but they are also subject to the scrutiny of an agreed body drawn from their peers who ensure that the required standards of practice are adhered to. Professionalization is a common strategy for distinguishing professional practitioners from amateurs. As such, it carries higher honorific value in society, greater political influence and more economic rewards.

It evolved a twin strategy of informed advocacy and educational research to pursue these goals.

Similarly, in America the National Parks and Recreation Association (NRPA) has defined a professional ethics code to achieve inclusion, group cohesion and standards of conduct. It requires members to pledge themselves to five principles (Clark 1995):

- Adhere to the highest standards of integrity and honesty in all public and personal activities to inspire public confidence and trust.
- Strive for personal and professional excellence and encourage the professional development of associates and students.
- Strive for the highest standards of professional competence, fairness, impartiality, efficiency, effectiveness and fiscal responsibility.
- Avoid any interest or activity that is in conflict with the performance of job responsibilities.
- Support equal opportunities.

Between the late 1980s and mid 90s leisure education experienced a gradual, but significant growth both in professional institutions and student numbers. Arguably, the leading examples of professional development were: National Parks and Recreation Association (NPRA, US, 1965); the Leisure Studies Association (LSA, UK, 1975); and the American Academy of Leisure Sciences (AALS, 1980).

The 1970s also witnessed the expansion of provision in higher education for leisure training. However, this was curtailed after the 1980s with the emergence of new academic fields concerned with play and entertainment, notably Sports Science, Tourist Studies and Event Management. Employment prospects in these fields have been robust as reflects their relationship to corporate capitalism, which until recently with the global liquidity crisis of 2008 has experienced a long spurt of growth while the public sector has been subject to new restraints. Additionally, the collapse of the leisure society thesis, the global deregulation of labour and the rise of what Schor (1992) refers to as 'the over-worked worker' stole the thunder from leisure educators.

The academic study of leisure bears the stamp of the Pragmatic approach and preoccupations. The influence of the Visionary tradition is evident in the philosophy of leisure education, especially with respect to the notion of work–life balance and the relationship between leisure and utopia. It is also apparent in the sociological and philosophical tradition in the connection of leisure forms and practice to empowerment, distributive justice, social inclusion and social reconstruction (Marcuse 1969; MacCannell 1976; Urry 2002). But because it concentrates upon the practical value of leisure for personal enrichment and social cohesion, and relies on quantitative methodology, the Pragmatic tradition has been ascendant in the organization of the academic training and study of leisure.

The academic study of leisure crystallized in universities long after the *Methodenstreit* debate. As we shall see in more detail presently, viewed internationally, research has tended to be dominated by nomothetic analysis, with high status placed upon quantitative method. Interpretive/qualitative methods have made a significant contribution in feminist, cultural and subcultural approaches to leisure. Nevertheless, they have been dominated by quantitative research methods. This reflects a strong prejudice in the field and arguably, in the wider social sciences, that hard-number based data is superior to interpretive analysis and qualitative data. This is especially true of the US in which the biggest concentration of academic resources for the study of leisure is situated. The pre-eminence of the US is so obvious and overwhelming that it is important to make a few comments abut the history of leisure education here before contrasting it briefly with other traditions.

The first university programme in parks and recreation was established at the University of Minnesota in 1937. However, until the 1940s, degrees in leisure and recreation were scarce. Between the 1940s and 50s, modest growth in university-level diploma and degree courses occurred. Doubtless this reflected the post-war sentiment to build a better, fuller type of society in which no-one had grounds to feel unacknowledged or excluded. Career openings were limited because the organized study of leisure and recreation was regarded to have a lower claim upon the public purse than education, economics, business, urban planning, health provision, crime control and welfare. Nevertheless, to the extent that public leisure and recreation provision were understood to make a positive contribution to these priorities, and to the degree that public financing of leisure and recreation was regarded to produce the good life, it was supported. State investment translated into job opportunities in the management of parks, heritage, children's play facilities, community leisure programmes and various other types of outdoor recreation. Managerial and strategic expertise in this area was regarded to be transferable; that is, while degrees and diplomas in leisure and recreation equipped people to enter these sectors the curriculum was not respected as presenting exclusive or preferential training in the principles of free time behaviour and management. People trained in the more established disciplines of Business Studies, Town Planning, Social Policy, Physical Education, Domestic Science, Hospitality Studies, Geography, Psychology, Sociology, and even Social Work, were viewed as being equally eligible for entry to the leisure and recreation sector.

From the start, the academic study of leisure has been dogged by the question of what theoretical and methodological tools have been custom-built, and what is borrowed, recycled or rebranded from the longer established and more powerful Social Sciences. Within the field of Leisure Studies there is a discernible reluctance to claim innovation or novelty. Kelly (1994: 87) submits that it is a 'dangerous over-simplification' to maintain that leisure possesses a unique set of meanings or that it has a monopoly over the orientation of freedom and intrinsic meaning. The main characteristic of the field continues to be making interdisciplinary connections rather than producing innovative findings from within.

Roberts (1987) has questioned if is possible to find *anything* distinctive about leisure theory and by extension, Leisure Studies. As such, despite claiming specialist expertise, the field is not in pole position to make claims about leisure. This is why academics in other disciplines and fields in the Natural and Social Sciences continue to be influential in adding to knowledge and the debate about leisure forms and practices. This produces a state of imbalance in the field. The more established disciplines often treat students of leisure with the condescension of a self-image composed in equal parts of privileged ancestry and assured posterity. Their perspective is regarded to be superior because it is based upon a longer history and a brighter future. The leisure society thesis interrupted this because it identified leisure as the future of the affluent societies. However, it was a brief interlude that punctuated the prevailing academic view that the academic study of leisure is the preserve of the scholarly misfit and the academic amateur. In the US, sensitivity to the issue of relevance produced a cogent impulse to professionalize leisure education and demonstrate outputs in therapeutic practice and model citizenship. Interest in qualitative questions of the phenomenology of leisure forms and the variety of experience attached thereto, was supplanted by evidence-based investigations of leisure outputs, often expressed in quantitative terms.

The pioneering work of Charles Brightbill and Allen Sapora at the University of Illinois acted as a template for developments in the field, especially with respect to the question of professional standards and the demonstration of relevance. The first professional course in recreation at Illinois was offered in 1932: 'Recreational Activities'. Convened by Jack Treece, it was taught within the Curriculum of Physical Education for Men. In 1937 a more professional course emerged: 'Principles of Recreation'. Confined to a second semester, 3-hour slot, it was an experimental course designed to attract students from Social Work, Physical Education, Urban Planning, Parks and others with an interest in outdoor recreation. The students were a motley crew, recruited from Literature, Biology, Social Work, Domestic Science and often possessing a personal interest in scouting, outdoor recreation and the voluntary sector. The course was closely tied to fieldwork, notably visits to the Works Progress Administration programme (WPA) established in the nearby town of Decatur under the directorship of Brightbill. The WPA programme was launched in 1935 as part of Roosevelt's New Deal. It was intended to provide economic relief and the expansion of cultural horizons for US citizens suffering from the Great Depression. Art, music, theatre and dance were funded by public resources as part of an egalitarian policy of economic relief and social reform. The WPA was one of the first major examples of the public use of creative industries for the purpose of social engineering. This carried over into the leisure and recreation curriculum at the University of Illinois.

The first graduate course in recreation was introduced in 1939: the 'Philosophy and Administration of Recreation'. It was taught by Hartley D. Price, a coach in gymnastics. This was a theory-based course which sought to explore models of public recreation as leaders of urban progress. The content was non-critical and insulated from the main currents of contemporaneous cultural and social theory. Leisure was presented as a social good which enhances personal and group life. The relationship of leisure to ideology, neurosis, power and manipulation did not figure on the horizon of this course. In this respect, leisure training reproduced the commonsense view. Expressed in the words of a later generation of leisure scholars, the mantra was: 'leisure is good' (Goodale and Godbey 1988: 1).

In 1940 a Bachelor of Science degree with a specialism in Recreation was established, under the leadership of one of Price's graduate assistants, Allen V. Sapora and the curriculum coordinator Ralph Johnson. In 1951, Charles K. Brightbill was appointed Chairman of the Recreation curriculum in the School of Physical Education. Two years later a Master of Science in Recreation was introduced. The curriculum was geared to state and federal employment opportunities. In 1957 the Department of Recreation and Municipal Park Administration was established within the College of Physical Education. At that time the staff complement consisted of four full-time faculty members and two graduate assistants. In 1975 the department was renamed the Department of Leisure Studies. Evidence of the early maturity of Leisure Studies in the US compared with other Western nations at this time is evident in the establishment of the Motor Performance and Play Research laboratory in 1966, the introduction of the PhD award in the Department of Recreation and Park Administration in 1972, and the creation of the Leisure Behavior Research Lab in 1974.

The history of the Illinois department deserves special consideration because it was a dynamic role model for the academic study of leisure in America. Charles Brightbill and Allen Sapora did not act alone, but the gravitas of Brightbill and the perpetual enthusiasm and networking skills of Sapora acted as a magnet for students and fledgling researchers in what, at this time, constituted a 'patch' rather than a 'field'.

Leisure and Recreation Studies became established in many American universities, notably Indiana, Clemson, Maryland, Chapel Hill, Texas A&M and Northern Iowa. But the roots were often justifiably seen as eccentric. For example, the Department of Health and Kinesiology at Purdue University traces its origins back to the recreation and athletics programme directed by Frank Curtiss a century ago. Strictly speaking this was not a pioneering course in leisure. Curtiss was an instructor in gymnastics. However, lessons in physical fitness and competitive athletics raised much wider questions about the use of free time. For example, Curtiss lectured on the corpuscular benefits of a structured sponge bath. This involved heating water to a temperature of 78 degrees and instruction on the correct order of body parts that required regimented ablution. The end result was not simply bodily pleasure and a satisifed state of mind, but a 'general elevation of the spirits' and the status distinction of presenting the combination of exercise and bathing as 'a natural tonic' for bones wearied by study and work (http://www.cla.purdue.edu/hk/history.htm).

Health/Kinesiology/Crime Control/Urban Aesthetics/Social Planning/ Social Theory/Philosophy – the origins of the academic study of leisure in America reveal a field of study emerging out of numerous fits and starts and a complex tangle of buds and offshoots, rather than coherent vision and a programmatic plan of action. Like the British Empire, the academic study of leisure in America was assembled in a fit of absent-mindedness. If Brightbill and Sapora acted as magnets, they drew disparate filaments from different traditions which encompassed the science of the body and the cultural value of the arts that conflicted with one another for precedence. Viewed from the perspective of academics in the largely rural universities that provided the energy and manpower for the scholarly study of leisure in the US, the stakes were high. By the 1940s, leisure was somewhat akin to the old-style Western frontier in American life – a constantly expanding imaginative horizon of human possibility and social engineering.

Conversely, from the standpoint of the key public funding departments in Washington D.C., the academics studying leisure were exotic parvenus, extolling an agenda of public benefits for leisure practice but lacking a table of proof or a compelling political and social programme. Washington D.C. preferred a policy of benign, limited indulgence to the hither and thither of academic ruminations and prognostications for leisure in America over outright, fully fledged support. American scholars of leisure were akin to their European counterparts: would-be conquerors of the work ethic and lifestyle planning, but without the support of the financial viziers whose cold assessment of the public balance sheet could turn their dreams into reality.

If one can use the word 'ferment' to describe American Leisure Studies after the 1940s, it was confined to the Plains, the West Coast and a smattering of Southern outposts. Nationally, it did not seriously engage with what non-white people and the disabled did in their 'free' time; it omitted to consider the relationship of leisure practice to resistance or the formation of deviant identity and oppositional subcultures; nor, with one or two exceptions, did a philosophy, or politics, for leisure in multi-ethnic, multicultural society prosper under its tutelage.

Do not think that the post-war pioneers of the academic study of leisure were oblivious to the slings and arrows of political and economic marginalization, cultural condescension and social ostracism. In their day, to propose that leisure, sport and recreation were worthy of serious academic study and public funding was to invite incredulity and even ridicule from many quarters. The pivotal importance of the work ethic was reinforced by the key institutions of normative coercion – the family, schooling, policing and religion. Students and scholars of leisure were non-conformists. Their non-conformity was of a rather disorganized kind. Despite the WPA programme, which explicitly identified leisure and culture with social engineering, the post-war pioneers did not develop a coherent position on the potential of leisure as a political solution to the problems of social division, sexual inequality and social integration. Questions of freedom, taken up and expressed most forcefully by the civil rights and feminist movements, turned on the issue of liberation rather than leisure. The pioneers followed the common sense precedent of regarding leisure as a state of mind insulated from the rest of society. There was no serious attempt to critically assess the role of leisure in organizing social conformity, dissent and other forms of identity. The question of the colonization of leisure by consumer culture and popular entertainment formed a backcloth to the development of Leisure Studies as a more serious, socially worthwhile use of free time. But there was no real effort to systematically relate leisure, consumption and popular entertainment to the financial and managerial imperatives of corporate capitalism. The recognition that leisure involves forms of monitoring, reconnaissance and other types of emotional labour that disrupt orthodox notions of 'time off' and 'free time', belonged to a later generation of scholars. Similarly, while the WPA initiative was partly inspired by anxieties about a possible relationship between idle hands and social unrest, the fledgling field developed no serious interest in deviant or illicit forms of leisure or in the role of gangs or underground cartels in supplying illegal demand. Respect for the virtues of American leisure was pre-eminent. In their free time, Americans enjoyed the benefits of democracy and full employment; they cultivated the traditions of community and enjoyed the pleasures of civilized relaxation. The wartime emergence of the US as the dominant Western power translated into massive popular support for the American way as the global template for all industrial societies.

Leisure Studies in the UK

In the UK, the provision of leisure training was much less advanced and professionalized. Voluntary organizations such as the National Trust (1895), Boys' Brigade (1883) and the Boy Scouts (1907) worked with a practical understanding of the relationship between physical education, disciplined leisure and personal wellbeing and social progress. However, it was mediated through the class structure. The idea of leisure education was so closely tied up with the notions of middle-class duties to the deserving poor, and middle-class anxieties about the underclass, that it constituted a philosophy or science of leisure in only the most tenuous way. Leisure training was ad hoc, and obeyed the principle of volunteering, which was usually expressed in the vocabulary and sentiments of Muscular Christianity and the Garden City movement with its idealized view of a balance between leisure, work and the rest of life. The most sophisticated courses in degree and diploma level courses in physical education, urban planning and education made reference to the question of the meaning of leisure. However, as with the US, there was a faint air of disapproval about the idea that theory might be relevant to leisure. The onus lay on a curriculum that emphasized practical knowledge for environmental and social issues. Interest in leisure as a focal point of identity and subcultural formation was growing. Hubble (2006) documents some of the empirical studies in the UK that respected the importance of free time behaviour and leisure forms in providing social coherence. An event like the abdication of King Edward VII in 1937, dominated the leisure talk in pubs and the home, and raised interesting questions of national identity, deference to tradition and the relationship between leisure and communities of resistance. However, as we shall see in more detail later, as with the tradition of non-conformity in American leisure studies, this response was unsystematic and failed to generate a theory of the relationship between leisure, consumption, power and social positioning.

The links in the UK between leisure studies and Geography and Sociology privileged qualitative over quantitative methodologies. The British tradition has always assigned more space for engaging with social and cultural theory. Social commentators and public intellectuals such as Raymond Williams, Richard Hoggart, E.P. Thompson and Stuart Hall were not clipboard researchers. They practised an approach that related questions of free time behaviour to culture, power and civilization. Since all were in varying degrees located on the Left, their work constantly touched upon the questions of social reform and social reconstruction. The connection between socio-cultural theory and leisure studies was much stronger in the UK than in the US. Because of this the movement to professionalize leisure studies was strongest where socio-cultural theory was concentrated: in universities. The quantitative tradition in British social and cultural study was much less developed in the US. This left the academic study of leisure with little to draw upon and an elective affinity with qualitative and interpretive analysis. One exception was the data generated by the Mass Observation movement between 1937 and 1949 (Hubble 2006). This was led by Charles Madge, a poet; Humphrey Jennings, a surrealist film maker and Tom Harrison, an anthropologist. It aimed to develop an anthropology of daily life based upon time diaries and day survey notes kept by ordinary people. Among the subjects it examined were:

The Pub as a Leisure Setting
Spare Time
Behaviour of People at War Memorials
Shouts and Gestures of Motorists
The Aspidistra Cult
The Anthropology of the Football Pools

Bathroom Behaviour
The Distribution, Diffusion and Significance of the Dirty Joke

Given the austere ethos of academic life in the inter-war and immediate post-war years, this range of interests in leisure and popular culture is extraordinarily refreshing. It was also audacious. The Mass Observation studies gathered an unprecedented collection of quantitative data on people's attitudes to the King's abdication, the frequency of copulation in the leisure resort of Blackpool, the micro-politics of family life, attitudes to embodiment and fashion and the perception of the class system. However, it is only a partial exception to the qualitative and interpretive tradition in the study of British cultural and social life. As an expression of quantitative methodology it was deeply flawed. The samples that it used were small, unrepresentative and inconsistent. It relied upon voluntary correspondence, peripatetic ethnographic methods and irregular interviews and surveys. Nevertheless, the material is valuable and offers an unparalleled research snapshot of everyday life in Britain between 1937 and 1949.

American Domination: Promises and Discontents

American Leisure Science has long been criticized as introspective and indifferent to cross-cultural experience and for perpetuating a perspective on leisure that is tantamount to the Americanization of the world. Introspective bias is doubtless present in every national tradition in the academic study of leisure. However, because of the strength and vitality of the field in the US, the size of the American population and the pre-eminence of America as the world's sole economic and military superpower, the ratio of bias is exaggerated. Valentine et al. (1999) reviewed 1352 articles published in the *Journal of Leisure Research*, *Leisure Sciences* and *Leisure Studies* and found low levels of cross-national analysis and high levels of ethnocentrism, particularly among North American scholars. Jackson's (2003) analysis of where North American scholars of leisure publish their articles supports Valentine et al.'s (1999) findings. He adds two qualifications. Firstly, 'elite' scholars in the US and Canada are less parochial and more cosmopolitan in orientation. Secondly, Canadian scholars at all levels have a greater propensity to engage with international issues than their American counterparts.

Similarly, an informal survey of the 'Top Ten Books in Recreation and Leisure' at the 2003 National Recreation and Park Association Congress in St Louis, Missouri, conducted by Robert Kauffman and David Zuefle, found room for only one book of European origin, Huizinga's (1944)

1. Thorstein Veblen (1899) *The Theory of the Leisure Class*
2. Sebastian de Grazia (1962) *Of Time, Work and Leisure*
3. Josef Pieper (1952) *Leisure, the Basis of Culture*
4. Mihaly Csikszentmihalyi (1990) *Flow*
5. Johan Huizinga (1944) *Homo Ludens*
6= Aldo Leopold (1949) *A Sand County Almanac*
6= Dean MacCannell (1976) *The Tourist*
7. Freeman Tilden (1957) *Interpreting Our Heritage*
8. Gary Cross (1990) *A Social History of Leisure Since 1990*
9   Charles K. Brightbill (1963) *The Challenge of Leisure*
10= Stefan Linder (1970) *The Harried Leisure Class*
10= Thomas Goodale and Geoffrey Godbey (1988) *The Evolution of Leisure*

Figure 6   NRPA top 10 books on leisure and recreation
Source: cited in Edington et al. 2004: 429

Homo Ludens. The rest originated in the US and focus overwhelmingly on US experience (see Figure 6).

Furthermore, the *Academy of Leisure Sciences*, one of the most prestigious global bodies in the academic study of leisure, currently has 70 fellows based in American universities, 10 in Canadian universities and only two from the rest of the world (China and the UK). In an age of globalization, mass communication and the international exchange of ideas, the membership is strikingly rooted in American dilemmas and issues.

Of course, many noted American scholars in the field engage seriously with global issues; one thinks of Geoff Godbey, Garry Chick, Karla Henderson, Dean MacCannell, John Kelly and Christopher Edington. That these figures stand out in the context of the American tradition is largely because they are exceptions to the rule. The American study of leisure and recreation is still dominated by graduates interested in American forests, American National Parks, the American coastline and what free time means in American cities. Comparative studies of leisure and recreation in other countries are rare. The participation of American scholars, such as Christopher Edington, Larry Neal, Susan Koch and Karen Barak, in international organizations, like the World Leisure Organization, helps to raise the profile of the emerging and developing world. However, it has not translated into a more global, ecumenical policy in the curriculum of what is taught in US leisure and recreation schools and published in US scholarly journals.

Naturally, American scholars can point to significant American *under-representation* in the curriculum and scholarly print culture of the academic study of leisure outside the US. American scholars do figure in European and Commonwealth courses on leisure and recreation, but there is also bias here to the contribution of national scholars and issues. In the era of globalization, mass communications have become universal. Access to the internet is a standard requirement of scholarly life.

Nowadays, academics may have more frequent and more meaningful exchanges with colleagues situated thousands of miles away, living and working in different time zones, than with members of the department in their own corridor. Notwithstanding this, all of the leading countries involved in leisure and recreation research have a strong natio-centric (or 'nation-centred') tendency; that is, they treat national issues and intellectual traditions as their milieux. International scholarly contributions and global questions are refracted through the lens of natio-centricism. But in the case of the US, national bias is pronounced (Jackson 2003).

To illustrate this in another way, consider the editorial composition and textual content of the leading British and American journals in the field. The leading British journal is *Leisure Studies.* The editorial board is dominated by British scholars. In 2008 all three Managing Editors had British citizenship. The editorial complement is divided in standard fashion into an Editorial Board of key participants who comment on editorial strategy, policy and referee papers, and a wider Advisory Board who focus on refereeing papers.

In 2008, of the seven members of the Editorial Board only one was not based in a British University (Andy Bennett, Griffith University, Australia). This would suggest strong natio-centrism, in respect of editorial strategy, policy and journal content. However, if one turns to the 32 members of the Editorial Advisory Board the picture is not so transparent. In 2008, 13 members were based in the UK, six were in the US, three were in Canada, three were in Australia and New Zealand, and the remainder were based in Europe. In addition, the journal has appointed five regional editors located in South Africa, the US, Australia, Poland and Japan.

Compared with the leading US journal, *Leisure Sciences,* this has a much stronger international dimension. Thus, in 2008 the Editors-in-Chief of *Leisure Sciences* were both American. Of the 31 Associate Editors, no less than 25 were based in the US; with four Canadians and two Australians bringing up the rearguard. The journal employs no system of Regional Editors and there is no European involvement at any formal level. Goodale's (1994) research into the content of articles published in *Leisure Sciences* found that over 50% of the material addresses variables associated with leisure or recreation activities and/or satisfaction or is devoted to testing relationships identified in earlier studies. The next most common type of article (30%) focused upon questions of testing and evaluation in leisure research. Of the remaining 20%, half addressed questions of theory, and half focused on historical issues.

Goodale (1994) deepened his analysis by examining seven topic categories which, he argued, predominate in the content of the journal:

1) Participation in and satisfaction with outdoor recreation including fishing, hunting and non-consumptive uses of wilderness.

2) Motivation in leisure practice, e.g. factors in group membership or the search for satisfaction in leisure activity.
3) Consumer behaviour, the correlation between motivation and fulfilment in vacation activity or the price paid for leisure commodities or programmes.
4) Ethnic and cultural differences in leisure and recreation behaviour.
5) The perceived value of recreation in relation to resource distribution.
6) Gender and feminist perspectives on leisure and recreation forms and practice.
7) Constraints on leisure and recreation participation and personal fulfilment.

The conclusion is that the material published in *Leisure Sciences* typically relies upon quantitative methodology and focuses on questions of observable practice. Comparative, historical and theoretical work is under-represented. Topics dealing with American parks, recreation and leisure predominate. Questions of the relationships between class, ideology, corporate manipulation and leisure, which require a bolder confrontation with the subject of the historical construction and contemporary distribution of power in American society, are not at the forefront of published research.

The editorial policy of *Leisure Studies* is less discriminatory. A mixed methods approach seems to be followed in which qualitative and quantitative articles are encouraged. The journal exhibits a stronger relationship with social and cultural theory. The cultural turn in Social Science after the late 1980s is reflected in published research on embodiment, consumer culture, the media and postmodern theory. The contents of *Leisure Studies* suggests a set of perspectives on leisure that treat the subject as politically contested terrain rather than a category of human behaviour with clear boundaries. Consider an edition (Vol. 8: Number 2) published in May 1989 as an example of the diet content supported by the journal. The edition contained 10 articles dealing with the interrelationships between Leisure Studies and cultural studies; leisure and pluralist theory; leisure, feminism and pluralism; leisure and neo-Marxism; leisure and subcultural formation; leisure and the arts; leisure, culture and history; leisure and embodiment; and patterns of co-operation in outdoor leisure and recreation.

It is not a question of the superiority of the British approach vis-à-vis the American approach. Each approach is valid and informative. For the purposes of the concerns in this section of the book, the salient issue is that there are sharp, demonstrable differences in approach to the academic study of leisure in both countries. In addition, globally speaking, the American approach is dominant.

Does American domination, and the bias of concentrating upon national questions in American leisure and recreation schools matter? There are two separate issues to consider. Firstly, while the US is the world's only superpower, and American leisure and recreation studies constitute the dominant force in global academic activity, it is still part of a fragile, interdependent, mobile world (Urry 2007). Many of the issues facing leisure policy-makers in America involve international relationships. Among other subjects, one can mention the pollution threat to the physical environment of the US, the supply of illegal drugs and contraband cigarettes to US consumers by drug gangs and cartels, sex trafficking from the emerging and developing world to US cities and the threat that international terrorism poses to leisure, recreation and sport settings. In all of these areas isolationism is not an option for American students of leisure and recreation or American citizens. To be sure, given US domination there is reason for arguing that leisure and recreation scholars should be asserting themselves more forcefully to play a leading part in supporting comparative research and developing a perspective on leisure and recreation that integrates national considerations and traditions with a global agenda.

Secondly, US pre-eminence is not just a matter of a research agenda and an orientation to international leisure forms and practice that emphasizes American dilemmas and issues. Americans have also tended to privilege quantitative methodology and the scientific model over qualitative, interpretive analysis. Until the 1990s, this resulted in the neglect of social, cultural, political and racial questions with respect to leisure forms and practice. American leisure was examined as naturalistic. Its historical routes and relation to power were underexamined. So Cheek and Burch (1976) in their influential structural functionalist approach, investigated leisure forms and practice in terms of the reproduction of core values in American society. Questions of the justice of these values and their inclusiveness for class formations, the gender divide and racial and religious groups in America were not dissected. Privileging quantitative over qualitative methodology possesses high status. For example, in 2005 the Institute of Scientific Information Journal Citations Report ranked *Leisure Sciences* 14th out of 51 journals in Environmental Studies (social science) and 21st out of 94 journals in Sociology with an Impact Factor of 1.045. By comparison, *Leisure Studies*, which tends to be weighted in favour of publishing articles using qualitative research and interpretive analysis, was unranked.

5

WHAT IS WRONG WITH LEISURE STUDIES?

Fred Coalter (1999) makes a useful distinction between *Leisure Studies*, which is the tradition of investigating leisure that has emerged from the UK, and *Leisure Sciences*, which is the corresponding US tradition. Leisure Studies is not ruled by a scientific paradigm but rather makes a virtue of a multi-paradigmatic approach to investigation. Data are not treated as unqualified, but as social in origin. This translates into a stronger interest in how power influences leisure participation and experience. The external conduct of individuals in free time is treated not simply as a matter of personal choice but also as the manifestation of how they are positioned in relation to class, gender, race, religion and status. The concept of leisure is perceived as inherently subject to interpretation, with much greater reliance on social and cultural theory. Power interests influence not only what people do in their free time but the ways in which their behaviour are measured and theorized. This means that greater significance is assigned to qualitative research and theoretical speculation since leisure is conceived of as a site of multiple realities as opposed to a single reality.

In contrast, Leisure Sciences follows a positivist cast to research that places a high premium upon quantitative evidence and statistical correlations. The relationship between the subject, doing the research, and the object, which is the focus of research, is regarded as subject to techniques of scientific control which result in objective knowledge. While difference and diversity are acknowledged, the Leisure Sciences approach tends to assume that leisure forms and activities can be compared and contrasted against a normative paradigm of leisure which provides a checklist of 'normal' leisure practice (Cheek and Burch 1976). It operates with what I once called 'a leisure without society' (Rojek 1985: 1) model, in which leisure practice is classified as a specialist area of human endeavour with unique laws and rhythms of behaviour that bear no necessary relation to wider determinate social and economic formations.

The division between Leisure Studies and Leisure Sciences revives the critical issues first raised in the old *Methodenstreit* debate. Within Social Science in the post-war period these issues were dramatically redefined by the so-called positivist dispute in German sociology. This refers to a series of debates about the appropriate methodologies to capture the various dimensions of social reality which occurred in Germany in the late 1950s and climaxed in the confrontation between Karl Popper and Theodor Adorno in 1961. Popper expounded 27 theses for a programme of critical rationalism. By the term critical rationalism he meant a scientific approach to the study of social reality based in empirically sustainable theories. The point at issue was to distinguish empirically verifiable knowledge about social reality from the more elastic and, for Popper, imprecise area of speculative theory.

Against Popper, Adorno contended that critical theory is not reducible to empirically-based scientific theory. It constitutes an independent paradigm. For Adorno, the application of the methods of natural science to the study of social reality simply reproduces the naturalistic fallacy of treating social relations as a naturally given. For example, a scientific approach to the relationship between wealth and leisure space may yield a good deal of valuable data about the bearing of high and low income to access to square feet of leisure space. However, it does not contextualize the research by relating it to the historical and social forces that produce inequality between individuals and groups in relation to scarcity. Critical theory is wary of a pure science of society (and leisure) because science fails to represent the antagonistic, conflict-ridden, contradictory nature of social reality.

Popper's response was that science is perfectly able to produce objective knowledge because its propositions are subject to the impartial judgement of scientists. In his (1945) account of 'the open society' he emphasized the importance of open, rational discussion for the accumulation and defence of scientific knowledge. Conversely, Adorno maintained that impartiality in the analysis of social reality is a pipe dream in societies divided by inequalities of class, gender, race and religion. The marketplace in scientific ideas is subject to the same antagonisms and contradictions that apply in the marketplace of commodities (Muller-Doohm 2005: 425–7).

The positivist dispute in German sociology did not refer directly to questions of leisure and recreation. But the ramifications of the dispute apply to the latter field, since they apply to the issue of the method and theory appropriate to grasping the nature of social reality. Take Cikszmenthayli's (1990) concept of flow. This is much cited in the literature on leisure. The concept refers to a psychological condition that derives from a complete fit between challenges and achievements. You might set yourself the goal of teaching yourself how to play a Coldplay song on your guitar. In the course of the process you may feel that you lose yourself in the music, that time passes without you recognizing it or that the music takes you to a different place. This is what Cikszmenthalyi means by the condition of flow. To repeat, this is a much cited, well-respected concept in the leisure literature. As we saw above, NRPA members listed the study in which the concept appears as the fourth most influential book published in the literature on leisure. In terms of the positivist dispute, Cikszmenthalyi's study is an expression of critical rationalism; that is, it applies scientific method to test social reality and produce theoretical propositions.

From the standpoint of critical theory, the objection to it centres upon the ethical content of behaviour. Without a discussion of the *lebenswelt,* the context in which the experience of flow is located, it is really a somewhat facile concept. It is a reprehensible truth that the Nazis experienced 'flow' in the programme of Jewish extermination (Bauman 1989). From Arendt's (1963) account of the trial of Adolf Eichmann for crimes against humanity, we know that Eichmann derived a powerful sense of work satisfaction and life justification by making the Nazi death trains carrying Jewish prisoners to the annihilation centres run on time.

These examples may appear to be extreme to students of leisure. The work of leisure Visionaries has been too successful in making us automatically associate leisure with positive, creative, legal, life-affirming experience. Maslow's (1973) discussion of 'peak experience' anticipated many aspects of Cikszmenthalyi's concept of flow. By this term he meant the experience of intensely joyful exciting sensation in which the individual experiences a sense of expanding into a wider unity. The examples he focused on were religious experience and other legal forms of subjective transcendence. However, cultural criminology presents a relevant critical counterpoint by proposing that peak experience is often the result of breaking the law. Episodes of mugging, violent beatings, theft, sadism, masochism, murder and serial killing produce the same intense joyful excitement and sense of expanding into a wider unity as described in Maslow's (1973) concept of peak experience or Cikszmenthalyi, in his account of flow. But they do so by reason of acts which invert the rules of society and stand them on their head (Katz 1988; Ferrell and Saunders 1995; Presdee 2000).

The concepts of flow and peak experience are meaningless unless the ends of action are demarcated and taken into account. Merely focusing upon individual flow relationships independently from the rest of society creates distorted analysis. This is because the personal coherence of a leisure relationship that produces flow experience is arbitrarily segregated from the antagonisms and contradictions in the rest of society.

Leisure Science proceeds without making ethical considerations an inherent issue of research. You might look at this or that social variable and relate it to an observable trajectory of leisure practice. Because the antagonisms, conflicts and contradictions of the social totality are not subject to critical scrutiny, the research findings are arbitrarily separated from the whole. Just as a day means nothing if it is separated from the notions of the week, the month and the year, the concepts of flow and peak experience are uninformative unless they are located in the aims of the individual and the context of society. The Leisure Science tradition is psychologistically informed and, on the whole, has no truck with this level of research.

In contrast, the Leisure Studies tradition is much more amenable to analysing leisure forms and practice as *located* structures and activities that reveal the distribution of power in society. This translates into a keener engagement with issues of conjecture and speculation raised in cultural and social theory.

Despite their contrasting approaches, Coalter (1999: 508) argues that Leisure Studies and Leisure Sciences have arrived at the same 'crossroads'. He cites influential scholars in the field from the UK such as Clarke, Critcher, Scraton, Veal and Rojek, and their counterparts in North America, such as Kelly, Mannell, Hemingway, Henderson and Bialeschki and Shaw, reaching the same conclusion that the two traditions must engage more intensively with the socio-cultural meanings of leisure and the relationship of individual and group leisure satisfaction with power.

Yet if Dustin and Goodale (1999) are to be taken at their word, the prospects of this happening in the US, which is the dominant partner in the international division of labour in the academic study of leisure, are dim. They argue that despite a good deal of segmentation in the field, the spirit of positivism is pre-eminent in US Leisure Sciences and this is reflected in the political agenda of the profession. In the words of Dustin and Goodale (1999: 479):

> Attempts at unification currently revolve around 'the benefits are endless' campaign, around the association of recreation with health, and around demonstrating the utility of parks and recreation as a medium for working with at-risk youth.

Despite the distinguished work of leisure historians such as Gary Cross (1993) and Benjamin Hunnicutt (1988), leisure anthropologists such as Garry Chick (1986), leisure feminists such as Karla Henderson and Deborah Bialeschki (1991) and leisure theorists such as John Kelly (1983) and John Hemingway (1999), positivism is the governing paradigm for the academic investigation of leisure in the USA. It carries with it a sense of complacency that antagonisms and conflict are subject to rational interrogation and control. This is often evident in the exaggerated confidence that positivist researchers articulate in relation to the problem-solving capacities of their methods.

> Positivism is an approach to the study of human life that seeks to uncover laws of behaviour based upon the scientific investigation and measurement of observable, external regularities in phenomena. Its interest in internal states of mind is limited to the manifestations of these conditions in behaviour that is manifest and subject to calibration.

It Helps with Those Troublesome Wrinkles Too

Consider the current philosophy of the *Academy of Leisure Sciences*, founded in the US in 1980 with a brief to pursue the intellectual advancement of leisure. At the time of writing (2009) the academy's White Paper 7 (published on their website, nd) lists the personal and public benefits of leisure. It groups them under five sub-headings based upon 'well-documented', although in this case, uncited, research:

1) Economic Benefits
   The leisure industry is now one of the biggest industries in the world. In quantitative terms, in four out of five of the top 50 states in the US, tourism ranks in the top three of all industrial sectors in the volume of income and employment it generates.

2) Physiological Benefits
   In so far as leisure is associated with physical exercise it maintains and improves health. Regular aerobic exercise offers cardiovascular benefits by reducing serum cholesterol and triglycerides, and high density lipids in the bloodstream and helping prevent and control hypertension. It also reduces spinal problems, neuropsychological functioning, increases the bone mass and strength of children, creates better connective tissue, increases lung capacity and nurtures a holistic sense of wellbeing. Physiological benefits accrue to individuals but they also benefit society by reducing stress, enhancing energy for work and reducing the burden on public welfare programmes.

3) Environmental Benefits
   The preservation of Wilderness and Heritage enhances culture and personal wellbeing. It encourages positive attitudes to sustainability and recycling. Taxation on sports and recreation licences multiplies the resources that are appropriated for leisure use. The development of leisure and recreation does not simply protect the environment, it enhances it, by bringing more and more acres and square yards into play functions.

4) Psychological Benefits
   The psychological benefits associated with leisure include: perceived sense of freedom; independence; autonomy; improved self-competence; improved sense of self-worth; greater self-confidence; improved leadership skills; better ability to relate to others; more tolerance and understanding; value clarification, enhanced creative ability; expression and reflection on personal spiritual values and orientation; increased cognitive efficiency; better problem-solving ability; greater adaptability and resilience; improved sense of cordiality and humour; greater joy from life; more balanced competitiveness; enhanced sense of personal place and fit; increased learning of history, culture, nature, cities etc.; more positive outlook; nurturance of a can-do attitude; and reduced sense of personal alienation.

5) Social Benefits
   The social/cultural benefits of leisure include: the development of pride in one's community and nation; the maintenance and transmission of the central values and positive identities in communities; the maintenance and enhancement of ethnic identities; meeting the unique needs of particular segments of society (the elderly, single parents, children, teenagers, the physically disabled, vagrants and the under-employed); producing healthy child development; the reduction of social alienation; facilitation of the recovery of institutionalized citizens; an easing of the burden of confinement; the reduction of substance abuse, crime and other social ills; and improved social integration.

This fulsome roll-call of benefits portrays leisure as the solution to the troubles of industrial civilization. Facetiously one might observe that it is surprising that the White Paper does not also submit that regular, serious leisure practice freshens your breath, whitens your teeth, helps with those troublesome wrinkles, and soothes those serious problems of latch-key children, civil negligence and instability in the business cycle! Throughout, the document makes first resort to over-kill in respect of its claims for leisure. This is coupled with indignation that the state has a disreputable history of under-appreciating and under-financing leisure services. As the 'Conclusion' to the White Paper (nd) puts it:

> In summary then, the 'social good' of leisure is truly staggering. Nevertheless, that 'good' is usually recognized and promoted strongly in public resource allocations only at some local units of government. State/provincial and federal programs that extol these benefits, such as urban and rural development programs, generally receive more lip-service than public funds, and this lip-service varies with the administration that is in office. (Academy of Leisure Sciences nd: 5)

It is not a question of the White Paper being wrong in respect of this or that claim about the good that leisure can bring. Rather all of the claims are so one-sided and presented with such relentless bland vigour that the issue of balanced judgement inserts itself in the mind of the undogmatic reader at every point. Leisure Services are presented uncritically as a universal panacea.

In this White Paper the Visionary tradition in the academic study of leisure has been allowed to blot out the real conditions of human striving, private competition, multi-national manipulation and state sponsorship of ideology in which the experience of leisure is situated and unfolds. A celebratory view of leisure that emphasizes the value of positive thinking and active engagement is not to be scorned. No worthwhile qualitative intervention in changing how people regard leisure and recreation has ever been achieved without mobilizing a utopian element. However, a view of leisure that consists only of good news or isolated statistical correlations, is not persuasive or helpful.

More than at any time in recent memory, as an alternative to paid labour, free time is colonized by emotional intelligence and emotional labour, the appropriation of positional goods and the compulsion to consume. This compromises common sense understandings of 'time off' and personal liberty. The rhetoric of the Academy with respect to leisure must be counter-balanced with an assessment of how people in the real world manage strategies to present credibility and competence and how they are situated in relation to scarcity. For it is the relationship of the individual to scarcity that is the material foundation of work and leisure experience. It is upon this data that the Leisure Science and Leisure Studies traditions will be most securely sustained and enriched.

If the SCASSMIL framework is to grow and prosper it needs to overcome many entrenched positions. These positions identify leisure as an unqualified social good and therefore recoil from arguments which suggest that some Western leisure forms and practice are connected to drug cartels and organized gangs operating covertly in Latin America, Russia, the Balkans and Africa. Globalization, deregulation and out-sourcing have produced a multiplier effect on the provision of illegal forms of Western leisure. Glenny (2008) charts the rise of sex trafficking, illegal drug distribution, contraband cigarettes and cyber crime in Eastern Europe since the fall of the Berlin Wall. The rise of a new class of billionaires in Russia and the Balkans is bound up with the relaxation of financial and trading restrictions. Deregulation has producer a multiplier effect in the number of cartels and organized gangs supplying Western markets with illegal types of leisure.

This requires new thinking about what students of leisure mean by the state and the corporation in Western societies. We shall come to these matters presently. Before reaching that point we need to get a little deeper into the changes that follow from adopting the SCASSMIL framework in how we see and do Leisure Studies/Leisure Science. For the framework does not simply mean that we have to take account of a greater number of axial factors in exploring leisure forms and individual and group trajectories of behaviour. It also means that we have to be cognizant of a much wider range of relationships and processes involving multiple equilibria of factors. What is involved here for the student of leisure is the subject of the next chapter.

6

MULTIPLE EQUILIBRIA:
A BALANCED APPROACH

The gap created by the collapse of the leisure society thesis has been partly filled by the attempt to reformulate what leisure means in relation to differentials of class, gender, ethnic and status inequality. This generated several paradigms in the study of leisure that aim to relate leisure forms and practice to power. I (1995, 2005) have written about these at length elsewhere. I do not propose to write about them in detail in this book. However, because I want to make the case that the study of leisure is caught in a bind between paradigms and needs to undergo an engineered paradigm shift, in which a different way of examining leisure becomes ascendant, I must make brief reference to what I take to be the dominant paradigms in the field. These paradigms are social formalism, Marxism, feminism, figurational sociology and post-structuralism/post-modernism. Since I have set out my (1985, 1995, 2005) stall on these paradigms elsewhere, it is sufficient to confine myself here to simply reprising some key features. Needless to say, the need for brevity means that I must eschew making the usual caveats and qualifications to my discussion which I would make were the publisher to allow me more space. What I am presenting here is a set of thumbnail sketches in order to further justify the propositions that the SCCA framework is too limiting and that paradigm change that recognizes the significance of what I call 'multiple equilibria' in leisure and recreation forms and activities is necessary.

'Paradigm' refers to a pattern of enquiry into human and natural relations. Thomas Kuhn (1962) defined it as a particular set of assumptions, conventions and methods that define a scientific approach to enquiry in a particular time and place. In a period of *normal science* the paradigm provides the exemplar for going about data gathering, formulating hypotheses and testing propositions. Kuhn contrasted this with scientific revolution when

(Continued)

there is a *paradigm shift* that problematizes the methods and propositions of normal science. The classical example is Galileo's theory of the heliocentric universe which not only conflicted with the exemplars of geocentric theory, but also challenged the power of the scientific establishments that espoused the geocentric perspective.

Social Formalism

This leisure paradigm is based upon the observation of leisure trajectories organized around causal relationships. Examples include Neulinger's (1981a) leisure paradigm, Csikzszentmihalyi's (1990) theory of flow, Wilensky's (1961) compensatory/spillover models of work and leisure, and Parker's (1981) extension/opposition/neutral models of work–leisure relationships. This paradigm tends to focus on national data and operate with a rational model of personal behaviour. For example, Neulinger (1981a) regards satisfaction in leisure as the result of perceived freedom and intrinsic motivation. Similarly, Parker's (1981) extension/opposition/neutral models identify causal relationships between work activity and leisure practice. Social formalism tends to abstract leisure trajectories from the context of leisure experience. The result is that questions of economics, culture and politics are under-examined. The main analytical defect of abstracting leisure trajectories from context is that causality is confused with correlation. Following Neulinger's (1981a; 1981b) paradigm, I may have a motivation to use my free time racing SUVs along coastal roads. However, it is questionable to refer to this motivation as 'intrinsic' since its roots lie in issues of gender, age, SUV subcultures, the advertising campaigns of SUV manufacturers, representations of masculinity and much else besides. My motivation to spend my perceived free time racing SUVs along coastal roads is therefore not exactly an autonomous matter. I may exercise choice, but I do so by being positioned in a particular set of relationships with respect to scarcity. In this respect, the position that I occupy was not selected by me and is not a condition of my own making. An adequate explanation of my leisure choice requires a framework of causal analysis that cannot be generated by the paradigm of social formalism. The latter is suited best to short-range analysis of correlations of behaviour in discrete, abstracted leisure trajectories.

Marxism

Marxism situates personal and group trajectories of leisure in a coherent social, economic and political framework. It does not abstract leisure trajectories from context. Instead it treats them as expressive of context. For Marxists, the primary contradiction in context is class inequality and struggle. While Clarke and Critcher (1985) identify cognate factors, notably gender, they analyse leisure experience and trajectories as based on class divisions. They see class as the governing determinant of relationship of the individual or group to scarcity. It is analysed as historically positioning and conditioning individuals and groups in relation to leisure choice and activities. Class membership determines access to domestic living space, access to private transport, cultural capital, work–life balance, leisure activities, educational success and life expectancy (Clarke and Critcher 1985).

The analytic reach of Marxism is far greater than social formalism. For example, my choice to race SUVs along coast roads in my free time, is analysed as a product of my personal choice in relation to my class background, gender and age. It is not a matter of abstracted 'self-actualization' or subjective 'life satisfaction'. Instead, subjective choice and action is theorized as inter-connected with objective social and economic forces. Where social formalism is neutral about questions of inequality and power in leisure forms and practice, Marxism treats them as pivotal. However, the strong emphasis upon class divisions and class struggle tends to either neutralize or subordinate other relationships having to do with age, race, ethnicity, locality, religion and much else besides. Class analysis is an enormously fruitful perspective to apply to leisure choice because it emphasizes the role of power and situated choice in relation to scarcity in the analysis of leisure forms and practice. However, it involves numerous assumptions about the causal primacy of class in history and contemporary socio-economic relations that limit its versatility and explanatory power.

Feminism

Feminist analysis treats embodiment as a type of property. Specifically, the female body is analysed as subject to male prerogatives in respect of power and reproduction. Despite decades of legislation on sexual inequality, men enjoy higher levels of pay than women for equivalent jobs. They outnumber women as Chief Executives of corporations, civil service leaders and governmental ministers. For most men the delineation between work and non-work is clear, whereas nurturing and child-rearing responsibilities are concentrated upon women. The result is that women's access to leisure resources is more constrained. The female body is ubiquitous in advertising, magazines, film and fashion. Despite the *fin de siècle* rhetoric of 'girl power' at the end of the twentieth century, the images of female embodiment that preponderate in the leisure industry focus on sexuality, dependence and reproduction. Sexual equality remains a mirage.

Feminism carries with it the requirement of a more dialogic type of analysis in leisure forms and practice. It is not simply a matter of isolating male power and subjecting it to critical appraisal. It is a matter of redefining the relationships between people in order to highlight the significance of emotional connections, mutual vulnerability and reciprocity. This redefinition extends beyond human relationships to embrace the relationship between individuals and planetary forces and threats (Shaw 2001; Henderson et al. 1996; Wearing 1998).

The development of socialist feminism, from within the feminist tradition, connected women's leisure directly with income, employment status and family situation in patriarchal, class-divided (male-dominated) society. This translated into policies of redistributive justice and social inclusion that focused on forcing the state to provide, *inter alia*, play and crèche facilities, 'women only' settings in sport, leisure and adult education as integral features of leisure and recreation policy and confidence building (Deem 1986; Green et al. 1987; Wimbush and Talbot 1988). However, as Henderson and Shaw (2006: 219–20) have recently noted, the unintended consequence of this was to skew the analysis of power so that males were assigned power and women were present as the subjects of male power.The inference of this criticism is that men's leisure and recreation is as much stamped by the mark of stereotypical sexual expectations as that of women. Henderson and Shaw (2006: 220) call for a shift towards what they call a relational model of the distribution of power between the sexes.

Feminism has played a key role in raising the significance of embodiment and establishing a dialogic/relational model of power in the study of leisure and recreation. However, in prioritizing the male prerogative in explanations of everyday life, it underscores the significance of divisions between women. In addition, the dialogic view of power extends social inclusion, but at the price of supporting a relativist view of society and culture.

Figurational Sociology

The figurational or process approach derives from the sociology of Norbert Elias (1978). It argues that the development of identity and human relationships in the West, have been subject to a 'civilizing process' that introduces and applies various regulatory mechanisms to the expression of aggression, sexuality and authority. The significance of leisure and recreation is that they offer settings in which to study the interplay between choice and routinization (Elias and Dunning 1986). In some cases this entails 'the controlled de-controlling of emotional controls' (Dunning 1999: 25). For example, boxing and wrestling allow the display of aggression in regulated settings in which violent behaviour is refereed. Similarly, horror films and pornography provide socially acceptable settings in which regulated aggressive and sexual emotions are de-regulated.

Dunning (1999) points to three leisure and recreation settings in which embodiment passes into the 'controlled de-controlling' of emotional restraints: Motility, Sociability and Mimesis.

- *Motility* is motor activity. Walking, dancing, running and exercising are pleasurable conditions of embodiment. They are concentrated in leisure forms and practice because these settings correlate with the 'controlled de-regulation' of bodily inhibitions and restraints.
- *Sociability* is the pleasurable enjoyment and emotional stimulation that follow from voluntary interaction with others. The pleasure generated by being in the company of others is often experienced as feelings of emotional closeness, fellowship or camaraderie. Elias and Dunning (1986: 121) describe this as 'leisure-*gemeinschaften*', by which they mean a form of leisure associated with pleasurable proximity and the voluntary exchange of experience and interests.
- *Mimesis* refers to *acting out* or *transposing* aggression and sexuality in socially acceptable settings. When we go to a horror film, watch a boxing match or swear with the football crowd, we are engaging in forms of leisure that involve the 'controlled de-controlling' of emotions. We give vent to emotions that are repressed in other settings such as work or shopping. There is a theatrical or dramaturgical quality to this process of venting repressed emotions. We 'play out' or *imitate* in socially acceptable ways, emotions that are restrained by the civilizing process.

The figurational approach makes significant contributions to paradigm shift, by insisting that all human relationships should be analysed in terms of a moving balance of power between continua. At the end of his life, Elias sought to change the name of his approach from 'figurational' to 'process' sociology – such was the decisive significance he and his followers attributed to analysing social life in terms of mobile balances of power between continua. However, it failed to develop a political position on leisure and recreation. This limited its capacity to contribute to action sociology and leisure and recreation policy. The failure to develop a political dimension resulted in the question of relevance. Figurational sociologists see themselves as taking the first small steps in establishing a genuinely scientific approach to the study of society. This is not a strong hand to play in a field that is crying out for instant solutions and to achieve strategies to tackle issues of inequality, injustice and social exclusion.

Poststructuralism

Poststructuralism departs from the emancipatory politics of the leisure society thesis and offers a reading of social life, leisure and recreation that is more heterogenous than that of Marxism, socialist feminism or figurational sociology. Instead of analysing power in society as divided between classes or the sexes it points to many fronts of domination and resistance. Class and gender are examined as discourses of power that construct regimes of authority that legitimate particular hierarchies of social positioning. Poststructuralism seeks to break with the so-called 'grand narratives' of modern social thought organized around nation, Empire, class, gender and race (Lyotard 1979). By treating them as representative orders which code behaviour, poststructuralism offers the methods of deconstruction and decentring to demonstrate the partiality of the power regime in which individuals and groups are positioned. For example, post-colonial thought that emerged from the poststructural moment exposes the moral codes and quasi-scientific framework of colonial authority that positions whites in a preferential relation to abundance compared to non-whites. Within the study of leisure and recreation the poststructuralist approach is used to expose the rhetoric of individual freedom and choice by contesting, disrupting, transgressing and reworking the codes of representation that maintain given regimes of social and cultural positioning (Aitchison 2003: 21).

Poststructuralism is the basis of an enhanced perspective for examining the complexity of leisure and recreation. Simple models of individual freedom, life-satisfaction, self-actualization and class or gender domination are themselves revealed as the expression of regimes of power. By defining the grand narratives that underpin social and cultural positioning as partial codes of representation, poststructuralism poses the possibility that the current order of leisure and society can be radically reformulated. However, decentring and deconstruction produce a vortex of power if they are allowed to become ends in themselves. Part of the responsibility of exposing the partiality of 'inherited' regimes of power is to unravel them and construct a social order in which justice, inclusion and empowerment obtain as genuine civil rights. This requires the development of a constructive approach to the politics of power. It is a step that poststructuralist writers have not made.

Leisure *Fini*?

It is no longer credible to behave as if there is a single meaning of leisure. More and more students of leisure have discarded the traditional notion of absolute voluntarism in leisure practice in favour of some sort of version of situated practice. Nearly all are congruent in rejecting the old notion in Leisure Studies that it is adequate to consider freedom and choice solely from the standpoint of the individual. However, as we saw in the thumbnail sketches of the vital perspectives in the last section, they differ somewhat in their accounts of the logistics of situated practice and the band-widths of regulation.

Recently, there has been candid frustration with the orthodox paradigms in Leisure Studies/Leisure Sciences and what the interplay between them is able to illuminate about leisure and recreation experience. For example, Blackshaw and Crabbe (2004: 40) reject positivist and 'implicitly positivist' paradigms in the field. They argue that positivist approaches, which I call social formalism, are unable to generate key questions about power because they are based on an uncritical view of the individual as free and self-determining. The 'implicitly positivist' perspectives that have emerged in reaction to positivism constitute a step forward because they situate leisure forms and practice in recognizable contexts of power. However, for Blackshaw and Crabbe (2004), the pebble in the shoe of these positions is that they are unduly partisan. Alan Tomlinson (1989) foreshadowed this argument long ago when he observed that the advent of the Cultural Studies perspective into the field of Leisure Studies/Leisure Sciences is cast in the bent of antagonism. It demands academics, students and professionals ask the question, 'Whose side are you on?' in respect of class inequality, patriarchy, state intervention and social transformation. In the hands of Blackshaw and Crabbe (2004) this argument is modified in important ways by the observation that buying into this or that critical perspective, be it Marxism, feminism, figurational sociology or poststructuralism, involves making all-or-nothing commitments to the epistemological and political features of each position and opposing contrasting positions that do not make the same commitments. Thus, if one accepts and utilizes the feminist argument that sexual inequality prevails at the material, representational and political levels in society, is it admissible to take the next step and maintain that men should be excluded from some leisure and sports settings to enhance female confidence? Similarly, if one accepts the Marxist argument that alienation and commodification are readily observable in leisure forms and practice under capitalism, must one accept the collateral Marxist propositions in respect of the centrality of class struggle, the 'false consciousness' of the proletariat and the concentration of the capitalist business corporation upon the extraction of surplus value? Blackshaw and Crabbe (2004) submit that the paradigm conventions of the field of Leisure Studies/Leisure Sciences mean that debate, research and teaching are trapped in a ping-pong match of perpetual criticism and counter-criticism organized around polarized positions that distort productive debate and exchange.

Ken Roberts (2004), who has hitherto hardly been noted as a writer who dwells on the *discontinuities* in leisure and recreation forms and practice, comments upon a similar impasse in his study of the leisure industries. His study is of great service in maintaining that the space in Leisure Studies/Leisure Sciences assigned to voluntary organizations and the public sector has been disproportionate. The commercialized sector of the leisure industry and the media matter too. It is rash to imagine that the multi-nationals in this sector are managed in the same way and have the same consequences. Such was the error of Adorno and Horkheimer (1944) in their famous unqualified criticism of the culture industry. A *Bertelsmann* is not a *Sony*, or a *News International* or a *Nike*. Multi-nationals may all have it in them to expropriate and achieve a quasi-monopoly of supply. However, as we shall see in Chapter 9, there are various, often highly ambiguous ways that they realize their financial objectives and the relationships that they build with their workforce, consumers, the state and the community.

What Is To Be Done?

I have attempted elsewhere to set out what I think should be done by outlining what I call an 'Action approach' to get out of the paradigm jam (Rojek 2005). I do not propose to repeat the arguments here. However, I think that it is worth addressing three issues that were perhaps under-played in my outline of the Action approach to the study of leisure. These refer to the virtue of eclecticism, the strengths of using a per-spective that analyses leisure in terms of multiple equilibria and the necessity of a political dimension in the Action approach.

Eclecticism

It used to be said of eclecticism that it is a bad thing which ought to be avoided. Its main defects are that it cuts corners and turns a blind eye to consistencies. Yet in the last twenty years a succession of contributions to social and cultural theory have maintained that the old paradigms have lost their resonance (Harvey 1989; Beck 1992; Lash and Urry 1987; 1994; Castells 1996, 1997, 2001; Giddens 1998). Social formalism is neo-liberal. It holds that individuals are free, that inequality is inevitable, that leisure and recreation practice is a matter of choice (rather than the exercise of intentionality in what I call 'positioning' to scarce resources) and that the duty of the welfare state is to produce and maintain a minimal safety net for the disadvantaged. Marxism and socialist femi-nism are collectivist and interventionist. They hold that individuals are constructed by and through inequality, that leisure and recreation forms and practice are socially, culturally and economically conditioned, that strong state involvement in everyday life is required and that egalitarian fiscal and public investment policies are necessary for the collective good. Poststructuralism approaches leisure forms and practice by situating them in regimes of discourse. The term discourse means a combination of power and knowledge that presents a given form of social ordering and identity politics as natural or without an alternative. Poststructuralists are typically disinterested in using the state or corporations to change leisure forms and practice. They regard strategies of change to be themselves forms of discourse. They emphasize the fragmentation, divisions and micro-politics of power.

There is something to be gained from all of these positions. As Blackshaw and Crabbe (2004) maintain, the problem is that the old way of conducting debate between these paradigms involves all-or-nothing commitments to this or that paradigm style and attempting to deal with opposing paradigms by taking what is best from them and eradicating the remainder. The Action approach calls upon students of leisure and recreation to treat eclecticism as a positive value. Social formalists are wrong to maintain that individuals are free and self-determining. The Marxist and socialist feminist reaction that individuals and groups are situated actors who practise leisure and recreation under the constraints of historical necessity and scarcity is accurate. However, by relating choice and freedom to context it does not follow that individuals and groups have *no* choice. As Wearing (1987) maintains, an unfortunate consequence of the contributions of socialist feminism and Marxism in leisure and recreation studies is to create subjects of analysis that are in most salient respects portrayed as docile, passive, victims of power. An eclectic approach to leisure and recreation seeks to reconcile the analytic gains made by positioning leisure choice and forms in relation to history and scarcity with a defence that leisure behaviour is intentional, albeit within the constraints of social positioning.

The old paradigm wars in the study of leisure and recreation were value-based. The challenge for students and researchers today is to move from value-based paradigms to evidence-based paradigms. The latter involve the cultivation of reflexivity about other positions and one's own position. It is not a question of being dogmatically or doctrinally attached to something. Rather, it is a matter of holding and applying the principle that everything is conditional, partial and should be put to the test. A separate set of questions is raised by the problem of choosing the best method to compare and contrast positions and also by the matter of the balance of power relationships between gatekeepers and the rest.

In social life we borrow from this or that individual or group the things that work better for us in life alone and life with others. The opportunities and threats presented to us by everyday life require us to be accomplished eclectics. An individual or group who runs against this current and insists on a closed consistency in social life may be admired, but they are also regarded by the majority as eccentric. This is one reason why organized religion based in the West in the twenty-first century faces an uphill struggle in maintaining faith among believers. Social life now revolves around give and take, sticking with things that work and abandoning things that don't work, remaining true of course to the ethical codes of care for the self and care for the other which recognize that we are differently positioned, and that some of us require more care than others. The cultivation of an eclectic approach to the analysis of leisure and recreation follows the same rule. But it does so with the caveat that researchers have a responsibility to subject assumptions and propositions to evidence and to desert assumptions and propositions that fail to measure up.

Multiple Equilibria

Simple unlinear models of causality tend to produce bipolar models. The best example in the study of leisure is the work–leisure pattern constructed by Wilensky (1960) that was later taken over and modified by Parker (1971). Traditionally, work is presented as the most significant variable that influences leisure practice and choice. There are many reasons for this. For most people, paid employment is the primary source of income and provides significant access to social networks. It follows that income regulates leisure choice and social networks influence the quality of leisure experience. Wilensky (1960) proposed that in industrial society most people are work-centred. He argued that this dominance results in two major types of work–leisure relationship. The *spillover/fusion* model consists of leisure activities which mirror work experience. For example, computer work carries over into internet browsing and computer games. The *compensatory/segmentation* model consists of leisure activities that make up for or offset work experience. In Parker's (1971) hands Wilensky's schema of work and leisure is redefined. Whereas Wilensky (1960) operates at the level of experience, Parker's analysis is pitched at three inter-connected levels: the individual, societal and philosophical.

Multiple equilibria refers to the constellation of relationships between factors upon which social action, and therefore leisure trajectories, are predicated. The presentation of self in specific leisure settings involves relationships

(Continued)

of knowledge, grooming, dress, discourse and much else besides. Behaviour in leisure settings involves significant preparatory emotional labour so as to achieve the impression of competence. Central to the concept of multiple equilibria is the proposition that relationships can move into a condition of disequilibria in which the impression of competence is compromised or fails. For example, if one makes a gaffe in a poker game it damages one's capacity to bluff an opponent.

At the level of the individual, he reproduces Wilensky's thesis that some patterns of work–leisure involve a spillover effect (which Parker calls *extension*); and others follow a compensatory/segmentation mode (which Parker calls *opposition*). To this he adds a third work–leisure pattern that he terms *neutrality* in which no causal relationship is evident between work and leisure.

At the societal level, Parker (1971: 83) identifies adjustments to industrial civilization that promote a *fusion* pattern between work and leisure in which working at our play and playing at our work sets the tone of group behaviour. Dress codes, language conventions and forms of what we now call emotional labour and impression management become congruent in the workplace and the leisure setting. The fusion pattern contrasts with the more traditional work–leisure pattern which Parker (1971: 83) calls *polarity*. As the term implies, this is a social formation in which play at work and work at play is not the norm. Work and leisure are chalk and cheese. Typically, the former is a sphere of inflexibility and regimentation, while the latter is less disciplined, standardized and more diverse and mobile.

Above and beyond the societal level, Parker (1971) identifies a third level of leisure that reflects back upon Pieper's (1952) philosophical designation of leisure as a state of mind, or condition of the soul. On this plane of analysis, the backdrop to the extension/fusion patterns is *holism;* that is, a personal philosophy predicated on the validity of what we would now call the work–life balance. According to this, work and life combine in a relationship of harmonious reciprocity that is mutually enhancing to exploit and develop a more complete and rounded personal and social philosophy. It is akin to the Pragmatist position which strives to find a balance between paid labour, physical exercise and an elevated state of mind as the *desiderata* of leisure in industrial society. According to Parker (1971) the counter to this is *segmentalism*. This is a view that maintains that work and leisure are separate matters and never the twain shall meet. Segmentalism is reminiscent of the Aristotlean view that identifies leisure as a state of mind that threatens to be corrupted by the world of work.

Even within the terms of the SCCA framework the arguments of Wilensky (1960) and Parker (1971) have been subject to criticism. As social formalists, they take work and leisure experience as given, instead of relating their qualities to the context of history and scarcity. The sample that Parker used to make his conclusions was quite limited. It does not support propositions that refer to the whole of culture and society (Veal 2004: 110). More pointedly, Moorhouse (1989: 23) submits that Parker's model simply correlates leisure and work with particular types of experience and is unable to establish genuine *causal* relationships between them. This is a serious criticism because it maintains that Parker provides no scientifically defensible case that certain types of work produce particular kinds of leisure practice.

From the perspective of the SCASSMIL framework the problems with the work of Wilensky and Parker multiply. Work and leisure practice are too limited as variables to illuminate work and leisure experience. The experience of work and leisure forms involves multiple equilibria arranged in a shifting cluster of relationships. Among the key equilibria are the position of the individual and groups in relation to scarcity, the development of emotional labour, age, gender, race, physical wellbeing, education, religion, politics and crimogenic cultures. In addition, there is a separate set of questions relating to the centrality of emotional intelligence and emotional labour in establishing and maintaining credibility and competence in interpersonal relations. These equilibria are positioned in complex, linear and non-linear relationships involving interplay between changing conditions of stability and instability. Among them, some processes of development emerge that become self-regulating, exceeding the capacity of individuals and groups to manage them.

The perspectives articulated by Wilensky and Parker need to adopt a much wider bandwidth of analysis that embraces globalization, multinational leisure corporations, state policy and licit and crimogenic cultures and their relationship to leisure forms and practice. Instead of presenting discrete variables such as work and leisure as correlating with specific kinds of experience, it is necessary to move analysis towards a perspective that is alive to multiple equilibria in which many variables co-exist in shifting relationships of stability and instability. In addition, one must allow that these equilibria operate at both the conscious and the subconscious level. For example, the attraction of leisure for many, is that it *symbolizes* freedom and choice. The subconscious association of leisure with freedom, choice and self-determination overrides the experience of leisure practice. In other words, if an individual's leisure experience is an anti-climax in producing fulfilling, enriching experience, it does not necessarily tarnish the cultural association of leisure as a transparent social good.

Politics

In my (2005) outline of the Action approach I argued for the necessity of maintaining a politics of leisure and recreation organized by a trinity of cardinal values: distributive justice, empowerment and social inclusion. There is no contradiction between this and supporting an evidence-based perspective on leisure. Indeed the evidence supports the necessity of preserving and developing all three values.

Let us consider one example to illustrate the point. It is now generally accepted that leisure and lifestyle choice affects the environment. Every time that we drive a car to work or take a day trip for pleasure we contribute to the production of greenhouse gases through the burning of fossil fuel; increase noise pollution; dictate land use patterns; and influence local patterns of health through vehicle emissions (Potter and Bailey 2008: 31). The UK government has set targets to cut greenhouse gas emissions by at least 12.5% by 2012 and carbon emissions by 60% by 2050 compared with 1990 levels. A recent document produced by the Department of Transport (DfT 2007) proposes that these targets will be achieved by a mixture of four policies:

1) Encourage environmentally friendly means of transport.
2) Improve vehicle fuel efficiency.
3) Reduce the fossil carbon content of transport fuel.
4) Increase the care that people take over fuel consumption while driving.

As Stradling et al. (2008: 140) note, measures two and three are supply-side issues predicated on the government achieving voluntary agreements with fuel and transport corporations. The remaining measures require an attitude-change in consumer lifestyles. They involve encouraging people to use public transport, switching to energy-saving vehicles and car sharing. There can be no mistake about the size of attitude change required to achieve these lifestyle changes. The twentieth century was the century of the car. Over one billion vehicles were manufactured, with an estimated 700 million cars in motion and the remainder occupying land space, parked in roads, garages, driveways and grass verges. The average car spends less than one hour per day in motion. In the UK 72% of adults hold a full driving licence, 81% of men and 63% of women, giving a total of 33.7 million licensed motorists who use 28 million licensed cars. According to the *British Social Attitudes Survey* only 18% of UK households do not own a car or van. Forty per cent own one car and 33% two cars. Nine per cent own more than two cars. Twenty-five per cent of households report one car between two adults, 39% report one car for every adult and 5% report more than one car for every adult (Stradling et al. 2008: 143–4).

Car use is a clear example of how leisure and lifestyle practice contribute to climate change. If we are to control pollution, reduce road congestion and manage noise pollution more efficiently, we must burn less carbon-based fuel. For students and professionals in leisure and recreation the challenge is first, one of education. Consumers must be *empowered* by acquiring knowledge of the relationship between leisure and lifestyle choice and environmental degradation. Students and professionals in the field of leisure and recreation should take a positive role in raising consumer consciousness about the environmental costs of driving for pleasure. At the same time, encouraging car drivers to share cars and switch to more efficient fuel-saving vehicles contributes to *distributive justice* by placing the burden of proactive change upon the richest strata in society. By exposing the risks to the totality of the population that arise from the lifestyle and leisure choices made by car-owners, more *inclusive* attitudes to co-operation, partnership and responsibility in leisure and recreation practice will be engendered.

In the twentieth century the leisure industry was based upon the idea of the consumer as a pleasure-seeking monad. The accumulation of clothes, vehicles, travel, cigarettes and alcohol was posited in terms of the experiential and status gains they delivered to the individual. For most of the twentieth century, in the West at least, the conduct of leisure and recreation was oil-rich, free of anxieties about global warming and located in the boundaries of nation-states in which individual and group security was not an issue. All of the signs are that the twenty-first century will be an era of peak energy prices, environmental instability and the omnipresent threat of terrorism. The days of the leisure monad are numbered.

The question of leisure and climate change calls for a new type of politics, which is globally sensitive, socially encompassing and moves beyond class, gender and race to focus on what might be called *total life risks*. It is far from being exhaustive. The menace of global terrorism calls upon professionals and educators in leisure and recreation to be alive to the uses of free time practice in inciting racial, political or religious hatred. Similarly, as we shall see at greater length in chapter 8, the strategy of global multinationals to maintain and enhance profit margins by switching the supply of dangerous types of leisure consumption (tobacco, alcohol) from the health-conscious developed countries to the emerging economies should be exposed and resisted by leisure educators and professionals. In addition, developing educational programmes to cope with infringement of intellectual property copyright law through illegal downloading, while recognizing the benefits of access for the emerging and developing world, is a major challenge for the field.

It would be wrong to suggest that these issues are not coded and conditioned by inequalities of class, race, gender and status. However, finding solutions to them requires an ecumenical approach that goes beyond a social inequalities perspective. One cannot divorce oneself from the values of one's own time, and the manner in which these values have been embedded at both conscious and subconscious levels, through the inflections of class, gender, race, status and the rest. In the present state of knowledge about human affairs, Elias's (1956) 'detour via detachment' is an illusion. Although compromised by attachments of which we are scarcely aware, and predisposed by the cultural codes and representations that surround us to take this or that view of where we have come from and what we must do, there is still a mode of reorientation for which it is worth fighting. It requires a politics of leisure and recreation that acknowledges common, global challenges to relations of production and consumption, and works to build common, global solutions. This task involves developing a framework that moves beyond regarding the nation-state as the primary regulator of leisure and recreation practice and engaging with the role of the global multinational in conditioning free time activities. We will address the questions of the state and the global multinational in the next two chapters of the book.

7

THE STATE

There would be no modern leisure without the state. Through its control of taxation, licensing, policing and propaganda, the state has imprinted its stamp upon leisure time. As Bailey (1978) and Coalter (2006a, 2006b) show, from the mid nineteenth century, state intervention into free time practice originated from an amalgamation of middle class anxieties about sanitation, health, work discipline, fitness to work, education and civic pride. Rational recreation was a movement founded in class control. The Victorian writer, Francis Fuller (1875: 717), expresses this perfectly, albeit also unconsciously, in a blithe, seldom quoted, little passage on the wisdom of encouraging the masses to use their leisure time in beneficial ways:

> It is a point of *self-interest* and *self-protection for us* to exert ourselves to improve the tone of popular amusements to induce *men* to cultivate the 'leisure hour' for the good of mind and body. Our *safety*, the *security of society,* of *our* homes, and families, in the long run, are concerned with *the form* in which *they* take their recreation. [emphasis added]

The provision of public swimming baths, urban parks, recreational grounds, libraries, art galleries, museums and so on, sprang from the anxieties of middle-class reformers like Fuller. The architects of the City Beautiful movement in the US were animated by similar misgivings (Wilson 1994). They understood well enough that class rule is provisional. In time, those denied and subjugated by the accidents of birth might redefine their position as an intolerable, retractable imposition of advantage and power. Their free time might then cease to be a matter of rest, recuperation and humble self-improvement. It could fester into a hot bed of opposition, resistance and rebellion. This is what Fuller foresaw, and it is why he urged public investment in leisure and recreation to produce, with rising living standards and additional public husbandry of welfare, the civic incorporation of working men and women. However, it would be a mistake to portray the capitalist state as relentlessly striving to keep the grievances of the working class at bay. A new note was sounded in public policy in the 1960s and early 70s when the state introduced a more positive concept of leisure founded upon supplying the needs of the community. In the midst of rising affluence, the leisure society thesis, the containment of work, leisure was reformulated as a part of the general fabric of social services. Public leisure policy ceased to be viewed as a front of class control. It was redefined as a transmission belt for cultural improvement in which the state took it upon itself to liberate the potential for civic enhancement inherent in free time forms and practices. As Coalter (2006b: 62) recognizes, this move was significant since it switched participation in leisure and recreation from a matter of personal choice into an issue of civic entitlement. In effect, this was a *de facto* extension of citizenship rights to cover the non-work sphere. It also offered official recognition that the condescension of high culture to the leisure of those positioned less advantageously in relation to scarcity was obsolescent (Eliot 1948).

Rational recreation and the interventions of the 1960s and 70s were essentially *donatory* types of state intervention; that is, the state sought to transform common customs and practices in leisure and recreation to comply with programmes of living devised by state apparatchiks. The programmes of living enjoined in each period were not the same. Rational recreation was heavily influenced by the doctrine of Muscular Christianity and respect for Empire. State intervention in the 1960s and 70s was secular and more populist. It tried to enhance the leisure and recreation of the people by increasing central and regional funding for the provision of education and the construction of facilities relating to the arts, sport and heritage. However, the moral atmosphere in which the state operated continued to be one of providing improvement and direction 'from above'. Politicians and civil servants, not the people, defined community needs and acted as the helmsmen for initiatives sponsored by the state. As a result, from the standpoint of the Left, state intervention into leisure and recreation was dismissed as unduly bureaucratic and 'managerialist'. The donatory ethos of state policy was regarded as redolent of a tokenisitic engagement with working class leisure forms and practices. The result was held to be the reinforcement of passive consumerism (Coalter 2006a: 165). For its part, the Right deplored leisure and recreation policies dedicated to redistributive justice and social inclusion because they were held to breed a culture of entitlement without corresponding responsibility (Roche 1992; Turner 2006; Taylor 2007).

The avid neo-liberal revival and the social democratic reaction to it, that has dominated conditions since the 1980s, has redefined the state as an enabler of leisure and recreation forms and practices and introduced the concepts of active citizenship and stakeholder culture. The

New Right programme of revitalizing public policy was built around *partnership* between the state, private capital and the community and the principle of value for money. The introduction of Compulsory Competitive Tendering (CCT) in the late 1980s was designed to break the bureaucratic stranglehold over the state provision of leisure and recreation (Henry 1993: 97–109; Aitchison 1997). Management objectives changed from catering for the leisure needs of the community to evidence-based, goal-driven management. Important accessories of this shift in state policy were the rise of audit culture to monitor and evaluate management outcomes and the sponsorship of event management strategies to achieve urban regeneration and enrich civic pride. Leisure and recreation were repositioned as shared resources in which individuals and groups are active citizens. Drawing upon a combination of theoretical influences from communitarianism (Etzioni 1997), social capital theory (Putnam 2000), stakeholder society (Hutton 1996) and Third Way politics (Giddens 1998) the concept of active citizenship involves developing emotional intelligence and using emotional labour to bolster civil society and empower communities. It is committed to social inclusion and extending responsible citizenship. At the heart of this programme is the concept of social capital. This signals a move from policy led by the goal of economic redistribution to policy shaped by the value of social and cultural relations between people. The chief correlates of strong social capital are robust social networks in the community, a vibrant civic infrastructure, common shared goals and high trust relations among members of the community and between the community, the state and business (Coalter 2006a: 169).

Social capital refers to voluntary labour that citizens give to enhance the community, improve the environment and protect the vulnerable (Putnam 2000). Examples include voluntary de-littering and street cleaning, visiting the elderly, providing after-school organized sport and leisure for youth and protecting the natural environment. Cultural capital refers to the beliefs, values and practices that define a culture and sub-culture (Bourdieu 1984). The way of life of a given culture and sub-culture is represented through dance, drama, literature, play-forms, sport, heritage preservation and many other forms of leisure and recreation. The cultivation and enhancement of these ways of life require significant voluntary labour in the shape of serious leisure types of activity (Stebbins 2002).

The movement to active citizenship assays an important change in the relationship of the citizen to common resources. In the era of nationalization and the public ownership of resources, citizens were presented as owning the commanding heights of the economy. In the 1980s deregulation and privatization dismantled the edifice of public ownership by using the argument that the state management of common resources is inefficient.

A new model of civic ownership emerged. It revised the position of active citizens as stakeholders in the relations that make up the quality of life. By, *inter alia*, caring for the environment, practising responsible recycling, developing a balanced diet, showing sensitivity to the disadvantaged, the active citizen strengthened social capital and hence, added to the stock of positive human relations. It also increased the value of competence, relevance and credibility and as such, boosted the significance of emotional intelligence and emotional labour in everyday life. Under the new model, economic investment in leisure and recreation resources that is disassociated from a sense of popular ownership is deplored, both by the state and the public. The knowledge, skills and practices of the community are regarded to be core assets in enhancing quality of life issues. As we shall see later in the chapter, this transition is indicative of a parallel shift in public management from state control to governmentality. The state has repositioned itself from acting as the ringmaster of leisure and recreation goals and the donator of resources, to being the enabling, positive catalyst that mobilizes social networks, bolsters civic infrastructures, builds shared goals and trust relationships with the people for the common goal of social enhancement. Leisure and recreation activities are identified as having a role to play in urban renewal, extending social inclusion, community enhancement, providing new employment opportunities and curbing anti-social behaviour (Scottish Office 1999). Public investment in them is justified as possessing much wider social, cultural and environmental objectives. Leisure and recreation are presented as resources for extending responsibility and building whole relationships in communities.

The Special Event

An important adjunct of stakeholding culture in leisure and recreation management has been the emergence of Special Event Management initiatives. The term 'special event' refers to:

> specific rituals, presentations, performances or celebrations that are consciously planned and created to mark special occasions and/or to achieve particular social, cultural or corporate goals and objectives. (Bowdin et al. 2006: 14–15)

Among the functions claimed for special events are, festive spirit, a sense of authenticity, hospitality and community enhancement (Getz 2005).

Special events refer to mass fundraising, audience-based activities in leisure and recreation. Examples include global consciousness-raising activities, such as Live Aid and Live Earth, international sports events (the Olympics, the FIFA World Cup), Drama, Dance, Film and Literary Galas/Festivals, Horticultural Shows and Heritage festivals (which cele-brate the values of national or regional cultures, such as the Carnival in Brazil or community culture such as the celebration of gay and lesbian lifestyle in the Sydney *Mardi Gras*). Special events fall into two categories: 1) one-off projects, such as Live Aid (1985), the Nelson Mandela 70th Birthday Concert aka Freedomfest (1988), Live 8 (2005) and Live Earth (2007) that focus on single issue topics like famine relief in Ethiopia and combating global warming; 2) cyclical events such as the Olympics, the Chelsea Flower Show, the Brazilian Carnival, New Orleans Mardi Gras, which are an established part of the leisure and recreation calendar. The preferred business model for special events is a partnership between the government, business and the community. They contrast with regular leisure and recreation services in carrying high publicity value (they are often covered live by the media) and follow an agenda of active citizen-ship (the 'can do' approach which submits that everyone is important and everyone can make a difference).

It would be stretching matters to submit that the Flower Festival has replaced the Leisure Centre. Notwithstanding that, at the national and international level, special events and event management have rapidly risen to become the jewels in the crown of modern public leisure provision. There are many reasons for this. Foremost among them is the power of the special event to attract intense coverage in the media and to exert a major demonstration effect in appearing to directly tackle problems of hunger, inequality and injustice. The shift from a citizen to a stake-holder culture that has occurred in state policy since the late 1990s redefines the citizen as an active agent in expanding social and cultural capital. Events management ties active citizenship to high public *causes célèbres* such as relieving poverty in the emerging and developing world, caring for the planet and fighting racial injustice. The special event signals a shift in leisure and recreation resourcing from the state acting as a donatory agent to a partnership between the state, the corporation and the community. The move to a partnership mode is justified as *enhancing* the relevance of output. Typically, the issue of relevance is presented as evidence-based as opposed to doctrinally defined. The adjunct of relevance is the *audit trail* in which resourcing is compared with measured outputs, usually employing quantitative methodologies.

The special event is calculated to appeal to the media age. Co-opting support from celebrities in the world of entertainment is standard practice. This enhances the brand of the good cause and, in its own right, steps up the media lens. However, it also produces a degree of slippage between the glamour of the event and the good causes which are its *raison d'être*. Giving, and participating, in a global concert can easily be confused with making a real difference in solving a problem. This is not to deny that special event funding makes a positive contribution to the management of social and economic problems. However, the scale of the development gap, AIDS infection, racism and environmental pollution require concerted, multilateral intervention. Ultimately this is a question of the Western electorate voting for progressive policies of distributive justice, social inclusion and empowerment. There is a danger that special events dissolve this political issue in more instantly attractive issues of entertainment and feeling good about making a 'contribution'. As such, they may be criticized for extending the old Roman idea of using bread and circuses to organize consent in the masses.

Special Events Management unhelpfully revives some aspects of the SCCA framework. In particular, it implies that there are simple, direct causal relationships between need and provision. In reality, the interface between need and provision involves multi-equilibria and determined strategy at the multilateral state structural level. This involves some tough long-term choices about resourcing and taxation which tend to get lost in the glamour, spontaneity and short intensity of the special event. In short, as a stateless solution to the world's problems, special events offer a useful adjunct. But they do not, and cannot, constitute, the primary front of intervention.

The State: Primary Layers

Before coming to the matters of *how* and *why* the state intervenes in free time activities, it is important to be clear about what is meant by 'the state'. For it is self-evident that intervention in leisure and recreation in the name of the state occurs at multiple levels, from the global and the national to the local (Roberts 2004). The first important distinction to

make is between the government and the state. The two are not synony-
mous. The government is the due, representative body of the electorate
that devises and articulates that national policy and strategy and, as Max
Weber (1948) argued, successfully claims the monopoly over the legitimate use of physical force within a given territory. The pretext, defence
and execution of these claims is not a matter of government. It is a matter of the state apparatus, of which the government is the head (although
in the case of the UK, the Monarch is the titular head).

In his classic study of the capitalist state, the late Ralph Miliband
(1969: 50) differentiated the main layers of the state thus:

• The Government

The elected representatives of the people who formulate policy and
strategy in the national interest.

• The Civil Service

The salaried, non-elected specialist, administrative staff who assist
the government in executing policy and strategy at both home and
abroad. It includes the operations of Embassies in representing the
national interest on foreign soil.

• The Judiciary

The salaried, independent body of legal experts who establish the
conventions of the law and manage the process through which the
law changes.

• The Military and Police

The specialist forces charged with enforcing the law, protecting the
integrity of the state and monitoring resistance.

• Parliamentary Assemblies

The various single-issue commissions and groups that advise on
government policy, and the conduct of the government, the civil
service, the judiciary, the military and the police.

- ## Sub-central Government

  This is a somewhat nebulous category, having to do with the state
  inspectorate that monitors provision and standards at the local level
  and charities that are recognized by the state and subject to the regulation of the Charity Commission. It also encompasses the local
  authority level. The latter is partly autonomous in the sense of being
  directly elected through local plebiscite and possessing local powers
  of taxation and policing. However, the ultimate guarantor and regulator of local government is central government, to whom the former
  is answerable for all matters of conduct.

Miliband wrote in an era in which the media power was less advanced than
it is today. So to his list we must add *the Press Office*. By this is meant the
media experts employed by the government to advise how policy and strategy should be sold to the people. In addition, the term encompasses the
various media specialists in the other branches of the state apparatus as
listed above, who have the task of spinning departmental initiatives, plans
and justifications to other departments, including central and local government, as well as the electorate and relevant international bodies of opinion.

In distinguishing between these layers in the state apparatus, Miliband
wants to depart from the notion that the state is a unitary mechanism
that works like a transmission belt to translate policy and strategy into
practice. To put it differently, he wants to draw attention to the fact that
the state apparatus involves interests that are independent of the
national interest and not necessarily subject to its sovereignty. As he
(1969: 50) puts it, it is in these layers

> in which 'state power' lies, and it is through them that this power is
> wielded in its different manifestations by the people who occupy leading
> positions in each of these institutions – the presidents, prime ministers
> and their ministerial colleagues; high civil servants and other state
> administrators; top military men; judges of the higher courts; some at
> least of the leading members of parliamentary assemblies.

Miliband's view of the capitalist state was forged in the furnace of
revitalized post-war Marxist theory. He regarded the state in class society as operating primarily and inevitably in the interests of the dominant class so as to ensure the predominance of this class.

Autonomy or Captivity?

There is a good deal of debate over the question of whether the state
is autonomous or, as Miliband (1969) maintains, captive to determinate

social interests. The classic statement of the captive state thesis is to be found in Marx and Engels (1846). They submit that the state is the tool of the capitalist class to exploit and develop economic, social and political class interests.[1] Writers like Karl Kautsky (1946, 2007) and Ralph Miliband (1969) take over this intellectual framework and argue that in modern capitalist society there is a close alliance between the capitalist class and the administrative class. In Kautsky's (ibid.) locution, this alliance has produced a type of 'state capitalism', in which the state typically operates to consolidate and advance the power of the capitalist class.

The captive state thesis is opposed by a wide flank of diverse writers who hold that the state in capitalist society is either partly or wholly autonomous from the interests of the capitalist class. The differences between these authors turn on the question of the degree of autonomy assigned to state power. For example, Gramsci (1971) follows Marx and Engels in maintaining that the capitalist state has an historical tendency to exploit and develop the interests of the capitalist class. State capitalism might be defined as the condition in which the capitalist class has achieved domination over both the economy and the state. Gramsci modifies this equation radically, by inserting what he terms 'civil society' between the state and the economy. Civil society is the social space occupied by voluntary social organizations and institutions like the media, leisure and education. They reflect upon both the state and the economy and articulate a cacophony of social interests that both support and take issue with capitalist authority. For Gramsci, the capitalist state operates most securely when it functions not via naked extortion or physical force but through the management of voluntary consent. To achieve this consent the capitalist class develops a 'complex unity' of rule that works through alliances along 'many fronts'. The capitalist class rules by nudging and pushing the state to engineer *hegemony* over rival social interests in the economy, the state and civil society.

Hegemony is a highly nuanced term in Gramsci's sociology. Its core meaning is the engineering of voluntary 'popular' consent through unifying different class interests around a common cause ('nation', 'Monarchy') and dividing class and social interests which are opposed to capitalist rule. However, around this core, several important distinctions are introduced and applied. Thus, hegemony establishes the 'horizon' of 'normal' conduct; that is, the scope of behaviour that is regarded as normal and tolerable. Closely aligned with this is the idea that hegemony positions actors

(Continued)

> not only to accept a given state of affairs, but to accept their ranking in this given state of affairs as legitimate. Then again, hegemony refers to the content and form of moral, political and intellectual leadership that enables 'a power bloc' of class to exert a 'field of force' over others who accept themselves as 'subjects'. The term 'power bloc' is itself a nuanced take on class rule, since it acknowledges that in complex, industrial democratic societies class interests rule through alliances and partnerships over others.

For Gramsci, struggle is inescapable in the business of winning hegemony over rival social interests. It is accomplished through partnerships between class interests that establish a power bloc of authority. As economic and political circumstances dictate, this power bloc takes advantage of rival social interests or makes concessions to them in order to achieve compliance via popular, voluntary consent. Gramsci's analysis of the state, then, establishes civil society as a field of contest in which state hegemony is asserted, applied and contested. Basic to his notion of state domination are the ideas of resistance and negotiation.

Poulantzas (1973, 1978) adopts a similar line of argument. He submits that the state is an instrument designed and employed to service ruling class interests. In order to be credible in winning compliance the state needs to represent itself as being autonomous from ruling class interests and to apply policies that make some concessions to the powers that are subject to ruling class authority. Thus, through struggle, popular interests are registered in the state apparatus and may translate in positioning disadvantaged groups more favourably in relation to scarcity. However, for Poulantzas the autonomy of the state is relative. In the long run the political sphere will re-establish the precedence of ruling class interests (Poulantzas 1978: 143). In effect, far from processes of bargaining and negotiation contributing to the liberation of subjugated strata, their real consequence is to conjure forth the image of advancing freedom which gives the illusion of progress. In this way, Poulantzas concludes, the working class colludes with the forces of oppression and regimentation that ensure ruling class domination.

The captive state thesis is now very unfashionable. Most commentators allow some autonomy to the state, the question is to what degree? In the fields of leisure and sport studies various contributors propose causal relationships between state action and leisure practice. For example, Hargreaves (1986), Sage (1998), McKay (1991) and Gruneau and Whitson (1993) make direct use of the concept of hegemony to analyse how the state invested and popularized sport as an articulation of 'respectable leisure' in order to blunt working class resistance and bind working class sentiments to a 'national-popular' agenda. Springhall (1977) and Yeo and Yeo (1981) note the same strategy in the state sponsorship of youth movements like the Scouts and the Boys' Brigade. Needless to say, these authors follow Gramsci in regarding the 'national-popular' agenda to be a mask for ruling class interests. The *esprit de corps* and nationalist fervour that organized sport and youth movements delivered elevates 'the national interest' above concrete divisions of class, race and gender. In this way, sport and youth movements were supported by the state to neutralize the potential of working class rebellion. These studies stop well short of affirming a determinist relationship between state action and individual conduct. The state may urge the individual to adopt this or that disposition in exercising voluntary choice, but it is for the individual to concede or reject the directions of the state. The premise that the intentionality of individual action is foundational is therefore preserved.

Control over policing, licensing and setting the public agenda, gives the state enormous power to shape leisure practice. However, this power and the concomitant issue of whether autonomy is absolute or relative, does not get to the heart of the emotional force that state intervention marshals and conducts. Emile Durkheim (1904: 72) argued that the state 'is above all, supremely, the organ of moral discipline'.

In modern times, this line of reasoning has been developed most cogently by Corrigan and Sayer (1985) in their analysis of the process of English state formation. Drawing co-extensively on the Marxist tradition, Corrigan and Sayer's (1985) analysis of the state is particularly relevant for our purposes because it gives due attention to the role of ritual, the creation and sponsorship of anniversaries, coronations and memorial days, heritage and representational culture, in general, in enhancing national identity. This application of representational culture made extensive use of theatrical form and dramatic spectacle to manufacture consent. Theatre and spectacle have their origins, and reach their fullest expression in everyday life today, in the sphere of leisure and recreation. The state sponsorship of national sports and cultural forms provides a collective representation of national values and national identity. For Corrigan and Sayer (1985) English state formation was crucially a process of *moral regulation*. Borrowing again from Durkheim, they present the project of making historical representations of the monarch of the day, Britannia, John Bull and other icons of English life 'timeless', as calculated attempts by the architects of statecraft to concentrate 'collective conscience'. Through these cultural mechanisms the earth-shattering changes wrought by industrialization and the rise of Empire were portrayed neutrally as 'the story of the people' rather than the machinations of the ruling class, intent upon preserving and bolstering class domination.

Moral regulation is state sponsorship of emotional bonds and cultural values that are building blocks of national character. In England, the Puritan *coup d'état* in the sixteenth century pursued the object of moral regulation through programmes of *moral cleansing*. Forms of leisure and recreation in dance, music and the theatre, which were not couched in the task of adding to the glory of God were censored or, in other ways, discouraged. This case does not exhaust the examples of moral cleansing. In Britain the state pursued the same task in the nineteenth and early twentieth centuries in sponsoring Christianity and recognized youth events. President Roosevelt's 'New Deal' legislation to combat the Great Depression in the US in the 1930s, embraced culture, leisure and sport as state-supported programmes of cultural and economic revival. Through the leisure pioneer Charles K. Brightbill, the leisure and recreation department of the University of Illinois at Urbana-Champaign developed close links with 'New Deal' regeneration projects in the region. In statist, including fascist-statist, societies in the twentieth century, organized leisure and recreation events and programmes were used as transmission belts of centrally approved indoctrination. Examples include the Nazi *Strength Through Joy* (*Kraft durch Freude*) programme which provided subsidized holidays, sponsored visits to the theatre, factory beautification, constructed sports facilities and developed the People's Car (the Volkswagen) for the masses (Baranowski 2004); and the Soviet Youth programme *Komsomol* (Communist Youth League) and the *Young Pioneers* tightly controlled by the Soviet Communist Party. Kassof (1965) reported that *Komsomol* had 19.4 million members aged between 14 and 28 in 1962; and the *Young Pioneers* (ages 10–14), 20 million members.

In the 1980s, Marxist (Van Moorst 1981; Clarke and Critcher 1985) and socialist feminist (Green et al. 1987; Wimbush and Talbot 1988) approaches to leisure identified the state as the central institutional lever of power in society. Through its control of schooling, workplace legislation, the media agenda and the distribution of public finance to local authority agencies and extra-Parliamentary bodies, like the Sports Council and the Arts Council, the state acted directly to influence leisure forms and practice. With hindsight, an evident lacuna in these approaches was an assessment of corporations and multi-national businesses in moulding leisure activities. The dynamics of globalization and its consequences, do not figure appreciably in these contributions. An unfortunate consequence of this is the emergence and crystallization of an analytic imbalance that tended to focus on leisure and recreation in one country. By the same token, the visionary and interventionist powers of the state are over-exaggerated. These approaches are firmly rooted in the SCCA framework in which radical socialism sees state control as the means to redress inequality and progressively regulate leisure forms and practice.

Had things turned out differently, the course of debate on the place of the state in leisure and recreation activity would have centred on the question of relative autonomy. Very likely, the voluntarism of individual and group behaviour in relation to the interventions of the state would have occupied the pedestal of enquiry. But things did not work out like that. As the 1980s unfolded, new poststructuralist interests in embodiment, bio-politics, representation, globalization and the dispersal of power within, and throughout society, directed analysis away from the state. Gradually, a focus on power, attached to the question of governmentality, supplanted the old accent upon the state as the central lever of power (Aitchison 2003). What is meant by the term 'governmentality'? And what are its consequences for the analysis of leisure and recreation?

Governmentality

The concept of governmentality is associated most closely with the work of Michel Foucault (1980, 1981, 1991). He does not supply a definition of governmentality. Instead he develops it incrementally through an interlinked series of studies of medicine, penology and the history of ideas. At the root of these studies is an interest in power. Foucault breaks with the neo-Marxist tradition that, through its liberal use of the concepts of 'domination', 'ideology' and 'rule', connects power with repression. This departure is not motivated by a wish to rehabilitate the social formalist perspective on power that portrays the individual as a free actor, exercising choice and responsibility. Instead, Foucault is concerned with two tasks. Firstly, he seeks to provide a more nuanced view of power that presents it as both constraining and enabling. Secondly, he aims to extend the idea of disciplinary power away from the state/class axis to encompass embodiment, therapy, pedagogy and correct government over oneself. We can get a better perspective of what is at issue here by adapting one of Foucault's concepts – Care for the Self – and introducing another – Care for the Other.

Care for the Self refers to *medical, psychological, cultural, political and social knowledge relating to individual wellbeing*. Examples would include greater knowledge of the health risks associated with poor diet, the threat to the environment posed by CO_2 emissions, the health benefits of regular exercise, the therapeutic value of leisure practice, and so on. The accumulation of knowledge about these matters enhances the capacity of individuals and groups to engage in productive emotional labour and enhance their perceived competence.

Care for the Other refers to *medical, psychological, cultural, political and social knowledge relating to behaviour that places others at risk*. The emergence of risk culture has popularized awareness that the pleasure-seeking activities of others produce collective risks and new responsibilities of risk management. Secondary smoking and the relationship between air travel, automobility and the carbon footprint are two examples of leisure-related activities that are understood to increase collective risk.

Since the 1970s, these two ethical principles have exerted a pronounced influence on everyday life issues and leisure choice. The transmission belts for this knowledge include organized education, but ordinary sociability in leisure and sport also plays a major role in expanding social consciousness. Each of these principles presupposes significant emotional intelligence and emotional labour by individuals. It is not just a matter of reconnaissance of questions of politics, culture, psychology and the environment which carries status. It is also a matter of monitoring presentational skills, hygiene, grooming and sensitivity to the needs of others to convey competence. The reconnaissance and monitoring of emotional intelligence is a significant occupation. On several occasions in this book I have noted that this in turn, raises tricky issues of what we mean by 'time off' and 'free choice' in leisure and recreation. It is exactly the pervasive nature of Care for the Self and Care for the Other and the permanent requirement to apply monitoring and reconnaissance behaviours that Foucault's concept of governmentality is designed to flag. The state is certainly complicit in raising popular consciousness about these ethical principles. But it is implausible to maintain that the power relations that give rise to them and their consequences may be confined to the state. The ethical principles of Care for the Self and Care for the Other are the products of many inter-connecting interventions, forms of knowledge and types of pedagogy. The concept of governmentality extends the analysis of power and influence from the activities of the state to encompass extra-state networks of power relating, *inter alia*, to discourses and traditions on health, responsibility, well-being, neighbourliness and sensitivity.

The concepts of emotional intelligence and emotional labour resonate powerfully with Foucault's discussion of governmentality. Historically, the state defined leisure and recreation as the reward for work. The trade union movement saw leisure and recreation in the same way. The struggle for holiday entitlement and statutory pensions was conducted as the reward for work offering the labourer opportunities for rest, recuperation and life-space for the cultivation of non-work interests. What was left out of account were the various ways in which leisure and recreation were gradually colonized by lifestyle and life-coaching concerns. To be regarded as a valued worker and good citizen it was incumbent upon the individual to radiate competence, relevance and credibility. Leisure and recreation became the life-space where data and relationships geared to achieving and exhibiting competence were accumulated. Through following the latest discussions on confidence, ease with others, fashion, grooming, psychological wholeness and correlative presentational skills, individuals and groups effectively committed themselves to a round-the-clock programme of life-coaching. This involved being conversant with the latest gossip and deeper perspectives about politics, health, relationships, education, justice and culture. The accumulation and demonstration of this information contributed to the individual being trusted as a rounded person. It also encompassed finding a mate and having a family. For the achievement and exhibition of competence depends upon having the right mate and the children with the right values, attitudes and codes of behaviour. Life-coaching was delivered by new specialist workers such as psychologists, psychiatrists, beauticians, colourists and lifestyle gurus. It extended to the media which, in addition to providing entertainment, became a portal for guidance and opinions about lifestyle and relationships. The colonization of leisure and recreation by life-coaching compromised traditional notions of 'time off' and 'freedom'. Leisure and recreation ceased to be the reward for work. They became a sphere of lifestyle in which individuals and groups were enmeshed in *another sort of governmentality* based upon the cultivation of emotional intelligence and the practice of emotional labour.

Foucault's work is often referred to as *decentring* our view of power; that is, by emphasizing the connection between power, discourse, knowledge and networks, Foucault de-couples power from the notion of a central struggle, whether it be conceptualized in terms of class, gender or race. It follows that to participate in leisure and recreation practice is to be caught up in networks of embodiment and emplacement that propel action and development in specific trajectories of behaviour. On this reading, those positioned more advantageously in relation to scarcity may enjoy privileges of access, but in the final analysis, they are also enmeshed in power relationships that condition embodiment and emplacement conduct.

The Limits of the State's Power

The decentring perspective forces us to amend the argument of state omnipotence. In complex, industrial society state power is always going to be significant (Gellner 1988). While the state legislates and polices behaviour, it is also entwined in discourses and traditions of knowledge, power and pedagogy that precede it and extend beyond the apparatus of regulation that it directly commands. Jürgen Habermas (1973) introduced the useful concept of *steering capacity* to refer to the room for manoeuvre possessed by the state to execute policy. In an interconnected world the steering capacity of the state depends on multilateral agreements between states and co-operative policies of policing and regulation. Reformist and progressive policies in leisure and recreation are easily compromised by the refusal of individual states to comply with multilateral agreements. We have already referred to the question of greenhouse gas emissions and the difficulties caused by the withdrawal of the US from the Kyoto protocol (pp. 43–4). Two other examples from leisure and recreation practice will serve to illustrate the challenges posed to state steering capacity by globalization and the informal economy: a) the drug trade and b) illegal downloading of intellectual property.

The Drug Trade

As we have already noted, the use of illegal drugs for the purpose of leisure and recreation is widespread in the West. The secluded and covert nature of illegal drug use means that there is some dispute about the extent of the practice. Mares (2006: 44) cites data collected by US government surveys which indicates that 46% of Americans over the age of 12 (94 million people) are estimated to have used an illegal substance. Illegal drug use is a common leisure and recreation practice throughout the West. Cannabis is the most widespread illicit drug of preference. In Australia 39% of the population are estimated to have used it. In the US the figure is 35%; in Denmark 31%; in England and Wales 25%; Spain 22%; Eire 20%; Holland 18%; France 16% and Germany 13%. The use of cocaine, ecstasy and amphetamines is concentrated in the US. Thus, 12% of the population in the US admit to having used cocaine. In Australia the figure is 4.3%; Spain 3.3%; England and Wales 3%; Holland 2.4%; Denmark 2%; Germany 1.5%; and Greece 1.3% (Mares 2006: 46). Parker et al.'s (1998) longitudinal study of illegal leisure in North West England, reported that 36.3% of all 14-year-olds had tried at least one illicit drug for recreational use. By 19 the figure had risen to 64.3% with marijuana, amyl nitrate and amphetamines predominating as drugs of favour.

Some of these figures contrast with estimates reported earlier in the book (pp. 72–6). This reinforces the point that gaining precise data is difficult because it is in the nature of the practice to be concealed and private. However, nobody involved in studying or managing the problem would dissent from the proposition that the practice of illegal drug use is significant and constitutes an appreciable component in the leisure/recreation spectrum.

Throughout Western economies the state has responded by legislation, policing, fining, sentencing and educational programmes. There is some evidence of stabilization and a slowing down in the rate of exposure to illegal substances. British Crime Survey data for the new millennium indicate that one third of the adult population have tried at least one illicit substance during their lifetime. For those over the age of 30 the figure rises to 50%. Between 2002 and 2007 there was a gradual decline of drug use of those aged between 16 and 24. At the same time, between 1997 and 2007 there was a doubling in the number of school children using at least one illicit drug, from 10 to 20% (Manning 2007: 53).

In the US the Office of Applied Statistics (http://oas.samhsa.gov/nhsda/98summHtml/TOC.htm) reports that monthly use of illicit drugs between 12–25-year-olds has fallen since the mid 1980s; while, for the age group between 26–34 there was an increase in use until the mid 1980s and then a decline. In contrast the use of ecstasy, Oxycontin and methamphetamines has increased dramatically. In some circles, the use of these drugs at the end of the 1990s and the start of the new millennium was described as an epidemic (Mares 2006: 133).

Policies of containment and education have modified patterns of illegal drug use, but they have not erased the practice from the leisure/recreation spectrum. Over the last thirty years the evidence suggests that there has been significant 'cultural accommodation' to the use of illegal drugs in leisure and recreation. This is evident in the social reaction to drug users in family, friendship and subcultural networks and the open treatment of illegal drug consumption through a diverse range of multi-media outlets spanning, film, television, magazines and novels (Parker et al. 2002). If one weighs data from the UK and the US, and compares it with comparative statistics from other Western societies there are clear common trends in the use of illegal drugs in leisure and recreation. Manning (2007: 53) gets it right when he summarizes thus:

From the middle of adolescence onwards a significant minority of young people acquire drug experiences, these experiences grow more frequent through late adolescence and much of this activity is centred around cannabis. On the other hand, there is some evidence that the rate of increasing exposure to drug experiences is slowing down and if we look beyond cannabis to other slightly 'harder' recreational drugs it seems that only around 10% of young people are regular consumers.

State policy to contain or reduce drug use is a mixture of unilateral and multilateral policing. The international drug trade between gangs and illegal cartels based in the emerging and developing world and the cash-rich metropolitan centres of the West is well established. The major world producers of opiates (heroin etc.) are Afghanistan, Thailand, Myanmar, North Korea, Colombia and Mexico; marijuana: Mexico, Colombia, Kazakhstan, Kyrgyzstan, Philippines, South Africa and Morocco; coca: Bolivia, Colombia, Peru; cocaine: Colombia; and hashish: Morocco (Mares 2006: 70). The gang and cartel culture in the illicit drug trade has demonized third-world drug barons and traffickers, such as Paulo Escobar in Colombia and Arellano Felix in Mexico. The use of extortion, money-laundering, torture and gang executions are well publicized features of international illegal drug chains. In countries where illegal drugs are produced and the traffickers are based, state policy is often compromised by organized intimidation and the importance of illegal drug revenues to the local population. Western states have limited powers to intervene directly and are, in any case, often compromised by the same pressures from drug barons and drug cartels.

Putting this to one side, it is a serious distortion to locate illegal drug production and trafficking solely in the developing and emerging world. In the UK in 1997 the police seized 149,996 kilos of cannabis plants and 164,000 LSD doses (Bean 2002: 7). The world's leading producers of ecstasy are Poland and Holland; LSD, the US; and high potency marijuana, the US (Mares 2006: 70). State law enforcement policies in respect of domestic drug production and trafficking have not broken the supply chain. The production and exchange of illegal drugs remains a significant component of leisure and recreation culture in the West. Both suppliers and consumers have been adept at taking evasive action. Some commentators detect the emergence of tolerance and relaxation in social attitudes to illegal drug use. Parker et al. (2002) propose that in the last three decades the West has lived through the 'normalization' in recreational drug use. This thesis has not been without dissent. For example, Shiner and Newburn (1997) submit that recreational drug cultures are marginal. In their interviews with young people in East London they found high levels of stigma are still attached to illegal drug use. Exposure to drug cultures may be widespread but this is not equivalent to cultural acceptance or cultural accommodation. Their research suggests that state policy against illegal drugs reinforces popular stigmas against illegal drug cultures and contributes to containment. Be that as it may, the persistence of recreational drug cultures is a strong example of the limitations of state power and a vindication of an approach to individual and group regulation which assigns importance of the concept of governmentality and the SCCASMIL perspective on leisure and recreation trajectories. Although they are illegal, recreational drug cultures are not *lawless*. On the contrary, they operate under regimes of power that are formulated in resistance to state policy and condition the form and content in which interpersonal exchange occurs.

Illegal Downloading of Intellectual Property

We have already noted the significance of illegal downloading and the piracy of intellectual property (see pp. 56–7). It merits further consideration because of the sheer scale of the practice in contemporary leisure and recreation. Music, film and software companies complain that they are losing billions of dollars per year. It is not simply a matter of file-sharing. A recent study commissioned by the industry group British Music Rights (www.bmr.org/page/submissions) reports that more than half of young people copy the songs on their hard drives to friends and swap CD and DVD recordings. The industry has focused on illegal online file-sharing. Multilateral agreements to impose criminal penalties and payment of damages cover 17 countries in Europe, Asia and North America and South America (Austria, Denmark, France, Finland, Germany, Ireland, Italy, Holland, the UK, Sweden, Switzerland, the USA, Japan, Iceland, Hong Kong, Singapore and Argentina). This has led to thousands of fines of US$3,000 or more imposed upon individuals and an international campaign against unauthorized P2P networks such as FastTrack (Kazaa), Gnutella (BearShare), DirectConnect, BitTorrent, WinMX and SoulSeek. In 2006 a US Senate resolution was passed to urge universities to clamp-down on illicit file-sharing across campus networks. The British Music Rights report maintains that home-copying is a bigger drain on revenue than file-sharing. Overall, 95% of their survey of 1,158 people had engaged in some form of copying, including downloading from a friend's hard-drive and copying from the radio.

The extent of illegal home-copying and file-sharing suggests that policing and legislation has a negligible deterrent effect. The concentration of policing and litigation in the developed world means that multilateral agreements have no substance in much of central Europe, South East Asia, Africa and Latin America. Software theft here does not have *carte blanche*. Public admonitions against copyright infringement and occasional example prosecutions are made. However, there are other priorities on the state agenda besides preventing the counterfeiting of intellectual property via file-exchange and home copying.

At the time of writing, most Western states are considering a shift in policy towards European law where private copying and downloading exceptions carry a fee to copyright holders in the form of compensation charged to the supplier. For example, if my University negotiates the right to download a DVD directed by Paul Thomas Anderson, or if I download the file from an Internet Service Provider, a fee is logged at source. But this implies a veritable panoply of effective data protection mechanisms that are not in place and which will be exceptionally difficult to organize on a multi-lateral basis. Currently, there is no tenable system for policing home copying or file-sharing. Everything hangs on an 'honesty box' policy in which the end-user is enjoined to come clean about the consumption of copyright material. There are no scientifically dependable research findings to establish if an honesty box policy works. We do know that where copyright material is offered on the net for legal downloading at a price voluntarily determined by the consumer there is a strong deflationary effect. In 2007 the UK band Radiohead offered their new album *In Rainbows* on the net for whatever price consumers would see fit to pay. The average price paid was £2.90 ($US 6.00).

Illegal downloading on the internet is a particularly compelling example of the limited powers of states to regulate the conduct of citizens. Many commentators argue that over the last thirty years civil society in democratic states has been subject to the deregulation of legal entitlements and protection and increasing and more intrusive forms of state surveillance justified in the name of an alien, terrorist threat (Bourdieu 1998; Bourdieu and Wacquant 2003; Smart 2003). At the same time, the internet has emerged as a major extension of the public sphere, offering new and often highly critical forms of information exchange, access to sensitive information and opportunities for sharing intellectual property. Illegal software exchange is one aspect of this. Currently, there is no effective mechanism of policing and the criminal proceedings initiated by copyright holders for illegal file-sharing and copying are widely regarded as low risk. The opportunities are so readily available that illegal software exchange has drawn millions into criminal activity. The cause of deterrence is not helped by the widespread belief that music and film companies, computer games suppliers and software manufacturers have been profiteering for decades. Illegal downloading is therefore justified as resistance against fat cat business corporations. Currently, there is no plausible national or multilateral state strategy to compensate copyright holders. Voluntary policing of piracy by the Internet Service

Provider (ISP) is mooted as one option. But it is a fanciful one since no ISP has the capacity to inspect and filter every file.

Another option that is widely discussed is black-listing suspected file-sharers and convicted internet pirates. In France President Sarkozy supports the Olivennes initiative, started in 2007, that requires ISPs to disconnect repeat infringers. In the UK the Gowers Review (HMSO 2006) into intellectual property law recommended enhancing government powers to penalize internet pirates. But these suggestions would address no more than the tip of the iceberg. The state is unable to enforce a comprehensive system of deterrence because no such system has yet been invented.

State Central

The reasons for the centrality of the state in the Marxist and socialist feminist analysis of leisure and recreation are straightforward. They derive from two of the key features of the modern state identified in Weberian sociology; that is, dual state monopolies over public economic and fiscal matters, and the legitimate use of physical force. Both in the academic study and popular culture, there is a strong association between leisure and voluntarism. Indeed, for many commentators leisure is the sphere of voluntary activity *par excellence* (Parker 1971; Neulinger 1981a). As I have observed elsewhere, this association is highly questionable (Rojek 2005: 17–30). However, because it is prominent and widespread we must take seriously the role of the state in planting and pruning leisure activities that contribute to moral wellbeing. Let us recall that Durkheim (1897) insisted that the state should be regarded as the *ultimate moral force* in society; that is, the conscience and mouthpiece of collective will. Because of this, the question of the moral significance of the modern state in legitimating leisure forms must be added to the twin monopolies identified by Weber.

But Durkheim and Weber wrote in an age before the arrival of the weightless world, globalization, multiculturalism and the recognition of common risks to the planet that encompass all individuals and groups, irrespective of the nation-state in which they are born and located. This new situation requires a shift from a perspective built around the notion of state monopolies over certain kinds of power, to a model of state-capital oligopoly, in which the power of individual states is counter-balanced and, in some cases, out-flanked by corporations and illegal cartels and gangs. The SCASSMIL framework is designed to capture this condition and follow it through in the study of leisure and recreation. How does this framework require us to modify the main features of the modern nation state identified by Durkheim and Weber? Let us consider each feature in turn.

Monopoly over Public Economics and Taxation

The state commands significant public resources. It has the power to identify leisure forms that enhance or diminish the public good and secure the economic resources to achieve its ends. State investment in sport, health education, recycling, reducing greenhouse gas emissions, control over illegal drugs and policing have a direct impact upon individual and group trajectories of leisure behaviour. However, in a weightless, globalized world in which a perspective of shifting multiple equilibria is more appropriate than closed, linear cause and effect models, the old idea of central state power does not hold much water. This can be illustrated in several ways. For example, it is one thing for states to recognize the contribution of leisure and recreation cultures to greenhouse gas emissions. It is quite another to reach binding agreements to achieve tenable global strategies to deal with the problem. As we have already noted (pp. 43–4) leisure and recreation practice in the US together with industrial activity, combines to make America a considerable net contributor to the problem of greenhouse gas emissions. By refusing to comply with the Kyoto Protocol (2005), the US significantly weakened the power of signatory nation-states to construct effective global policies on global pollution.

Similarly, there may be good economic and legal reasons for states to curb the activities of businesses and corporations. However, in the age of instant mass communication the transnationality of leisure and recreation supply chains goes hand in glove with low fixed capital requirements, flexible adaptation to market conditions and high degrees of invisibility or at least, semi-transparency, with respect to state control. For example, if nation-state A decides to impose a levy on ISPs located within the territorial boundaries over which they have jurisdiction in order to generate funds to reward copyright holders whose intellectual property rights have been illegally infringed, it is within the capacity of ISPs to relocate to state B or C in which levies do not exist and, through this means, maintain and enhance profit margins.

Equally, in an age of globalization multi-nationals are relatively impervious to state fiscal policy. If state A seeks to curb inflation by raising corporation tax on products of leisure and recreation that are regarded to be harmful, global multi-nationals simply borrow money in nations that offer more favourable interest rates or transfer central operations to a national base that is more tax-efficient. Globalization provides capital with extraordinary flexibility. Financial resources and loan arrangements can be switched around the world at the press of a button. Similarly, production functions can be transferred from high wage economies to low wage economies, thus limiting the power of unions to defend workers' rights. Many of the economic strategies to tackle the leisure and recreation problems facing individual nation-states demand levels of co-operative resolve between nation-states that have so far, been difficult to muster. The modern state operates in a cat's cradle of global economic power in which multiple equlibria between corporations and cartels, gangs and leisure and recreation consumers is effectively invulnerable to the central rule of law. It is not simply a matter of the speed and visibility at which some of these relationships change. It is also a matter of the absence of a central organ of legislative and policing power that possesses credibility in regulating the global stage.

Monopoly over the Legitimate Use of Physical Force

The same argument applies to international policing. Bilateral and multilateral policing arrangements over leisure and recreation practice and much else besides are of limited value if some nations adopt unilateralism. For example, it is one thing for Western societies to issue denunciations of illegal drug use and take policing measures to curtail the practice. As we saw earlier in the chapter (pp. 148–51), there is some basis for proposing that these policies have stabilized some types of illegal drug use in leisure and recreation cultures. However, this is counter-balanced by the counter-strategies of drug cartels and gangs to develop new centres of production and re-model supply chains beyond the radar of state detection and also to launch drugs which create new markets.

Similarly, toughening up the laws against sex workers in nations with high per capita income provides a fillip to sex tourism and the emergence of open ghettoes of sex work in the emerging and developing world. Hitherto, child prostitution in these regions has been conventionally analysed as the result of poverty, illiteracy and low employment opportunities (Lim 1998). Globalization has added consumerism to the menu. The desire for prestige commodities has motivated some parents to nudge their children into prostitution (Lau 2008). The number of child prostitutes currently working in Thailand is estimated to be between 60,000 and 200,000 (UNICEF 2005). The conclusion is inescapable. Globalization does not eliminate illegal forms of leisure and recreation in the economically advanced nations. However, the demand for foreign currency in the emerging and developing countries generates new markets for sex and drug tourism with significant finance provided by Western consumers.

Of course, the effect of transferring significant investment to the emerging and developing world has consequences for economic power in some sectors of the semi-periphery and periphery.[2] For example, the annual *Global Entertainment and Media Outlook* (2008) published by the Pricewaterhouse Corporation predicts that GDP in Europe, the Middle East and Africa will grow 6.8% per year from $ 570bn in 2007 to $792 bn in 2011; the US will grow by 4.8% a year from $601bn to $759bn. The Asia-Pacific will grow 8.8% per year from $333bn to $508bn, with Latin America increasing from $51bn to $85bn. Global leisure and entertainment markets have traditionally been divided between the cash-rich West and the cash-poor East. We are now at a juncture in the global media and leisure industry where the purchasing power of West and East is predicted to converge. Hitherto, convergence has been largely one-way.[3] The media corporations and leisure forms of the West have colonized the East. What has been happening since the 1980s is a two-way convergence process with Eastern companies, like *Sony* and *Tata*, gaining capital share of Western production, and Eastern leisure forms becoming normalized in the West.

The evolution of a global economy in leisure, media and entertainment produces leaky policing. For the police force in a given territory face not only the threat of domestic supply chains of illegal leisure commodities re-defining themselves, but new sources of production and exchange in territories beyond their jurisdiction. Arguably, from the moment of the industrial revolution it was ever so. But the digital order and air transport network enhance the flexibility and contribute to the semi-transparency of illegal leisure and recreation channels of supply. In the era of the internet there is no credible system for police to monitor and detect illegal activity. 1.3 billion people now have domestic access to the internet. This is expected to climb to 1.6 billion in 2010. Seventy per cent of all Americans are internet users; 63% of British; 50.3% of French; 10.6% of Chinese and 3.6% of Indians (CNNIC; OFCOM; Internetworldstats.com).

Turning to the subject of air travel, in 2004 overseas visitors made a record 27.8 million visits to the UK. Over 2003–4 there was a 16% increase in the number of visits to the UK by overseas visitors. The number of visits abroad by UK residents almost doubled between 1984 and 2004, to a record 64.2 million. Two thirds of the visits were classified as holidays. Just under half of them were package holidays (www.statistics.gov.uk). This immense transport flow is conducive to drug couriering, sex trafficking and other types of illegal leisure practice. Police resources simply cannot match this level of trans-national production and market saturation. In these conditions it is not a question of the state ceasing to possess a monopoly over the legitimate use of force. Rather, the question is, can this force have genuine credibility in a digital order where communication and exchange is so transparently beyond the police's powers of detection?

Monopoly over Moral Regulation

It is not within the gift of any single nation-state to control or police the international chains of supply that provide resources to markets in the economically developed regions of the world. But surely individual nation-states can set the moral agenda and conventions of leisure and recreation practice in the territories over which they have jurisdiction. Can we not see in the toughening up of drink driving laws and the ban on public smoking in the West, clear evidence of the state's resolute moral force? Finding on one side or the other of the issue is one of degree.

Despite increasing medical knowledge of the relationship between the leisure pursuits of tobacco smoking and alcohol consumption, both activities remain major causes of preventable death in the West. According to Sir Richard Peto, Professor of Medical Statistics at Oxford University, tobacco has killed 6.3 million people in the UK during the last half-century. Between 1950 and 2000, 42 per cent of deaths in middle age (35–69) in UK men were caused by smoking. Over the same period of time, smoking was responsible for 16% of deaths in middle-aged UK women. Although the percentage that smoke is now decreasing, in 2000 smoking was still responsible for 35 per cent of cancer deaths among men in England and Wales, and 42 per cent in Scotland. The proportion of deaths in middle-aged men caused by tobacco in the UK has fallen from half 40 years ago to approximately a quarter in 2005. The proportion of UK middle-aged women killed by smoking has declined from 25 per cent 20 years ago to a fifth in 2005 (http://info.can cerresearch.org/news/pressreleases/2005/march/69657). In the EU it is estimated that around 80–90% of all lung cancer deaths in the 35–54 age group are attributable to smoking. Generally lung cancer death rates, including among the new member states, are falling. However, Portugal, Greece, France and Spain show no evidence of a decline across the 35–54 age range (Didkowska et al. 2005). The redistribution of the advertising and marketing resources of major Western tobacco companies to the emerging world has resulted in increasing rates of smoking in China, India, Pakistan, and many African nations. Tobacco consumption here is marketed as signifying maturity, independence and sophistication. MacKay et al. (2006) predict that tobacco will kill one billion people in the twenty-first century. Ten times the number in the last century, if current trends continue.

Alcohol-related deaths provide a similar challenge for Health and Leisure professionals. In the UK the alcohol-related death rate between 1991 and 2005 almost doubled from 6.9 per 100,000 to 12.9. Death rates are much higher for men than women. In 2005 the male death rate was 17.9 deaths per 100,000, compared with 8.3 deaths per 100,000 for women (www.statistics.gov.uk). In the US, alcohol is estimated to cause 75,000 deaths per year. The majority of deaths (72%) involve young males (under 35 years of age). About half the total deaths result from acute conditions (child maltreatment, fall injuries, fire injuries, homicide and motor vehicle traffic injuries). The remainder are associated with physical conditions such as acute pancreatitis, liver cancer, hypertension, stroke, liver cirrhosis and esophageal cancer (US Center for Disease Control and Prevention www.cdc.gov). US research into alcohol advertising campaigns discovered a direct correlation between advertising and youth drinking. Young people, aged between 15 and 26, who reported seeing more alcohol adverts drank more, on average, with each additional ad seen increasing the number of drinks consumed by 1 per cent (Snyder et al. 2006).

It is not so much that the modern nation-state has no moral power to encourage responsible drinking in leisure and recreation cultures. Rather, it is that its power is impeded by civic liberties of free choice, resistance and counter-balanced by corporate advertising and sales campaigns that augment the attraction of alcohol as a leisure resource for various target groups. In the light of this there is surely reason to reconfigure Durkheim's thesis that the modern state is the *ultimate* moral force in society. In the post-war period the expansion of the media has vastly enlarged the public sphere. It now encompasses newspapers, magazines, radio, television and the internet. All of these provide multiple channels of communication which counterbalance the press office of the modern nation-state. They provide data on care for the self and care for the other which frequently contrasts with the official line on policy. Some idea of the scale of unregulated information flow can be gleaned if we note that *YouTube* hosts 100 million daily video streams and more than a billion songs are shared on the internet everyday (IDC 2007).

The state has regulatory powers to curtail media exchange. However, the instantaneous, automatic nature of media transmission means that these powers are often invoked after the fact; that is, data transmission occurs before the regulatory tracking powers of the modern state can jam exchange.

With this level of popular access to underground and global fronts of resistance, policing faces formidable obstacles. Parker et al. (2002) partly base their thesis of the normalization of illegal leisure and recreational drug cultures around the transparent incapacity of the police to comprehensively enforce legislation. With the advent of the digital order, and the wide availability of the desktop, the laptop, the mobile phone and a variety of hand-held communication devices, the problem with respect to the illegal downloading of copyrighted intellectual property, will inevitably be magnified.

For all of these reasons it is necessary to reformulate the thesis that the state is central to leisure and recreation. Globalization brings a variety of new equilibria into play, some of which have high levels of flexibility in relations of production, exchange and consumption. The significance of the state is not in doubt. But students of leisure and recreation must learn to see its power as counter-balanced and, in some cases, outflanked by multi-nationals, illegal cartels and gangs. The range of influences that bear upon us in leisure choice and activity are expanding. In many cases, the state writ to regulate these influences is nullified by technology and the distribution and flexibility of leisure and recreation supply chains. The state faces a tall order in regulating invisible or semi-transparent sources of supply and demand in leisure and recreation.

8
CORPORATIONS

A major lacuna in Marxist, socialist-feminist, figurational and poststructuralist accounts of leisure forms and practice is the role of the corporation. This is surprising. As Ken Roberts (2004: 21) maintains, over the last one hundred years the corporation has unequivocally become the main leisure provider. Multi-nationals like Nike, Sony, Disney, Apple, Virgin, Calvin Klein, Cisco, Time-Warner, Exxon-Mobil, BP, Thomson, British-American Tobacco, Stella Artois, Ford and General Motors have become pervasive. The synergy between leisure forms and brand culture is so strong that some types of leisure and recreation activity and identity are now constructed around brands. Nike, Volkswagen, Harley, Apple and Corona have become *cultural icons* that signify particular lifestyle values and attitudes to leisure. These brands do not simply differentiate products, they also signify much deeper values of liberty, self-assurance, social awareness, belonging and personal standing. Moreover, while the influence of states upon leisure practice is bounded by territorial limits, multi-nationals relate to the entire globe as their market.

In this chapter I do not propose to trace the connections between multi-nationals, leisure forms and cultural icons. Others, albeit usually working outside the field of Leisure Studies/Science, have already made significant contributions in this direction (Goldman and Papson 1998; Holt 2004). Instead, I seek to address a particular aspect of corporate culture: the business of selling leisure products that are known to be bad for you. As Roberts (2004: 202) observes, 'people spend far more time and money on drink, tobacco, drugs, gambling and television than on taking exercise.' Leisure corporations position people to make these choices. Throughout the book, I have argued that principles of Care for the Self and Care for the Other have contributed to the enlargement of emotional intelligence and emotional labour with respect to issues of health, recycling and the work–life balance. Self-coaching and coaching others in the practice of responsible consumption has become a standard feature of what might be termed a progressive lifestyle. Frank (1997) traces the emergence of this shift in the structure of capitalism back to the 1960s counter-culture. Under pressure from consumers seeking more accountability, transparency, distributive justice and informality from corporations, capitalism began to restructure its relationship with consumer culture. Marketing and advertising departments started to re-gear their businesses to recognize the demands of consumers for enlarged corporate awareness about inequality, environmental risks, social justice and empowerment. Yet in the midst of the emergence of the 'new capitalism', many corporations in the leisure and recreation field continue to manufacture products that carry demonstrable risk to health, wellbeing and the environment.

In what has come to be known as 'the new capitalism', corporations have learned from consumer rights groups and fair-trade movements (Sennett 2006). They have developed visionary doctrines of corporate responsibility to build their brand and offer stateless solutions to key social and environmental problems. This has been particularly attractive to corporations involved in the leisure and recreation field which produce commodities that are associated with technological manipulation, environmental pollution, dietary risk and addiction. The development of responsible programmes of investment in environmental and social issues enhances the image of the brand. For example, Microsoft, Cisco, State Street and Randstad have launched a European-wide initiative to target over 20 million 'at risk' groups for education in IT literacy. The justification is to increase employment skills and extend social inclusion. Similarly, Coca-Cola has developed an ethical doctrine of conservation and environmental protection, notably by supporting initiatives that bring safe water and sanitation to communities in need. Exxon Mobil has developed a programme of reducing oil spills from marine vessels, contracting greenhouse-gas emissions, contributing to the local community and safeguarding the environment.

What strategies do leisure corporations that produce addictive commodities that carry a health risk use to maintain and grow market share? How do they respond to responsible consumerism that encourages informed and up-to-date responses to the work–life balance? This chapter uses two case studies from the tobacco and alcohol industries to explore these questions. It seeks to demonstrate how leisure corporations have devised and implemented principles of corporate responsibility to mask the physical and social risks of the products that they produce; and it also addresses how globalization has been exploited by these corporations to enlarge growth in the emerging and developing world.

Tobacco and Leisure

Globally speaking, the commercial redistribution of harmful leisure commodities has reached an interesting juncture. The business strategies of leading Western tobacco companies, notably Imperial Tobacco, British American Tobacco and Phillip Morris, to re-position their commodities in the global marketplace reveal much of the sneaky logic and moral double-dealing that leisure corporations involved in products that carry physical, social and environmental risks employ to defend and enhance market share. At the heart of this is the planned, industrially organized popularization of cigarette consumption throughout the markets of the emerging and developing world. Currently, multiple, mutually reinforcing advertising and branding strategies are being intensively applied by dominant Western multinationals in Africa, South East Asia, Latin America and Eastern Europe, to persuade consumers that tobacco smoking tallies with personal sophistication (especially for the female market), cultural achievement, weight loss and Western-style independence. In a word, smoking is being portrayed as a suitable leisure activity for those who dream of a better life or who are in the throes of experiencing upward mobility. Three sets of interrelated ethical and political problems are posed here. They have to do with (a) health risk, (b) environmental degradation and (c) the cost–benefit ratio of inward investment strategies from the developing and emerging world.

Health Risk

To come first to the question of health risk: the World Health Organization (WHO) (2004) estimates that five million people die each year worldwide from tobacco-related diseases. Approximately 1.3 billion people smoke cigarettes, of whom one billion are men. In developing countries it is estimated that 50% of men and 9% of women are smokers, as against 35% of men and 22% of women in the developed world (Mackay and Eriksen 2002).

The health risks associated with tobacco smoking are well documented and disputed by only a statistically insignificant number of physicians, scientists and politicians. The World Health Organization (2004) maintains that tobacco is the second major cause of death in the world. Approximately one in ten adults die from tobacco-related diseases every year. If current smoking patterns continue, smoking will account for 10 million deaths per annum by 2020, of which three quarters are estimated to be concentrated in the developing world (Mackay and Eriksen 2002). Eighty-four per cent of all smokers live in the developing world. Half of all smokers, approximately 650 million people, will eventually die as a result of tobacco – a greater figure of preventable and premature deaths than is accounted for by AIDS, illegal drugs, road accidents, homicide and suicide combined. China is estimated to suffer a million deaths per year through the effects of tobacco, a figure that is projected to double by 2025 (Peto and Lopez 2004).

Environmental Degradation

Turning now to the environmental dimension of smoking, tobacco production is associated with deforestation and soil degradation. In poorer countries, regulations on tobacco advertising and tar levels tend to be significantly higher than in brands sold in the US and Western Europe. More than 40 developing countries do not require health warnings to be printed on cigarette packs. Of those that do, 73% are ambiguously worded and frequently published in English rather than in the local language (Tobacco Warning Labels and Packaging Fact Sheet 2000). Singapore, Brazil, South Africa and Thailand are leaders in the developing world in applying comprehensive tobacco control laws covering bans on tobacco advertising, sponsorship, developing smoke-free public environments and implementing effective health education campaigns. However, they are exceptions to the rule. Tobacco production threatens water supplies since tobacco cultivation uses a lot of water and it has pesticides applied to it (Madeley 1999). It also contributes to the physical pollution of the environment, although it has proved difficult to quantify by how much.

Economic Cost–Benefit Ratio

Moving on now to the cost–benefit ratio associated with the developing and emerging world's support for tobacco production, in 2002 the three largest tobacco multinationals – Japan Tobacco, Philip Morris/Altira and British American Tobacco – had combined trade revenues of US$121 billion. To put this into context, the World Health Organization estimates that this sum is greater than the combined GDP of 27 developing countries (WHO 2004: 6). Not surprisingly, the leading Western tobacco companies constitute a significant interest group, influencing national and international policy on aid, debt relief and international treaties on the regulation of tobacco use. In 2003, the 171 nations comprising the World Health Organization approved a historical Framework Convention on Tobacco Control. This applied a ban on global tobacco advertising, promotion and sponsorship. The tobacco industry lobby, especially the Philip Morris Corporation, in the US successfully delayed ratification by the American government and supported it with a donation of $57,764 to the Republican Party. Under American pressure, restrictions on cigarette advertising were eased, a pro-tax element for non-smokers was abandoned and the ban on descriptive terms like 'low tar', 'light' and 'mild', was relinquished. It should be noted here that tobacco companies have provided a major source of campaign funds for George W. Bush's Republican Party. Alterman and Green (2004: 123) report that in 1997, Republican candidates and committees received $20.2 million, or 81% of the tobacco industry's contributions.

With respect to investment in the developing world, tobacco companies have enjoyed high levels of success in introducing aid and relief packages to developing countries with friendly policies in respect of Western investment in tobacco production. Investing in tobacco production has been presented as creating jobs, boosting revenues and expanding exports and foreign exchange. The health costs of tobacco-related illnesses and premature death have been systematically underplayed. The cost–benefit ratio of tobacco production is subtly engineered to favour the interests of Western investors. Inward investment of seed, tools, curing barns and delivery systems is offset by a system of nuanced loans to small farmers for fertiliser and insecticides. The result is that local tobacco producers are trapped in a cycle of debt that makes them vulnerable to the initiatives and imperatives of Western tobacco companies. The World Health Organization has alleged that tobacco multinationals routinely engage in price fixing and credit busting for producers that refuse to comply with the tobacco cartel (WHO 2004: 4).

The conclusions are inescapable. In the last two decades, Western tobacco multinationals have identified developing and emerging markets as a primary investment and marketing opportunity. They have sought to maximize margins by concentrating on markets where anti-smoking lobbies are weak, the history of litigation against tobacco companies is negligible, public health education programmes are inadequate and the popular cultural association between smoking and Western status is strong. They have exploited the image of tobacco as a sign of maturity, sophistication and choice in lifestyle and leisure. Advertising of cigarettes often develops this in very crude ways. For example, in Africa brand names include Diplomat (Ghana), High Society (Nigeria), Sportsman and Champion (Kenya) (Maxwell Report 1997). In the developed countries this type of one-sided brand identification would be challenged and almost certainly prohibited. To put it bluntly, since the 1960s Western tobacco multinationals have defined the developing and emerging world as a soft market. Why?

The Struggle for Responsible Consumption of Tobacco in the West

The economically developed countries do not, any longer, constitute an attractive market for tobacco corporations. According to *ASH* (Action on

Smoking and Health 2004) demand is projected to fall for the foreseeable future. In 2010 the consumption of tobacco tonnage is predicted to be 10% lower than the 1998 figure. In contrast, consumption in the developing and emerging economies is anticipated to increase to 5.09 million tonnes – a 1.7% growth rate between 1998 and 2010. Some 80% of this increase in demand is projected for the Asian market, especially China. The representation and theming of smoking as a leisure pursuit in developed Western economies has changed dramatically in the last forty years. There is nothing new in this.

Jason Hughes's (2003) outstanding study reveals the astonishing historical range of representations and symbols associated with smoking. For example, historically speaking, it was linked with high fashion, modernity, science, sexuality, cultural advancement and cool. Incredibly, it was also popularly believed to have medicinal value. At various times it was presented as a cure for both the plague and cancer, on the grounds that smoke must 'obviously' blast away all harmful deposits and residues in the body caused by other aspects of diet, stress and urban-industrial existence.

Yet from its introduction to Europe from the New World, smoking had its share of vociferous detractors. In England, in 1604, King James 1 published a treatise against smoking entitled *A Counterblast To Tobacco.* In the same century, Michael Feoder vich, the first Romanov Czar, declared smoking to be a deadly sin, and worked up a variety of punishments for the possession of tobacco. During the same period, Pope Clement VIII advocated excommunication as a punishment for anyone found smoking in a holy place. However, these measures fell on stony ground.

By the early twentieth century, smoking rivalled only alcohol consumption as a popular leisure pursuit in the Western economies. There were many reasons for this. Smoking constituted a form of popular conspicuous consumption, in Veblen's (1899) sense of the term, since it was cheap, and therefore available to the masses, as well as the privileged leisure class. In a nutshell, it made a social and cultural virtue out of waste that was affordable to the non-leisure class. This signified social standing and cultural distinction by demonstrating individual freedom, from having to scrimp and save. More often than not this was a symbolic freedom. Smoking was a way of representing and theming status distinction. If you were wealthy enough to burn your money away by inhaling tobacco smoke it provided transparent evidence that you were a person of substance, a man or woman to be reckoned with, or at least were well on the road to being regarded as such.

Smoking was also associated with quantifiable physical and psychological effects such as easing nervous tension, managing irritability and impatience, assisting contemplation, easing discussion and managing stress. It was not commonly associated with a risk to health and was therefore taken up and practised by millions as a positive leisure pursuit.

It was not until the *US Surgeon General's Report* in 1964, that the health risks associated with this pastime were popularly appreciated.[1] This document established irrefutable links between tobacco smoking and many avoidable diseases, such as lung cancer, cardio-vascular degeneration and respiratory disease. Anti-smoking campaigners seized upon this to call for a ban on smoking. Gradually, the status of smoking was redefined, although looking back the process was remarkably gradual and uneven.

In the US the *Federal Cigarette Labelling and Advertising Act* (1965) required manufacturers to print health warnings on cigarette packets. In the same year, the UK outlawed cigarette advertising on television. In 1970, the US followed suit. In 1971 the UK government negotiated a voluntary agreement for tobacco companies to print health warnings on cigarette packets. The anti-smoking and health lobby turned their attention to banning smoking in public places. In 1973 US federal law introduced mandatory non-smoking compartments on domestic flights. In 1987, the law was extended to apply a total smoking ban on flights of less than two hours. In 1990 the US went further by banning tobacco smoking on inter-state buses and all domestic flights with a duration of less than six hours. In 1992 the US Supreme Court made the historic ruling that warning labels on cigarette packets do not protect US companies from lawsuits. In 1999 the UK hospitality industry introduced a Voluntary Charter on Smoking in Public Places that advised pubs and restaurants to introduce signs informing staff and customers of the health risks associated with smoking. There have been many high profile, costly and successful legal actions brought against tobacco companies by victims of smoking-related diseases in the West. In 2000 a US jury awarded damages of nearly $145 billion against five US tobacco companies after a class action in the state of Florida. In 2003 the advertising and promotion of tobacco smoking was banned in the UK. New York followed California and Delaware in introducing a state-wide ban on smoking in public places. Ireland took the same action in 2004. The UK government implemented similar plans for a ban on smoking in pubs, cafes and restaurants to be applied in England and Wales in 2006.

The reason for this dramatic and unambiguous public stigmatization of a long-standing, popular leisure pursuit in Western countries has to do with the repudiation of the libertarian argument in favour of smoking. After health risks were unequivocally established in 1964, the libertarian response was that the practice must therefore be redefined as a matter of personal conscience. If individuals chose to put their medium- or long-term health in jeopardy by smoking it was up to them.

This may be read as an expression of the old functionalist argument in Leisure Studies that leisure practice is a matter of individual choice, freedom and self-determination so long as its consequences do not hazard the wellbeing of others (Parker 1981). The basic idea is not new. In the industrial era it goes back to J.S. Mill's (1859) famous defence of liberty that individuals are free to pursue their own wants, desires and interests so long as they do not impinge upon those of others.

In the 1980s and 1990s tobacco companies responded to this argument by dramatically increasing the number of brands, promoting filter and tar-reduced cigarettes, thus suggesting that some products were 'healthier' than others (Glanz et al. 1996: 30). This was pursued in the name of extending consumer choice. Enlarging the range of brands was portrayed as contributing to the *individualization* of consumer culture. By extending choice, the tobacco companies argued that they enhanced the freedom of consumers to manage the health risks associated with consuming the product.

Secondary Smoking

In the West, it is precisely this libertarian principle that has now ceased to be tenable with respect to smoking. For medical research and public health policy in the 1990s, and the new century, has established a causal link between secondary smoking, illness and premature death. This took time to develop among researchers and medical practitioners. A causal connection between secondary smoking and preventable illness and premature death had been mooted as early as the 1970s. However, the evidence was inconclusive (Jackson 1994). As the 1980s unfolded a variety of studies researching the health hazards of passive smoking were published (Eriksen and Le Maistre 1988). In medical and public health circles, by the 1990s it was no longer a question of smokers dicing with only their lives. It was now an issue of being responsible for threatening the wellbeing of the Other: the wellbeing of non-smoking partners, children, workmates, consumers and other social categories are imperilled by the smoker's habit.

In the West, the age of 'live and let live' with respect to smoking has passed. It is now popularly recognized that what the smoker does can damage the interests of others by causing preventable illness and premature death. At the same time, parallel research into the public costs of smoking-related illness through hospitalization and days off work firmly embedded the practice as a health hazard in popular opinion. This is why it is now being discouraged by public health professionals and governments and the law is being extended and applied to ban it in public places such as work settings, restaurants, cafes and bars.

The adverse legal, political and public opinion conditions that apply to cigarette smoking in the West have forced tobacco companies to adopt a defensive management strategy in this territory and look for investment opportunities elsewhere. The emerging and developing world has been identified as an economically attractive and politically and culturally soft substitute. The ways in which the tobacco companies have sought to reposition a leisure practice that is now labelled as dangerous in the West in these markets are clever, but I think, morally reprehensible. The tobacco companies deny that they target women and children in the developing world as primary markets. But the ways in which their advertising and marketing departments link glamour, power and freedom with cigarettes makes these groups vulnerable.

At the 12th World Conference on Tobacco and Health in 2003, significantly increased smoking rates were reported among women in Bangladesh, Cambodia and Malaysia. Girls aged 15 and 16 are more likely to smoke than boys in Bulgaria, Denmark, Ireland, Italy, Malta, Norway, Slovenia and the UK (www.womensnews.org). Promotional strategies associate smoking with cultural sophistication, weight-control and Western styles of freedom to choose. Smoking is portrayed as an extension of choice, flexibility and freedom. Since smoking is globally more common among men than women, to the tune of 47% of all men smoking compared with 12% of women, the decision to smoke for women is celebrated by tobacco companies as a statement of female empowerment.

In 2003 the website of the Women's Health Project in Johannesburg, South Africa highlights the advertising campaign for Winston cigarettes. The billboards show a young, attractive blonde woman sitting on a park bench holding a cigarette in her hand with the message: 'Do I look like I would cook you breakfast?' The message operates through connotation, but it is perfectly plain. Smoking is connected with escape from the world of female submissiveness and male domination. It castigates male domination and celebrates female emancipation. Yet this celebration cannot be concerned with human rights, since the balance of medical opinion strongly suggests that the well-established consequence of smoking is appreciably increased risk of preventable illness and premature death. The connotation with choice and freedom must therefore be spurious since the medically well-documented effect of smoking is to damage health, but at the level of the individual and the community. So what is going on here?

The British American Tobacco Online Company Report 2004 (www.bat.com)

I think it is worthwhile to get deeper into the business strategy and marketing initiatives of the tobacco companies in peddling the message to the emerging and developing markets that smoking is good for you.

Because that is what these strategies and initiatives are designed to do: they aim to negate or obfuscate the influence of medical and campaigning groups that identify smoking with illness and premature death, and redefine smoking with a positive, feel-good message that privileges cultural connotation over physical risks to the body. The health issues for the smoker and others are understated in favour of cultural connotations that associate smoking with individualism, freedom, power and achievement. Consider the British American Tobacco website, a representative example of the business genre that tobacco corporations wish to present to the world today (www.bat.com).

Paul Adams, the Chief Executive, begins the online company report for 2004 with the banner headline of spectacular economic growth. The company achieved 29% growth per annum in the five years prior to the end of 2004, compared with an average minus 3% loss in the *Financial Times* Share Index. The company mission statement is organized around three central pillars: 1) to grow the business; 2) to improve the quality of the product and 3) to embed principles of corporate social responsibility throughout the business and its markets. The phrase *corporate social responsibility* is particularly significant and I shall come back to investigate it more closely presently.

Adams's report concedes that British American Tobacco products constitute a health risk and that trading in them can be seen as controversial. Against this, he notes that tobacco products remain legal. The business strategy is to increase profit margins by improving productivity and increasing market share, not encouraging growth in the number of global smokers. In support of this, Adams points out that the number of global smokers has remained static at about one billion for some time.

But this is misleading. The question is not the size of the total number of smokers in the world, it is rather the *distribution* of smokers between the developed world and the rest. Popular knowledge and lifestyle coaching about health risks related to smoking and the anti-smoking movement are most advanced in the West. As a result, the market for British American Tobacco in such countries has been contracting for some time. In 2004 British American Tobacco sales declined in Germany, France, Canada and Japan; but this was offset by strong performance from Russia, India and Pakistan. China is identified as an attractive market for investment, because the country already accounts for one third of all tobacco sales. It is in the emerging and developing markets that rapid growth is underway. It is also here where the line between consumer choice and the effects of corporate promotion is decidedly vague.

Adams submits that growth is achieved by offering consumers high quality products and choice. But in the emerging and developing markets the choice to smoke is firmly associated with the acquisition and signification of status. Through branding, marketing and advertising, tobacco companies seek to consolidate this connection. Smoking is linked with freedom and maturity, which in turn, problematizes the issue of personal choice. At one point in his online report, Adams submits that the growth in the numbers of smokers in emerging and developing markets is evidence of social and economic progress. As an economy develops, he argues, consumers trade-up for quality goods. Increasing the numbers of consumers who smoke quality brands is therefore presented as evidence of personal, social and economic advancement.

It amounts to a bizarre appropriation and partial distortion of Walt Rostow's (1956) old 'take-off' thesis in modernization theory. Rostow argued that there is a unilinear sequence of stages that modernizing nations go through before production and consumption capacity reach 'take off' into sustainable progress. Adams sees industrialization going through a parallel unilinear sequence. As the emerging and developing countries achieve economic lift-off, consumer sovereignty to dispose of surplus as and how they please is asserted. The turn to tobacco is presented as part and parcel of a libertarian doctrine that cherishes individual freedom, economic growth and modernization. A blind eye is turned to the well-documented risks to health and mortality associated with tobacco consumption. Indeed, Adams portrays British American Tobacco as adding value to consumers. By offering quality brands manufactured and sold in an ethos of *corporate social responsibility*, Adams positions his company as improving the quality of life in emerging and developing markets.   But what does corporate social responsibility mean in this context? Before coming to this question, we should turn to a parallel case study of a corporate leisure sector associated with the production of recreational commodities that carry demonstrable physical and social risks.

Alcohol and Leisure

The Anheuser-Busch Group of companies (AB) account for 57% of US ale beverage consumption. In 2005 it shipped 1010 million barrels more than 2.5 times its closest domestic competitor. The Group has 48.8% of US market share. It includes the Budweiser, Bud Light and Michelob brands. Its version of corporate responsibility expressed in its company report and website (www.anheuser-busch.com), accepts the case of the environmental and health lobbies that its product base can be harmful. It emphasizes the duty of producers to be informative and consumers to be cautious and respect health risks in their consumption patterns.

Budweiser Means Moderation is the strap-line for one of its most popular brands. AB claims to have invested in alcohol awareness and education initiatives since the early 1900s. Through community-based programmes, partnerships and personal responsibility campaigns AB claims to have participated in the 37% reduction in drink-driving fatalities claimed by the US Department of Transportation from 1982 to 2000. The AB war on underage drinking is singled out as a particularly notable success. The 1999 'We All Make a Difference' campaign reinforced personal responsibility and warned consumers of the dangers involved in alcohol abuse, drink-driving and underage drinking. AB works directly with the National Social Norms Resource Center to underwrite education programmes at US colleges and universities which stress that college students of legal age must drink responsibly if they choose to drink. AB has developed a variety of responsible environmental and community initiatives including recycling, solid waste reduction, 'partners in progress' programmes with minority and women-owned vendors, mobile health screening units, animal rescue campaigns, breast cancer research, disaster relief and support for Paralyzed Veterans of America (PVA). It has developed a high profile entertainment and leisure park programme through its *Busch Gardens* parks in Williamsburg, Va. and Tampa, Fla. These investments enhance the brand by a) disassociating it from negative connotations of health risks and mortality; and b) associating it with positive denotations of social responsibility and environmental concern.

However, drinks producers in the West now work in a climate of well-publicized scientific data showing unimpeachable correlations between alcohol consumption, ill-health and mortality, where there are significant lobbying forces organized to educate the public about the risks involved in immoderate consumption. Just like tobacco companies, drinks producers are responding to these restraints on trade in Western markets, by spatial distribution into emerging and developing markets. The world's fastest-growing and largest beer market by volume is China. AB has made significant market investment to build recognition of its Budweiser brands there. It has a 27% equity position in Tsingtao, the largest brewer in China and producer of the Tsingtao, brand. AB also owns 50% of Mexico's leading brewer, Grupo Modelo, which has a 56% share of the Mexican beer market.

Although beer outsells hard liquor and wine in the US, its rate of growth has been depressed by the increasing popularity of these beverages with the US consumer. AB consolidated sales declined by 0.5% in 2005. The 2006 company plan is committed to enhancing domestic beer volume and market share growth, including new product development, packaging and promotions. Although the ethic of responsible drinking is redoubled, the aim of the 2006 plan is to increase volume sales. With respect to the domestic market this means that a) either more people need to consume the AB brands or b) the current market needs to consume in greater volume i.e. by drinking more. Revenues can also be increased globally by entering new markets. AB may do this under the banner of 'responsible drinking'. However, there is no guarantee that consumers in the emerging and developing world, where a lower proportion of Gross National Product is devoted to health awareness and education campaigns, will observe the health warnings.

A variety of chronic physical conditions and diseases are associated with the excessive consumption of alcohol. They include acute pancreatitis, liver cancer, stroke, oesophageal cancer, gastroesophageal haemorrhage, liver cirrhosis and hypertension. Among the acute conditions are alcohol poisioning, child maltreatment, fall injuries, fire injuries, homicide, motor-vehicle traffic injuries and suicide. According to statistics supplied by the US Center for Disease Control and Prevention (www.cdc.gov) excessive alcohol consumption is the third leading preventable cause of death in the US. Approximately 75,000 alcohol attributable deaths occur in the US every year, with on average, thirty years of life lost per individual. The majority of deaths (72%) involved young males (under 35 years of age). About half of the total deaths resulted from acute conditions.

AB's ethic of responsible drinking is designed to minimize the potential negative impacts of alcohol misuse on individuals, their families and the wider community. However, its *business*, what it does to stay in operation and make a profit, is producing a leisure commodity that is associated with addiction, illness, the lowering of inhibitions against aggression and sexuality and premature death. Especially among youth groups, moderation and alcohol do not go hand in hand. Advertising campaigns deliberately target the youth market by the glamorization of alcohol through links with sexual imagery, low price strategies in clubs and bars and the inducement of DJs to consume greater quantitites. Research by Snyder et al. (2006) in the US, discovered a direct correlation between advertising and significant increases in youth drinking. Young people aged between 15 and 26 who reported seeing more alcohol advertisements drank more on average, with each additional ad seen increasing the number of drinks consumed by 1 per cent. Similarly, young people living in media markets with greater alcohol advertising expenditures drank more, with each additional dollar spent per capita increasing the number of drinks consumed by 3 per cent. To express it differently, a 20-year-old male who saw few alcohol ads and lived in a media market with minimal advertising expenditures per capita is estimated to average nine alcoholic drinks per month, compared to 16 drinks per month if he saw many ads. All the pious, self-righteous disclaimers and justifications in the world will not disguise the fact that the advertising campaigns of leading alcohol companies like

AB play a major role in encouraging young people to drink. Among youth groups exposure to alcohol is associated with alterations in brain development, poor academic performance, risky sexual behaviour, increased likelihood of addiction, sexual harassment and increased probability of fatal alcohol-related accidents, including car crashes.

The hypocrisy of the alcohol industry's ethic of responsible drinking can be illustrated from another angle if one looks at point-of-sale pricing incentives. Supermarkets offer significant price reductions for bulk purchase. In 2008 Morrisons supermarket were selling a 24-can pack of Carlsberg lager for £10.98. This comes down to 45p (or US$ 1) per 440 ml can. The bulk purchase of other brands of beer and spirits are offered at swingeing price cuts. Drinks producers maintain that they have no control over point-of-sale pricing. But this is a specious argument since producers form an organic relationship in the supply of alcohol. If a supermarket chain offers cut-price reductions on some brands as a loss leader, alcohol producers might voluntarily cut supply or the state might intervene to force prices up.

Corporate Social Responsibility and Neat Capitalism

Neat capitalism is an approach that recognizes that social responsibility and environmental awareness are central to progressive business practice. Of course, capitalist corporations had always cultivated a philanthropic side to their operations. In the late eighteenth century in Britain, Robert Owen developed the New Lanark community in Scotland which was regarded as a model of employer–worker relations. Cadbury's developed Bourneville in Birmingham (1895) and William Lever, Port Sunlight (1888) in the North West of England, as model housing estates for workers. Henry T. Ford employed 'social workers' to monitor the patterns of consumption among his workforce and indeed, the system of industrial management known as Fordism assumed that employers recognized a responsibility to regulate standards of consumption (and therefore leisure) as well as plan and maintain the production process. But none of this was based in an equal partnership with the consumer. Instead it sought to offer a sort of *consumer pedagogy* or life-coaching philosophy to consumers. By investing in good works and worthy causes, usually in the fields of social causes and heritage, capitalist corporations aimed to build the brand and proselytize their commitment to standards of respectable society.

The business form of neat capitalism that emerged in the 1960s was quite different. It was based in listening to consumers and learning from them. Strictly speaking the partnership was not equal since corporations held economic assets, power over cultural production and political influence that consumers could not hope to match. Conversely, consumers had significant cultural power on exposing the deficiencies and limitations of the traditional model of capitalism, and turning them into public issues. Neat capitalist corporations began to identify a range of organizational responsibilities that extended beyond achieving an acceptable rate of return for shareholders. These had to do with improving the environment, raising awareness about health risks, producing adequate standards of employment, involvement in campaigns against world hunger, disaster relief and reducing needless bureaucracy and red tape. Corporations like Virgin, the Body Shop, Microsoft and Apple positioned themselves in the market as 'big citizens'. They often turned to charismatic business owners or chief executives to function as the public face of the corporation. So Steve Jobs is the 'face' of Apple Macintosh; Anita Roddick was the embodiment of the business values of the Body Shop; and Sir Richard Branson is the public face of the Virgin group of companies. This contrasted sharply with the traditional business culture of capitalist corporations organized around suits, hierarchy, officiousness and impersonality.

It also paid business dividends. Between the 1970s and the present day, neat capitalist companies often achieved spectacular rates of economic growth. Richard Branson's Virgin group began from a first floor record shop selling cut-price records above a shoe shop in central London in the early 1970s, to a multi-national empire which by 2005 consisted of over 200 companies, with businesses in leisure retailing, soft drinks, air travel, music recording, personal investment packages, mobile phones and insurance. As a result, traditional corporations began to re-engineeer their businesses to adopt the rhetoric and some of the business practices of neat capitalist corporations.

But what do you do if you are the chief executive of a leisure corporation that produces commodities for a global market which scientific research has identified as causing preventable illness and premature death? This was the dilemma for the major tobacco and alcohol companies in the 1990s. They developed a philosophy of corporate social responsibility that accepted the health and premature mortality risks involved with consumption of their products, but defended the sovereignty of consumer choice and recognized a variety of corporate responsibilities with respect to society and the environment. In the case of British American Tobacco these responsibilities were developed along eight distinct fronts of action: youth smoking prevention; sustainable development; environment, health and safety; responsible tobacco production; biodiversity; eliminating child labour; enhancing the community; and supporting globalization and business integrity. Building leisure parks, preserving the environment, spreading organized education and culture to disadvantaged areas drew some of the opprobrium generated by producing commodities that carry a scientifically proven risk to health and mortality.

It would be wrong to attribute simple bad faith or cynicism to the principle of corporate social responsibility. It is better than doing nothing. But it should not be used to whitewash the risks to health and the environment associated with cigarettes. British American Tobacco is typical of leading Western tobacco companies in noting the risks, but countering them with the arguments that a) tobacco smoking is legal and b) consumer sovereignty and choice are impregnable. Knowledge about the hazards of secondary smoking now make each of these arguments harder to apply in Western markets. Successive Western states have recognized the legality of smoking but taken steps to unequivocally publicize the risks to health and banish smoking from public places. To justify the intensification of the business activities of the tobacco companies in the emerging and developing markets, in the context of the general and unambivalent public reaction against smoking in the West, is a somewhat generous application of the term 'corporate social responsibility'. Clearly, the tobacco companies have turned to these new markets because the culture of trading conditions in their staple markets has been adversely affected by anti-smoking and public health campaigns. New and emerging markets offer a more attractive base for the exploitation and development of the business. Where should leisure educators and professionals stand on this question? What ethical issues does it raise?

Disaster Capitalism: The Shock Doctrine and Leisure

Multinationals exploit leisure practice as a major field for brand-building. By presenting product coaching as free choice they reinforce the *repressive desublimation* that Marcuse (1969) and others wrote about it in the 1960s and 70s. Recently, the emergence of the special event as a global leisure form has added a new layer of complexity to the concept. By contributing to events like *Live Earth* and *Live 8* individuals add to personal competence and credibility by flagging empathy for environmental and Third World issues. These extend beyond the requirements of workplace and personal friendship networks to signify aspirations of global conscience and world citizenship. It is not that people are necessarily insincere in making these commitments. Rather, it is that the scale of environmental and Third World issues requires much higher levels of personal commitment and expenditure than participation in global special events generally achieves. The global special event affords highly public opportunities for displaying a personal 'can do' attitude in a context in which durable solutions require co-ordinated, multi-lateral action among states and citizens. Marcuse (1969) argued that consumer culture tends to co-opt consumers to identify with the status quo. Might it be that the global special event takes co-option to a new level by using the field of leisure as a forum for gestural politics that provide individuals and groups with the satisfaction of making a difference while leaving the structural dynamics that create global environmental and Third World problems intact? These dynamics relate to the age-old business of capitalist corporations pursuing the imperative of maximizing surplus value by driving down costs and maximizing profits.

The involvement of multi-national corporations in these events raises a separate set of questions having to do with the economic relationship between stateless solutions to global problems and corporate enhancement. Neat capitalism places high value upon relevance. The neat capitalist corporation does not merely supply commodities that people want, at a price which they can afford, it mobilizes corporate clout to publicize and tackle wider questions of social inclusion, empowerment and distributive justice. As we saw in the discussion of capitalist corporations involved in producing leisure commodities that carry high health and mortality risks for consumers, the ethic of corporate responsibility often disperses profits to worthy causes. It is not that the corporate involvement in literacy campaigns or cleaning polluted lakes and waterways is negative. Rather the issue is the line between producing relevant stateless solutions to global problems and brand-building.

Should leisure educators and professionals operate on the assumption that capitalism is inherently bad? Strong state power is required to regulate economic activity. However, time and again, capitalism has proved to be more effective in wealth generation, flexibility and innovation. As we have seen above, in extending their remit from matters of corporate governance to corporate responsibility, multi-national corporations have started to routinely offer stateless solutions to global problems and the challenges faced by individual nation-states. Many of these solutions relate directly to leisure forms and practice. At issue here are new forms of brand-building, corporate coaching to encourage responsible consumption and other lifestyle values, the creation of leisure and amusement parks and the financing of a variety of special events.

The rise of corporate stateless solutions requires the expansion of corrective multi-lateral agreements between states to provide a framework of regulation that while being conducive is sensitive to the agenda of citizenship rights issues having to do with distributive justice, empowerment and social inclusion. That said, the impetus for multi-nationals to extend their remit to topics of corporate responsibility is, arguably, intrinsic to the impetus of globalization. As corporations become more comfortable with regarding the world as their market, they are very likely to extend their sphere of influence to propose stateless solutions to issues of natural disaster management, inequality in education, climate change, gang culture and so on. For it is questions like this that have a direct bearing upon the vitality and growth prospects of their market.

The two examples given above focus upon the opportunities for re-gearing exploitation in global leisure and recreation cultures. Students of leisure and recreation should be aware that there are dangers in tarring capitalism with the same brush. Naomi Klein's (2007) *shock doctrine thesis* is an example in point. It is a bold thesis from which students of leisure and recreation have much to learn. She contends that global capitalism exploits shocks like the natural disasters of the tsunami catastrophe (2004) in Southern Asia and Hurricane Katrina (2005), or sluggish economic development in the West in the 1980s, to revitalize principles of market fundamentalism. Citing the so-called 'shock therapy' developed by the Nobel laureate and University of Chicago free market economist, Milton Friedman, she argues that since the 1970s, neo-liberal regimes have seized upon economic or natural shocks to the system to provide licence for the introduction of authoritarian market solutions that are eventually reinforced by the intensification of policing and punishment to reproduce compliance. Her book is suggestive in the most inspiring way. Her accounts of state thuggery and planned repression in Chile, Argentina, Russia and the Allied occupation in Iraq are compelling and horrifying. She demonstrates that, without doubt, right-wing regimes in these countries have attempted to impose crude free market economics and monolithic lifestyles of work, family and leisure upon the population. At all levels, from organized politics to recreation, dissent and resistance have been ruthlessly attacked, with state-administered assassinations freely used as an ultimate resort. Klein's account proposes that state-sponsored authoritarianism and inequality are the corollaries of the totally free market. This implies that Friedman's economic shock therapy tends only in one direction. What Klein neglects is that Friedman's free market position was a reaction to state-sponsored solutions to another kind of shock. The Keynesian reforms of the inter-war and post-war years were a response to what was perceived to be the catastrophic failure of the market to generate full employment, economic growth, social justice and prevent war. Since the 1980s, there has been a powerful swing away from this in the economic and social policies of the neo-liberal renaissance. However, neat capitalism may be interpreted as partly bucking this trend. For while neat capitalist corporations have retained a business focus. They have developed a variety of stateless solutions, often in partnership with consumers and non-government organizations to provide benefits for individuals and groups who are defined as being 'at risk'.

In addition, neat capitalist corporations like Exxon Mobile, BP and Coca-Cola have developed environment-friendly business models to limit and in some cases, reverse the environmental degradation caused by industrial practice. Many multi-nationals accept that their activities play a big part in global pollution. It may be that an important calculation here is that the public response to the trading prospects of multi-nationals will be adverse if climate change produces economic dislocation or food and water shortages. Be that as it may, in this respect, the evidence is that most of the big multi-nationals are not pursuing the shock doctrine *à la* Milton Friedman.

Leisure educators and professionals must offer a more nuanced model of the multiple equilibria between the corporation, the state and the consumer to counterbalance Klein's thought-provoking but somewhat monolithic thesis. The SCASSMIL framework outlined in this study may be considered as a resource to this end. Although committed to distributive justice, empowerment and social inclusion, the SCASSMIL framework does not pre-judge the behaviour of either the corporation or the state. Instead, it recognizes that each of these institutions consists of multiple equilibria located in a social and economic context based on organized inequality. The SCASSMIL framework does not pretend to be the last word in examining the relationships between the corporation, the state and the consumer. However, it does try to attune researchers, teachers and students to the many-sided character of leisure institutions and the shifting, transnational balance of power relationships within and between field activities.

IT'S STILL
LEISURE, STUPID[1]

Back in the days when the Visionaries and Pragmatists occupied their respective positions of influence, the study of leisure appeared luxuriously straightforward. Leaving aside the business of whether leisure is best regarded as a state of mind, or a dynamic set of forms and practices, among academics, leisure was presented as a simple category: the sum total of what people do in their spare time. Since the necessity to submit to wage labour was held to be the prime restraint upon time-use in industrial civilization, Visionaries and Pragmatists tended to equate spare time with free time.

A simple, but erroneous stream of associations was set loose by this train of thought: less work equals more leisure; and more leisure equals more freedom. This became the delta from which the SCCA approach to leisure and the leisure society thesis eventually spread and irrigated academic debate and research. This tradition provided an important counterpoint to perspectives that viewed work to be the inevitable central life interest for the majority in industrial civilization. It influenced generations of students and managers in the field of leisure and is, to this day, immensely powerful and seductive.

Although I have argued that the SCCA framework is now obsolescent, the perspective should be given its due in invigorating the field of Leisure Studies/Science. The SCCA framework encouraged people to take leisure seriously, rather than dismiss it as the trivial or 'less serious' side of life.[2] It raised the important question of organizing social life around fulfilment and life satisfaction rather than the work ethic. But it could not answer it. The SCCA framework was too permeated with the old chain of association that less work equals more leisure; and more leisure equals more freedom.

The move from the SCCA to the SCASSMIL framework is a jump from simple causal relationships that play the role of the master-key in the whole of life (notably the work–leisure relationship), to relationships of multiple equilibria involving changing balance of power ratios and a mixture of stable and unstable factors and links. This alters the way in which leisure is conceptualized and analysed. The question of leisure is no longer primarily about freedom from work. Competence, relevance and credibility require emotional intelligence and emotional labour that precedes the working day, are adapted to changing conditions during the working day and do not cease when the working day ends.

The significance of emotional intelligence and emotional labour in the conduct of life is hidden somewhat by the contemporary emphasis on flexible accumulation and postmodernism (Harvey 1989). In the weightless world individuals are analysed as possessing high mobility, using new technologies to switch from one economic or emotional market to the next and being highly responsive to new conditions (Coyle 1999). What this obscures is that to be adept in the weightless world individuals and groups have to develop considerable personal and collective *weight* in conveying competence, relevance and credibility. This weight is of a particular kind. To borrow and adapt Burns and Stalker's (1961) famous distinction between mechanistic and organic forms of organization, where production is hierarchical and regimented, where consumption is based upon predictable reproduction of demand and work organizational values emphasize loyalty and conformity, a mechanical form of organization, in which responsibilities and tasks are clearly demarcated, is often fitting. The worker is work-centred and can treat the work production process as atomized from the wider society. Globalization and delayering have combined to force these forms out to the periphery of the organizational landscape. Organic systems are more suitable to this new landscape. They consist of production based around flexible responsibilities and tasks; an orientation to the market that is sensitive to adaptation and the re-definition of demand; and organizational work values that emphasize making a difference to culture and society as well as achieving business targets. The organic form is the foundation of neat capitalism. It assumes a form of personal directedness to work that brings with it amiability, cordiality, professionalism and, crucially, knowledge and sensitivity about how the work process fits in with the social, cultural, psychological and environmental issues that make a difference to the global quality of life. In keeping up with the times, monitoring changing national and global conditions, noting how the wind is blowing with respect to social and economic relations and indicators of personal prestige, the individual enhances work-directedness.

Leisure is not fettered by the employment contract. It is a setting in which the accumulation of emotional intelligence and the practice of emotional labour roam from this topic to that, in modes of self-directed play or inquiry, to produce attitudes and knowledge about changing times and new directions in social, economic, cultural bodily and psychological relations that enhance competence, credibility and relevance.

This way of reading the generation of competent, relevant, credible prestige challenges conventional meanings of freedom. The SCASSMIL framework submits that freedom is an empty concept, unless we ask the questions, freedom from what? and, freedom from whom? Once these questions are accepted as not merely reasonable but necessary, the status of leisure changes.

In this book we have interrogated these questions to argue that analysis of leisure must proceed upon the basis that both leisure forms and practice and readings of leisure are positioned. The issue of positioning relates to power, expressed in many forms, chief among which are class, gender, race, ethnicity, nation, coding and representation. The SCASSMIL framework sets the cat among the pigeons in breaking the old chain of association that less work means more leisure; and more leisure means more freedom. Instead, it indicates that less work means a weaker claim upon scarce resources, and more leisure, if disconnected from questions of distributive justice and social inclusion, tends to end in more standardization, impoverishment of the imagination and the woe of entrapment without an alternative.

In contemporary society, competence and credibility are integral to our prestige as relevant, competent, mobile actors so that any place and any time is open to their accumulation and refinement. Competence, relevance and credibility are part of building a 'big picture' of the good and valued citizen. This is an evasive set of personal qualities, but one that is now pivotal in contemporary life. To be perceived as a good copper broker, policeman or long-haul traffic manager, it is no longer enough to know the mechanical details of your job. You need to convey an organic relationship with a range of wider issues having to do with culture (increasingly visual culture), society, economics, politics (especially the politics of embodiment) and psychology. It is a question of attitudes, outlook, bearing, background assumptions, a sense of proportion and discretion, ethical values and social principles. These qualities are partly the expression of our relationship to scarcity, mediated through relations of class, gender, race, ethnicity and status. Over and above the issue of positioning in relation to scarcity, every individual imposes his or her stamp upon these qualities through emotional intelligence and emotional labour. The things from which we derive pleasure and, in some cases, a sense of 'flow', have consequences that may be usefully transferred to other settings, such as work or politics. Leisure time and space is rather like Swiss cheese: although outwardly coded and represented as 'free' it is punctured with holes or 'eyes' which channel data about competence, relevance and credibility at the most unexpected times and in the most improbable places. Leisure is a regime, not a vacuum of pure voluntarism.

Specialization and Leisure: The Challenge from Within

Visionaries and Pragmatists were amateurs. They lacked training in Leisure Studies/Science and, generally, their interest in leisure was an off-shoot of more deeply rooted branches of study, such as Philosophy, History, Sociology or Urban Planning. Leisure scholars such as Thorstein Veblen, John Dewey, Johan Huizinga, Josef Pieper and Sebastian de Grazia all belong to this category. They have been succeeded by a new generation of scholars, many of whom have degrees in Leisure Studies/Science, and behold leisure as their specialized field of academic enquiry. In a word, what has happened is the professionalization of Leisure Studies/Science. Yet with this professionalization, an unanticipated type of specialization has emerged and crystallized.

Earlier in the book, we reviewed the salient features of professionalization (see pp. 97–103). The process of professionalization involves fashioning a code of ethics that governs practice, the claim of a monopoly relationship over a given field of enquiry or practice and specialist training in the knowledge base. The development of undergraduate and postgraduate degrees in Leisure Studies/Science and the creation of national and international professional associations are important indicators of professionalization. At the same time, professionalization is associated with the specialization of knowledge and practice. As amateurs, Visionaries and Pragmatists drew no distinction between fields of enquiry. The philosopher John Dewey thought nothing of developing a politics of leisure, based in the state funding of leisure forms and practice, as the inevitable consequence of his philosophical enquiry into the meaning of leisure. It is more difficult to do this today because the field is divided up into specialists in leisure theory, leisure policy, leisure psychology, therapeutic leisure and so on.

If one turns to the question of new degrees and the founding of new professional associations in the field of free time practice, one quickly learns that specialization has produced much deeper divisions in training and types of enquiry which have segregated some fields that were once housed under the canopy of leisure. In particular, the emergence of sport and tourism as specialized types of leisure has produced new academic power groups that challenge the traditional reading of leisure as 'spare' or 'free' time. The North American Society for the Sociology of Sport (NASS) was founded in 1978; The British Association of Sport and Exercise Science (BASE) followed in 1984; the Council for Australian University Tourism and Hospitality Education (CAUTHE) emerged in the late 1980s; and in the UK the Association for Tourism in Higher Education (ATHE) was founded in 2000. The UK Universities and Colleges Admission Service (UCAS) reported that in 2007 4,156 students were accepted for Hospitality, Leisure and Tourism degrees compared with 9,842 for Sport Science.

It is surprisingly difficult to acquire accurate figures for the number of students enrolled in dedicated Leisure Studies courses in the UK, Australia and the US. In the UK the figures are combined with hospitality and tourism. I have been unable to find a reliable source that separates them. In Australia the Department of Education, Employment and Workplace Relations does not separate the statistics on enrolment for sport, leisure and tourism.[3] In the US, as of February 2008, the National Recreation and Parks Association accredits 89 programmes. However, some large leisure programmes such as those at Illinois and Penn State are not included because the Faculties have elected not to seek accreditation. The best estimates that I have received suggest that there are about 200 Leisure Studies, Parks and Recreation programmes in the US, with Penn State and Texas A&M each having over 400 undergraduate students.[4] One of the reasons for imprecision about student numbers is that the field does not possess an organization like the American Psychological Association or the American Sociological Association that tracks undergraduate and postgraduate numbers.

What can be said with confidence is that the growth in Leisure Studies and Sciences has been comfortably out-paced by Sports Studies/Science and Tourism Studies. Student numbers in Leisure Studies/Science have been either static or shrinking. One of the main reasons for this is that the employment opportunities for graduates in Leisure Studies/Science are concentrated in the public sector. Since the 1980s, investment in the public sector of recreation has been capped or reduced. The private sector offers more work opportunities for graduates in Sports Studies/Science and Tourism Studies. The attraction of these newer fields is boosted by their media profile. Special events like the Olympics or the FIFA World Cup receive blanket media coverage throughout the world and, for young people, provide a glamorous image of careers in sport and tourism. By contrast, Leisure Studies graduates operate in Departments of Parks and Recreation as part of the standard complement of local public services. There is no equivalent global, honeypot attraction like the Olympics in the field of leisure.

The new fields that have developed around Sport and Tourism have produced their own distinctive approaches to theorizing free time and analysing non-work practice. Both fields command significant media attention and are the focus of multi-national and public interest in ways that Leisure Studies/Science do not match. For example, sport and tourism have been closely associated with global issues of human rights and responsibilities that have swiftly become *causes célèbres*. The struggle against apartheid in South Africa focused upon the role of sport in representing collective identity and expressing ethnic and racial cleavages. More generally, colonial and post-colonial history contains many examples of how sport was used to control subjects, dramatize the politics of exclusion and operate as an instrument of social healing and nation-building (Rowe 2004; Horne 2006). Similarly, tourism has highlighted wider questions of climate change, sustainability and political/racial divisions. By comparison the association of leisure with the good life and a healthy work–life balance seems insipid and vague. In terms of student numbers and public profile Sport Studies/Science and to a lesser extent, Tourism Studies, have now, in some respects, eclipsed Leisure Studies.

Sport, Tourism and Leisure: The Rules of the Game

What does it mean to maintain that in some respects Sport Studies/Science and Tourism Studies have eclipsed Leisure Studies/Science? This is a complex question. In terms of student numbers, more people study sport and tourism than leisure at university. Because the demand for study of these subjects is greater, the number of teachers involved in supplying classes and research is higher. The books and journals devoted to sport and tourism outnumber those in leisure because a greater number of people are studying in these areas and the demand for data relating to them is higher. This carries over into the employment market. More sport and tourism graduates means more influence for these subjects in the private and public sectors. In addition, this translates into a higher profile for matters of sport and tourism in public affairs. Graduates of Leisure Studies/Sciences are primarily employed in the unfashionable public sector. Their activities are often subsumed under broader agendas of 'culture' and 'community'. The questions of how to live with more leisure and how to use leisure for personal fulfilment and social enrichment tend to be left to private discretion.

In the course of all of this it is easy to suppose that leisure has been left behind. The agendas for teaching and research in sport and tourism seem solid and transparent whereas those of leisure are vague and obscure. The output goals of building sports capacity that will enable a country to compete more effectively in the next Olympics or creating sustainable tourism are easier to understand and measure than the airy-fairy commitment that many scholars and students of leisure have to contribute to the good life.

Richard Giulanotti (2005: xii–xiii) offers five identifying characteristics of sport from which clear teaching and research questions can be extrapolated. According to him, sport is:

1) *Structured*, by rules and codes of conduct which govern the terms of engagement and duration of events. This means that there is a universal pattern to sporting events, so that they can be readily understood irrespective of cultural, religious, racial, ethnic, or political distinctions.
2) *Goal-oriented*, by the tangible achievement of results, such as winning a game, breaking a record and so forth. This means that sports events involve clear winners and losers.
3) *Competitive*, by clear opponents involved in a contest to achieve transparent ends.
4) *Ludic*, that is, it involves absorption, tension, excitement and mirth.
5) *Culturally situated*, in the sense that although sport is rule-bound and conforms to universal codes of practice, it is inflected by cultural distinctions. This means that sport is an extraordinarily powerful vehicle for expressing national or group identity.

In the field of tourism, the Global Code of Ethics for Tourism published by the World Tourism Organization (1999) (reprinted in Wylie 2000: 189–95), provides a clear guide to tourist behaviour from which an analogous research agenda can be extrapolated. Tourists are:

1) *Visitors*, who should conduct themselves in harmony with the attributes and traditions of the host communities in respect of laws, customs and cultural practice.
2) *Guests*, who are entitled to the respect and protection of host communities in respect of personal safety, cultural integrity and religious practice.
3) *Stakeholders,* in the common heritage of mankind. Tourism must respect the equality of men and women, safeguard the natural environment and protect artistic, archaeological and historic heritage.
4) *Investors*, in the financial infrastructure of host communities. Responsible tourism expands economic, social and cultural benefits and raises the general standard of living.
5) *World citizens,* with a right to direct and personal access to the discovery and enjoyment of the planet's resources. Tourists should benefit, within the compliance of the law, to have freedom of movement within their own countries and from one nation to another in accordance with Article 13 of the Universal Declaration of Human Rights.

Compare this with the definition of the main characteristics of the 'multidimensional construct of leisure' expounded by Edington et al. (2004: 37–9). Leisure is:

1) *Freedom*, involving the choice of individuals and groups to follow self-determined forms and practices which are not curtailed by the obligations of work, family or home activities.
2) *Perceived Competence*, involving the application of skills and abilities that enable successful participation in a leisure form or practice. Satisfying leisure experience occurs when skills and abilities are commensurate with the challenges of intended leisure experience. Commensurability is a matter of individual and group perception. It does not matter if the perception is accurate or reality-based.
3) *Intrinsic Motivation,* involving the fulfilment of self-determined individual or group goals. When this condition is met, individuals and groups become engrossed in forms and practices that offer satisfaction, enjoyment and gratification.
4) *Positive Affect*, involving a feeling of being in control or having primary influence over experience.

From a sociological perspective, this definition is problematic. It does not acknowledge that the meaning of the individual and group is itself externally conditioned and varies along comparative and historical dimensions. Thus the meaning of an individual who is a member of a *Sunni* population in Iraq in terms of entitlement, responsibility, emotional intelligence, emotional labour, competence and credibility is significantly different to an individual from the *Shi'ite* or *Kurd* population in the same country. A great many errors derive from operating with a universal model of individual and group needs and perception of freedom. Not the least of them is that the beliefs, values and aspirations of one culture and religion can be projected willy-nilly upon all cultures and religions.

Notwithstanding that, Edington et al.'s definition is useful in sensitizing teachers, researchers and students to the analytical and practical difficulties that follow from investigating a field in which the content of forms and practice are elastic and the perception of freedom is multidimensional. The sports player and the tourist are complex, but at least their identities are coherent. The parameters of leisure are more elusive. As a result, the rules governing social encounters in leisure are frequently harder to discern or grasp. We have already noted Turner's (1982: 37) observation that leisure often involves *entering* new symbolic worlds through play, experimentation and diversion and *transcending* social limitations through ideas, fantasies, words and social relationships. Sport, tourism and leisure are all expanding fields. But leisure expands exponentially because the only rules governing human creativity are the laws of human creativity itself.

The Revitalization of Leisure Studies: Leisure as a School of Life

We are coming to the end of the present discussion. The study of leisure began with the ideas of Visionaries and the caveats of Pragmatists intent upon building the good life in urban-industrial society. Many scholars of the day celebrated the leisure society thesis as the culmination of this tradition. It now looks more like an aberration. Today, few submit that automation and ethical management are converging to abolish manual labour or that leisure is set to replace work as the central life interest. Debate and research have shifted gear. Leisure is now examined as a scarce resource and a core component of the work–life balance. This raises a separate set of questions about the positioning of leisure forms with respect to class, ethnicity, race and gender, the role of leisure in social and personal health and wellbeing, the relationship between emotional intelligence, emotional labour and leisure forms and practice and the value of leisure as an instrument of resource allocation. Within the field, dedicated research groups have emerged and combined to investigate these matters. They have incorporated and adapted several theoretical approaches from more established social sciences to help them in their various tasks.

The old idea that leisure study is about what pleasure-accumulating individuals and groups do in their free time has been modified by a new research agenda having to do with the multiple meanings of pleasure, the social, economic and political context in which time is coded and represented as 'free', the use of leisure in enhancing personal and group direction, and the ideological connotation of freedom in a society based upon organized inequality. In the process the prestige and power of Leisure Studies/Leisure Science has changed.

The innocence of the old SCCA framework has given ground to the new preoccupations of what I have called the SCASSMIL era. These issues involve the development of a political economy of leisure, a critical psychology of free time practice and a global sociology of leisure forms and practices. Freedom and pleasure are slowly being redefined as socially and economically conditioned human qualities rather than timeless, natural capacities that occur universally regardless of comparative and historical criteria of authority and power. In the SCCA era, leisure was regarded to be an enchanted glade that one enters after the door of work is closed. What is limited at work, is plentiful in leisure. What requires subordination at work is permitted to flourish in leisure. The bane of life is left behind and replaced with opportunities for boundless pleasure accumulation, rest and relaxation.

This polarized, distorting way of looking at work and leisure bred unicorns and dragons. Generations of leisure scholars have chased boundless freedom and self-determination only to discover the multi-faceted positioning of individuals and groups in relation to scarcity. It is as if we have been constantly looking for something that only exists in fancy and poetry: freedom, choice, self-determination and spontaneity. For decades we have been engaged in little more than chasing our own tails. This has contributed to questions of relevance and justification in the public. Why persist with Leisure Studies/Science when its assumptions seem to be so obviously wrong-footed and its theoretical and practical achievements, compared with Sport Studies and Tourism Studies, are so thin and paltry?

The SCASSMIL framework calls for a reorientation of the field. This is a question of moving from simple causal models of leisure choices and trajectories of behaviour to more complex perspectives that approach leisure experience as the product of relations between multiple equilibria. We must learn to regard leisure not as a state of mind, but as a condition that is the product of interrelations between many factors, some of which are distanced far away from the immediate location of pleasure accumulation, rest or relaxation. But the reorientation implied by the SCASSMIL framework involves more than this.

Leisure is a primary setting for coaching about the people skills and global vision that boost personal prestige. Through play and relaxation we assimilate data and encounter role models that have the potential to add to emotional intelligence and enhance our emotional labour capacities. Leisure provides an unparalleled mechanism for learning and adaptation that transfers to more structured settings, like work, and confers competitive advantage to individuals and groups. This is quite different from being free. In leisure we are conscious of our need to adapt, our capacity to learn and our ability to imagine.

The revitalization of Leisure Studies is never going to happen if we rely on the second coming of the leisure society thesis. That thesis was fundamentally flawed in failing to address the development gap or engage with the conflation of leisure and consumerism. The former required a level of resource distribution that was not tolerable for Western democracy, while the latter made the demand for paid employment impregnable. This is another way of saying that the leisure society thesis held a faulty view of scarcity. It failed to address the persistence of class, race, gender and status relations in positioning individuals and groups unequally in relation to scarcity. In societies based upon organized inequality where the majority possess labour power as the only, or primary, asset of economic wherewithal, competence, relevance and credibility are the trinity for full social membership and meaningful participation in civil culture. The revitalization of leisure studies is based in unlocking how leisure forms and practice enhance the storage capacity and repertoire of accomplishments necessary to achieve competence, relevance and credibility. This means linking leisure directly to emotional intelligence and emotional labour.

The Ancient Greek word for leisure is schole. Etymologically speaking, it is the root of our word 'school'. Aristotle understood that to be an epicure of leisure requires discipline and preparation. 'We do without leisure [*ascholoumetha*]', he writes (1941: 56), in a discussion of what our priorities in life should be, 'only to give ourselves leisure [*gar hina scholazomen*]'.[5] Aristotle was wrong to identify true leisure with the world of elite culture. How could he have foreseen the immense redistribution of time and wealth achieved in the urban-industrial age?[6] Yet he was right in his positioning of leisure in the scale of human priorities. To truly enjoy leisure we must harness ludic discipline to gain wisdom from scarcity, rather than feast or play as pleasure-accumulating ends in themselves. In proposing that the revitalization of leisure rests upon linking it directly to emotional intelligence and emotional labour, I am casting back to the roots of the term in Ancient Greece. Leisure is not consumption activity, since this is ultimately driven by the capitalist goal of ceaseless accumulation. Nor is it activity designed to distract one from the cares and predicaments of work, since this merely reinforces the domination of the work ethic by condemning leisure to a subsidiary, compensatory function. Leisure is a school for life. The end of schooling is to maintain and enhance competence, relevance and credibility. The successful attainment of this end requires perpetual emotional intelligence and emotional labour. Freedom is for the birds.

NOTES

Chapter 1

1 This example is borrowed from Norbert Elias. Elias deliberately untied his shoelaces and walked in city streets in order to discover the effect on pedestrians. This is reminiscent of Harold Garfinkel's (1967) famous 'breaching experiments' which called upon students to examine the taken-for-granted assumptions and rules of everyday life by deliberately disrupting them. It is very unlikely that Elias knew about Garfinkel's work at the time. For an account of the content of Elias's shoelace experiment see Moerth, I. (2008) 'The Shoe-Lace Breaching Experiment', http://soziologie.soz.uni-linz.ac.at

2 I introduced A&B analysis into the study of leisure because I was interested in how we might analyse trajectories of behaviour in leisure locations without falling back on the preconceptions of race, gender and class (Rojek 2005: 24–7). This is very much a mind game about the dynamics of social relationships in leisure settings. It is not intended as a plea for a new direction in the methodology of leisure studies! I simply wanted to illuminate quantitative issues in trajectories of leisure behaviour. Their significance, I fancy, is often obscured by the quite natural tendency of researchers and students working in particular traditions of leisure study to foreground qualitative issues.

Chapter 2

1 Deregulation refers to the relaxation of state rules governing the financial and employment requirements of corporations. Out-sourcing refers to the strategic decision to allocate resourcing responsibilities to specialized private contractors. Naomi Klein (2007), in her provocative and informative book, noted that the Pentagon has awarded key munitions supply contracts to private companies as a strategy for controlling the cost of the Armed Services and enhancing evidence-based efficiency. One of the main beneficiaries is Halliburton Energy Services, based in Houston, Texas. Dick Cheney, the Vice President in George Bush's administrations, served as Chairman of the Board and Chief Executive Officer of Halliburton between 1995–2000.

2 Richard Florida (2002) provides an influential modern take on this line of argument. He submits that leisure resources are a primary consideration in choices about contemporary business location. Under the new capitalism (or what I call neat capitalism), the creative class does not simply want high income and prestige, they want access to beaches, golf courses, cultural centres, nature parks and other leisure and recreation resources. For Florida, leisure capacity is now a major element in business recruitment and location strategy.

3 Invasive and mephitic forms of leisure are orientated around a) gaining risky leisure experience that may pose a threat to personal wellbeing and mortality;

and b) posing a risk to others. The chains of supply of illegal leisure resources is, by definition, covert. Katz (1988) has suggested that part of the attraction of criminal activity is the simple offloading of repressive controls required by modern civilization. This also applies to illegal forms of leisure practice. Another source of attraction here might be the hidden or 'secret' character of these leisure lives.

Chapter 3

1   The father of structuralism was Ferdinand de Saussure (1974). He argued that a sign is the basic unit of language. Every language constitutes a system of signs. *Parole* (the individual act of communication) is the expression of language. For Saussure the system of language was founded upon a series of recognized differences combined with a series of different ideas. His work therefore raised important questions relating to the generation of meaning and representation. In the field of leisure these ideas have been developed most eloquently and insightfully by Dean MacCannell (1976). MacCannell's theory of markers is pivotal in understanding the laws of representation in modern tourism.

2   'Crackpot realism' is a phrase coined by C. Wright Mills (1958). He used it to refer to the nuclear arms struggle in the Cold War. Mills viewed this as a crackpot way to allocate resources since its end point was nuclear annihilation. The phrase can be extended to a number of different settings. The audit trail in the modern university, which aims to measure educational outcomes quantitatively, is one that comes to mind!

3   Sayyid Qutb is widely regarded as the father of Islamic fundamentalism. His (2008) attack on Western permissiveness offers a counterpoint to Islamic programmes of modernization. His execution and defence of the traditional values of Islam have been a major resource in the terrorist *jihad* against the West over the last thirty years.

Chapter 4

1   By the term 'second nature' I mean the social and psychological resources that we assimilate and which become a condition of practising as a competent, relevant, credible actor. Our 'first nature' refers to our genetic inheritance and human drives. Second nature is learned *social* behaviour that has been accumulated over millennia and which now helps to define human behaviour as distinct.

Chapter 7

1   As Marx and Engels (1970: 8) put it:

> Through the emancipation of private property from the community, the State has become a separate entity, beside and outside civil society; but it is nothing more than the form of organization which the bourgeois

necessarily adopt both for internal and external purposes, for the mutual guarantee of their property and interests ... Since the State is the form in which the individuals of a ruling class assert their common interests, and in which the whole of civil society of an epoch is epitomized, it follows that the State mediates in the formation of all common institutions and that the institutions receive a political form. Hence, the illusion that law is based on the will, and indeed on the will divorced from its real basis – on *free* will [emphasis in original].

For Marx and Engels then the concept of freedom in capitalist society is adapted to fulfil the interests of the dominant class.

2   Wallerstein's (1974, 2004, 2006) core, periphery and semi-periphery model has its detractors. The model is regarded as too rigid and as lacking clarity. Within core countries there are peripheral and semi-peripheral regions. However, notwithstanding these criticisms I have found Wallerstein's division of the world to be a very helpful way of reading globalization. Wallerstein divides the globe into:

1)   Core countries, consisting of advanced urban-industrial economies, sophisticated financial sectors, highly developed education sectors and serious global military capacity.
2)   Periphery countries, composed of emerging urban-industrial economies, weak financial sectors, under-developed education sectors and weak global military capacity.
3)   Semi-periphery countries, consisting of developing urban-industrial economies, with medium-sized financial sectors, emerging education sectors and medium-sized global military capacity.

3   The terms 'one-way' and two-way' convergence were introduced by Eric Dunning and Earl Hopper (1966) in the context of the debate over industrialism and convergence. 'One-way convergence' refers to the magnetizing effect that one developed social and economic system has in producing replicas of itself in emerging social systems in terms of social institutions, economic levels of development, political parties and personality types. 'Two-way convergence' refers to the exchange of institutions between social systems in terms of social institutions, economic levels of development, political parties and personality types. Dunning and Hopper (1966) were taking issue with Kerr et al. (1962) who submitted that the American system of urban-industrial market society is constructed around an implacable logic of industrialization that all industrializing nations are fated to obey. Instead of converging to one (American) type, Dunning and Hopper contended that industrialization involves a permutation of exchange in which social institutions, political systems and personality types from competing systems are exchanged. Many aspects of this debate, which also drew in the acerbic John Goldthorpe (1971), can usefully be reconsidered in relation to the modern debate on globalization.

Chapter 8

1   The US Surgeon General's Report was preceded by a Report from the *Royal College of Physicians* (1962) which drew broadly similar conclusions.

Chapter 9

1   The phrase is a play on the phrase 'It's the economy, stupid.' Coined by the Democrat Party campaign strategist, James Carville in the 1992 presidential campaign, it was successfully used by Bill Clinton to imply that the presidential policies of George W. Bush neglected the domestic economy by focusing too much on foreign policy issues.

2   Emile Durkheim was responsible for tarring leisure with the brush of being 'less serious'. He viewed leisure, sport and recreation as fulfilling a subsidiary, compensatory function in industrial society. As he (1893: 26) put it: 'It appears in the nature of things [that] sport and recreation develops side by side with the *serious life* which it serves to balance and relieve.'

3   I am indebted to my friend A.J. Veal for correspondence that clarified these matters for me. Tony is in no way responsible for the interpretation that I have put upon these figures here.

4   Garry Chick provided me with very useful data on American programmes in leisure and recreation. Garry is in no way responsible for the interpretation that I have put upon these figures here.

5   For this reading of the Ancient Greek roots of the term 'leisure' I am indebted to Michael O'Loughlin's (1978) study of the literary celebration of civic and retired leisure. This book is little known in Leisure Studies/Science, yet it is a treasure trove of insights about the ancient and modern meaning of leisure.

6   Throughout the book I have emphasized that human beings are positioned in relation to scarcity. I have also quoted favourably Fred Hirsch's (1976) theory of positional goods which argues that even in an epoch of abundance new relations of scarcity are bound to develop around prestige and honorific values. So in referring to the immense redistribution of time and wealth achieved in the industrial-urban age I am not offering an apology for the current distribution of scarcity. Rather I am making the point that never in human history has so much surplus been shared out to so many. To say this does not gainsay that inequality is still a welt on the face of industrial capitalism. For the Third World, in relation to the advanced industrial economies, it is more than this. It is an abomination.

REFERENCES

Academy of Leisure Sciences (nd). 'White Paper 7: The Benefits of Leisure.' http://www.academyofleisuresciences.org/alwsp/.html

Action on Smoking and Health (2004). 'Factsheet Number 4: Smoking and Cancer.' www.ash.org.uk.

Adorno, T.W. and Horkheimer, M. (1944) *Philosophische Fragmente*. New York, Social Studies Association.

Aitchison, C. (1997). 'A decade of Compulsory Competitive Tendering (CCT) in UK sport and leisure services: some feminist reflections.' *Leisure Studies* **16**(2): 85–105.

Aitchison, C. (2003). *Gender and Leisure*. London, Routledge.

Alterman, E. and Green, M. (2004). *The Book of Bush*. New York, Penguin.

Althusser, L. (1969). *For Marx*. Harmondsworth, Penguin.

Althusser, L. (1971). *Lenin and Philosophy and Other Essays*. London, New Left Books.

Andrew, E. (1981). *Closing The Iron Cage*. Montreal, Black Rose Books.

Arendt, H. (1963). *Eichmann in Jerusalem*. Harmondsworth, Penguin.

Aristotle (1941). *Nicomachean Ethics*. New York, Random House.

Aristotle (1962). *The Politics*. Harmondsworth, Penguin.

Armstrong, G. (1998). *Football Hooligans*. London, Berg.

Aronowitz, S. and DiFazio, W. (1994). *The Jobless Future*. Minneapolis, Minnesota University Press.

ASHE (2007). *Annual Survey of Hours and Earnings*. www.statistics.gov.uk

Australian Government (2004). *Tobacco Smoking Fact Sheet*. www.symphu.health.wa.gov.au

Bailey, P. (1978). *Leisure and Class in Vicotrian England*. London, Routledge & Kegan Paul.

Bailyn, B. (1974). *The Ordeal of Thomas Hutchinson*. Cambridge, Harvard University Press.

Balthorpe, J., Forrest, S. and Newman, M.E.J (2004). 'Technological Networks and the Spread of Computer Viruses', *Science* **304**, 5670: 527–9.

Baranowski, S. (2004). *Strength Through Joy: Consumerism and Mass Tourism in the Third Reich*. Cambridge, Cambridge University Press.

Baudrillard, J. (1981). *For a Critique of the Political Economy of the Sign*. St Louis, Telos.

Baudrillard, J. (2004). *The Gulf War Did Not Take Place*. Sydney, Power Publications.

Bauman, Z. (1989). *Modernity and the Holocaust*. Cambridge, Polity.

Bauman, Z. (1997). *Legislators and Interpreters*. Cambridge, Polity.

Bean, P. (2002). *Drugs and Crime*. Cullumpton, Willan.

Beaven, B. (2005). *Leisure, Citizenship and Working Class Men in Britain 1850–1945*. Manchester, Manchester University Press.

Beck, U. (1992). *Risk Society*. London, Sage.

Bell, D. (1974). *The Coming of Post Industrial Society*. Harmondsworth, Penguin.

Blackshaw, T. (2003). *Leisure Life*. London, Routledge.

Blackshaw, T. and Crabbe, T. (2004). *New Perspectives on Sport and 'Deviance'*. Abingdon, Routledge.

Blyton, P. and Jenkins, J. (2007). *Key Concepts in Work*. Sage, London.

Borzello, F. (1987). *Civilizing Caliban*. London, Routledge.

Botterill, T. and Brown, G. (1985). 'Leisure Studies in the USA.' *Leisure Studies* **4**(3): 251–74.

Bourdieu, P. (1984). *Distinction*. London, Routledge.

Bourdieu, P. (1998). *Acts of Resistance*. Cambridge, Polity.

Bourdieu, P. and Wacquant, L. (2003). *Firing Back: Against The Tyranny of the Market*. New York, New Press.

Bowdin, G., Allen, A., O'Toole, W., Harris, R. and McDonnell, I. (2006). *Events Management* (2nd edition). Oxford, Elsevier.

Bramham, P. (2002). 'Rojek, The Sociological Imagination and Leisure.' *Leisure Studies* **21**(3/4): 221–34.

Bramham, P. (2006). 'Review of "Leisure Theory: Principles & Practice".' *Leisure Studies* **25**(4): 479–80.

Brewer, D., Potterat, J., Garrett, S., Muth, S.Q., Roberts, J.M., Kaspryzk, D., Montano, D. and Darrow, W. (2000). 'Prostitution and the sex discrepancy in reported number of partners.' *Proceedings of the National Academy of Sciences* **97**(22): 12385–8.

British American Tobacco (2004). '"Who We Are": Corporate Social Responsibility and Social Report 2004/5', www.bat.com

Bryman, A. (2001). *Social Research*. Oxford, Oxford University Press.

Bryson, J.R., Daniels, P.W. and Warf, B. (2004). *Service Worlds*. London, Routledge.

Burns, T. and Stalker, G.M. (1961). *The Management of Innovation*. London, Tavistock.

Campbell, R. and O'Neill, M. (eds) (2006). *Sex Work Now*. London, Willan.

Castells, M. (1996). *The Rise of the Network Society*. Oxford, Blackwell.

Castells, M. (1997). *Power of Identity*. Oxford, Blackwell.

Castells, M. (2001). *The Internet Society*. Oxford, Oxford University Press.

Cheek, N. and Burch, W. (1976). *The Social Organization of Leisure in Human Society*. New York, Harper & Row.

Chelala, C. (1999). 'Tobacco Corporations Step Up Invasion of Third World.' *Third World Network*, wwfw.twnside.org.sg

Chick, G. (1986). 'Leisure, Labour and the Complexity of Culture.' *Journal of Leisure Research* **18**(3): 154–66.

CIA World Fact Book. www.cia.gov/library/publications/the-world-factbook/

Clark, D. (1995). 'A New Code of Ethics for NRPA.' *Parks & Recreation Magazine* **30**(8): 38–43.

Clarke, J. and Critcher, C. (1985). *The Devil Makes Work*. London, Macmillan.

Clayre, A. (1974). *Work and Play*. New York, Harper & Rowe.

Clutterbuck, D. (2003). *Meeting Work-Life Balance: A Guide for HR in Achieving Organisational and Individual Change*. London, CIPD.

Coalter, F. (1999). 'Leisure Sciences and Leisure Studies: The Challenge of Meaning.' In E. Jackson and T. Burton, *Leisure Studies: Prospects For The Twenty-First Century*. State College, Venture Publishing. Pp. 507–19.

Coalter, F. (2006a). 'Public Policy & Leisure.' In E. Kennedy, and H. Poussard, *Defining The Field: 30 Years of the Leisure Studies Association*. Brighton, Leisure Studies Association. Pp. 59–72.

Coalter, F. (2006b). 'The Duality of Leisure Policy.' In C. Rojek, S. Shaw and A. J. Veal, *A Handbook of Leisure Studies*. Basingstoke, Macmillan-Palgrave. Pp. 162–84.

Cohen-Geweric, E. and Stebbins, R. (eds) (2007). *The Pivotal Role of Leisure Education*. State College, Venture.

Corrigan, P. and Sayer, D. (1985). *The Great Arch*. Oxford, Blackwell.

Coyle, D. (1999). *The Weightless World: Thriving in the Digital Age*. Oxford, Capstone.

Critcher, C. and Bramham, P. (2004). 'The Devil Still Makes Work.' In J. Veal and A. J. Haworth (eds) *Work and Leisure*. Routledge, London. Pp. 34–50.

Cross, G. (1993). *Of Time and Money: The Making of Consumer Culture*. London, Routledge.

Csikszentmihalyi, M. (1975). *Between Boredom and Anxiety*. San Francisco, Josey Bass.

Csikszentmihalyi, M. (1990). *Flow: The Psychology of Optimal Experience*. New York, Harper & Row.

Csikszentmihalyi, M. (1998). *Finding Flow: The Psychology of Engagement With Everyday Life*. Harcourt Brace Jovanovich, New York.

Cunnen, C., Findlay, M., Lynch, R., Tupper, V. (1989). *Dynamics of Collective Conflict: Riots at the Bathurst Bike Races*. Sydney, The Law Book Company.

Daniels, B. (1995). *Purtians at Play: Leisure and Recreation in Colonial New England*. London, St Martin's Press.

De Graaf, D. and Jordan, D. (2003). 'Social Capital: It's About Community.' *Parks and Recreation* **39**(2) (no page references available).

De Graaf, J. (2004). *Take Back Your Time*. San Francisco, Berrett-Korhler Books.

de Grazia, S. (1962). *Of Time, Work and Leisure*. New York, The Twentieth Century Fund.

De Saussure, F. (1974). *Course in General Linguistics*. London, Fontana.

Deem, R. (1986). *All Work and No Play*. Milton Keynes, Open University Press.

Dewey, J. (1916). *Education and Democracy*. New York, Free Press.

Didkowlska, J., Manczuk, M., McNeill, A., Powles, J. and Zatonski, W. (2005). 'Lung Cancer Mortality at Ages 35–54 in the European Union.' *British Medical Journal* (331): 189–91.

Donnelly, P. (1986). 'The Paradox of the Parks.' *Leisure Studies* **5**(2): 211–32.

Dumazedier, J. (1967). *Towards A Society of Leisure*. New York, Free Press.

Dumazedier, J. (1974). *Sociology of Leisure*. Amsterdam, Elsevier.

Dumont, L. (1986). *Essays On Individualism*. Chicago, Chicago University Press.

Dunning, E. (1999). *Sport Matters*. London, Routledge.

Dunning, E. and Sheard, K. (2005). *Barbarians, Gentlemen and Players* (2nd edition). Abingdon, Routledge.

Dunning, E.G. and Hopper, E.I. (1966). 'Industrialization and the Problem of Convergence: a Critical Note.' *Sociological Review* **14**(2): 163086.

Durkheim, E. (1893). *The Division of Labour*. New York, Free Press.

Durkheim, E. (1897). *Suicide*. London, Routledge & Kegan Paul.

Durkheim, E. (1904). *Professional Ethics and Civic Morals*. London, Routledge.

Dustin, D.L. and Goodale, T.L. (1999). 'Reflections on Recreation, Park, and Leisure Studies'. In E. Jackson and T. Burton, *Leisure Studies: Prospects for the Twenty First Century*. State College, Venture. Pp. 477–86.

Edington, C.R., Huson, S.D., Dieser, R.B. and Edington, S.R. (2004). *Leisure Programming: A Service Centred and Benefits Approach,* (4th edition). New York, McGraw Hill.

Elias, N. (1956). 'Problems of Involvement and Detachment.' *British Journal of Sociology* **7**(3): 226–52.

Elias, N. (1978). *The Civilizing Process*. New York, Pantheon Books.

Elias, N. (1983). *The Court Society*. Oxford, Blackwell.

Elias, N. and Dunning, E. (1986). *The Quest for Excitement*. Oxford, Blackwell.

Eliot, T.S. (1948). *Notes Towards A Definition of Culture*. London, Faber.

Eriksen, M. and Le Maistre, A. (1988). 'Health Hazards of Passive Smoking.' *Annual Review of Public Health*: 47–70.

Etzioni, A. (1997). *The New Golden Rule: Community and Morality in a Democratic Society*. London, Profile.

Ferrell, J. and Sanders, C. R. (1995). *Cultural Criminology.* Chicago, Northeastern University Press.

Ferrell, J. (1999). 'Cultural Criminology.' *Annual Review of Sociology,* 25: 395–418.

Fleming, I. (1996). 'The Professionalization of Leisure Management in Western Europe.' *Managing Leisure* **1**(4): 248–52.

Florida, R. (2002). *The Rise of the Creative Class.* New York, Bantam.

Foucault, M. (1975). *Discipline and Punish.* Harmondsworth, Penguin.

Foucault, M. (1980). *Power/Knowledge: Selected Interviews and Other Writings 1972–77.* Hemel Hempstead, Harvester.

Foucault, M. (1981). *History of Sexuality, Volume 1.* Harmondsworth, Penguin.

Foucault, M. (1991). 'Governmentality'. In G. Burchell, C. Gorden and P. Miller (eds) *The Foucault Effect: Studies in Governmentality.* London, Harvester Wheatsheaf.

Frank, R. (2003). *What Price The Moral High Ground.* Princeton, Princeton University Press.

Frank, T. (1997). *The Conquest of Cool.* Chicago, Chicago University Press.

Fuller, F. (1875). *How To Elevate The People.* New York, National Association for the Promotion of Social Sciences.

Garfinkel, H. (1967). *Studies in Ethnomethodology.* Englewood Cliffs, New Jersey, Prentice Hall.

Gartman, D. (1994). *Auto-Opium.* London, Routledge.

Gellner, E. (1988). *Plough, Sword and Book: The Structure of Human History.* Chicago, Chicago University Press.

Gershuny, J. (2000). *Changing Times: Work and Leisure in Postindustrial Society.* Oxford, Oxford University Press.

Getz, D. (2005). *Event Management and Event Tourism* (2nd edition). New York, Van Nostron Rheinhold.

Giddens, A. (1986). *The Constitution of Society.* Cambridge, Polity.

Giddens, A. (1994). *Beyond Left and Right.* Cambridge, Polity.

Giddens, A. (1998). *The Third Way.* Cambridge, Polity.

Giddens, A. (2000). *The Third Way and its Critics.* Cambridge, Polity.

Giddens, A. (2007). *Europe in the Global Age.* Cambridge, Polity.

Giulanotti, R. (2005). *Sport: A Critical Sociology.* Cambridge, Polity.

Glanz, S. A., Slade, J., Bero, L. A., Hanauer, P. and Barnes, D.E. (1996). *The Cigarette Papers.* Berkeley, University of California Press.

Glenny, M. (2008). *McMafia.* London, Bodley Head.

Glover, T. (2004). 'Social Capital in the Lived Experience of Community Gardeners.' *Leisure Sciences* **26**(2): 1–20.

Godbey, G. (1978). 'The Professionalization of Recreation and Parks in the Public Sector.' *Leisure & Society* **1**(2): 269–84.

Goffman, E. (1959). *The Presentation of Self in Everyday Life.* Harmondsworth, Penguin.

Goldman, R. and Papson, S. (1998). *Nike Culture.* London, Sage.

Goldthorpe, J. (1971). 'Theories of Industrial Society: Reflections on the Recrudescence of Historicism and the Future of Futurology.' *Archives of European Sociology* **12**: 263–88.

Goleman, D. (1995). *Emotional Intelligence.* New York, Bantam.

Goodale, T. (1994). 'Leisure Sciences: Impractical? Impenetrable?' *Parks and Recreation* 12/1/1994.

Goodale, T. and Godbey, G. (1988). *The Evolution of Leisure.* State College, Venture.

Gorz, A. (1978). *Farewell to the Working Class.* London, Pluto.

Gramsci, A. (1971). *Selections From the Prison Notebooks.* London, Lawrence & Wishart.

Gratton, C. and Taylor, P. (2004). 'The Economics of Work and Leisure'. In J. Veal and A.J. Haworth (eds) *Work and Leisure.* London, Routledge. Pp. 85–106.

Gray, R. (1981). *The Aristocracy of Labour.* London, Macmillan.

Green, E., Hebron, S. and Woodward, D. (1987). *Women's Leisure, What Leisure?* Basingstoke, Macmillan.

Greenwood Parr, G. and Lashua, B. (2005). '"Students'" Perceptions of Leisure, Leisure Professionals and the Professional Body of Knowledge.' *Journal of Hospitality, Leisure, Sport and Tourism Education* **4**(2): 16–26.

Gruneau, R. and Whitson, D. (1993). *Hockey Night in Canada.* Toronto, Garamond.

Habermas, J. (1962 tr. 1989). *The Structural Transformation of the Public Sphere.* Cambridge, Polity.

Habermas, J. (1973). *Legitimation Crisis.* London, Heinemann.

Hall, S., Critcher, C., Jefferson, T., Clarke, J. and Roberts, R. (1978). *Policing The Crisis.* Basingstoke, Macmillan.

Hargreaves, J. (1986). *Sport, Power and Culture.* Cambridge, Polity.

Harmer, P., Williams, P., Gunsch, G. and Lamont, G. (2002). 'An Artificial Immune System Archiecture for Computer Security Applications.' *IEEE Transactions on Evolutionary Computation* **6**: 252–80.

Harvey, D. (1989). *The Condition of Postmodernity.* Oxford, Blackwell.

Haworth, J. and Veal, A.J. (eds) (2004). *Work and Leisure.* London, Routledge.

Hayward, K.J. (2004). *City Limits: Crime, Consumer Culture and the Urban Experience.* London, Routledge Cavendish.

Headey, B., Wooden, M. and Marks, G. (2004). *Structure and Distribution of Household Wealth in Australia.* Melbourne Institute Working Paper wp2004n12, Melbourne University Institute of Applied Economic and Social Research.

Heeley, J. (1986). 'Leisure and Moral Reform.' *Leisure Studies* **5**(1): 57–67.

Hegel, G.W.F. (1807 tr. 1977). *Phenomenology of Spirit.* Oxford, Oxford University Press.

Hemingway, J. (1999). 'Leisure, Social Capital and Democratic Citizenship.' *Journal of Leisure Research* **31**: 150–65.

Henderson, K., Bialeschki, M., Shaw, S. and Freysinger, V. (1996). *Both Gains and Gaps: Feminist Perspectives on Womens Leisure.* State College, Venture Publishing.

Henderson, K. and Bialeschki, M. (1991). 'A Sense of Entitlement to Leisure as Constraint and Empowerment for Women'. *Leisure Sciences* **13**(2): 51–65.

Henderson, K. and Shaw, S. (2006). 'Leisure and Gender.' In C. Rojek, S. Shaw and A.J. Veal. *A Handbook of Leisure Studies.* Basingstoke, Macmillan: 203–15.

Henry, I. (1993). *The Politics of Leisure Policy.* Basingstoke, Macmillan.

Hill, J. (2003). *Sport, Leisure and Culture in Twentieth-Century Britain.* Basingstoke, Palgrave Macmillan.

Hirsch, F. (1976). *The Social Limits to Growth.* London, Routledge & Kegan Paul.

HMSO (2006). *Gowers Review of Intellectual Property.* London, HMSO.

HMSO (2008). *British Crime Survey.* London, HMSO.

Hochschild, A. (1983). *The Managed Heart.* Berkeley, University of California Press.

Holt, D. (2004). *How Brands Became Icons.* Cambridge, Mass., Harvard Business School.

Horne, J. (2006). *Sport in Consumer Culture.* Basingstoke, Palgrave Macmillan.

Hubble, N. (2006). *Mass Observation and Everyday Life.* Basingstoke, Palgrave Macmillan.

Hughes, J. (2003). *Learning To Smoke.* Chicago, Chicago University Press.

Huizinga, J. (1944). *Homo Ludens.* London, Routledge.

Hunniccutt, B. (1988). *Work Without End.* Philadelphia, Temple University Press.

Hutton, W. (1996). *The State We're In.* London, Vintage.

IDC (2007). IDC Predictions 2007. http://cdn.idc.com/downloads/204631.pdf

Imbush, E. and Talbot, M. (eds) (1988). *Relative Freedoms.* Milton Keynes, Open University Press.

International Federation of the Phonographic Industry (IFPI) (2006). *The Recording Industry Report 2006*, http://www.ifpi.org.

Jackson, E. (2003). 'Leisure Research by Canadians and Americans.' *Journal of Leisure Research* **35**(3): 292–315.

Jackson, P. (1994). 'Passive Smoking and Ill Health.' *Sociology of Health & Illness* **16**(2): 424–47.

Jenkins, P. (1994). *Using Murder: The Social Construction of Serial Homicide.* Hawthorne, NY, Aldine de Gruyter.

Kammen, M. (1999). *American, Culture, American Tastes.* New York, Basic.

Kaplan, M. (1960). *Leisure in America.* New York, Wiley.

Kaplan, M. (1978). *Leisure: Perspectives on Education and Policy.* West Haven, National Education Association.

Kassof, A. (1965). *The Soviet Youth Program: Regimentation and Rebellion.* Cambdridge, Mass., Harvard University Press.

Kasson, J.E. (1978). *Amusing The Masses.* New York, Hill & Wang.

Katz, J. (1988). *Seductions of Crime.* New York, Basic Books.

Kautsky, K. (1946). *Social Democracy versus Communism.* New York, Rand School Press.

Kautsky, K. (2007). *The Road To Power.* New York, Center for Socialist History.

Kelly, J.R. (1983). *Leisure Identities and Interactions.* London, Allen & Unwin.

Kelly, J.R. (1994). 'The Symboloic Interactionist Metaphor and Leisure.' *Leisure Studies* **13**: 81–96.

Kerr, C., Dunlop, J., Harbison, F. and Meyers, C.A. (1962). *Industrialism and Industrial Man.* Glenoce, Free Press.

Keynes, J. M. (1931). 'Economic Possibililties for Our Grand Children'. In *The Collected Writings of John Maynard Keynes Vol. 9: Essays in Persuasion (1972).* London, Macmillan.

Klein, N. (2001). *No Logo.* Flamingo, London.

Klein, N. (2007). *The Shock Doctrine.* London, Penguin.

Kuhn, T. S. (1962). *The Structure of Scientific Revolutions.* Chicago, University of Chicago Press.

Lash, S. and Urry, J. (1987). *The End of Organized Capitalism.* Cambridge, Polity.

Lash, S. and Urry, J. (1994). *Economies of Signs and Space.* London, Sage.

Lau, C. (2008). 'Child prostitution in Thailand.' *Journal of Child Health Care* **12**: 144–55.

Lim, L. (ed.) (1998). *The Sex Sector: the Economic and Social Bases of Prostitution in South East Asia.* Geneva, International Labour Office.

Linder, S. (1970). *The Harried Leisure Class.* New York, Columbia University Press.

Linklater, A. (1998). *The Transformation of Political Community.* Cambridge, Polity.

Lyng, S. (ed.) (2004). *Edgework.* London, Routledge.

Lyotard, J.F. (1979). *The Postmodern Condition.* Manchester, Manchester University Press.

MacCannell, D. (1976). *The Tourist.* New York, Schocken.

Mackay, J. and Eriksen, M. (2002). *The Tobacco Atlas.* Geneva, WHO.

Mackay, J., Eriksen, M. and Shafey, O. (2006) *The Tobacco Atlas, 2nd ed.* Geneva, WHO.

Mackenzie, J.M. (1984). *Imperialism and Popular Culture.* Manchester, Manchester University Press.

Madeley, J. (1999). *Big Business, Poor Peoples.* London, Zed.

Mangan, J. (1985). *The Games Ethic and Imperialism.* Cambridge, Cambridge University Press.

Manning, P. (2007). 'Introduction: An Overview of the Normalization Debate'. In P. Manning. *Drugs and Popular Culture.* Cullumpton, Willan. Pp. 49–55.

Marcuse, H. (1964). *One Dimensional Man*. London, Abacus.
Marcuse, H. (1969). *An Essay on Liberation*. Harmondsworth, Penguin.
Marcuse, H. (1978). *The Aesthetic Dimension*. London, Macmillan.
Mares, D. (2006). *Drug Wars and Coffee Houses*. Washington, CQ Press.
Marinetto, M. (2007). *Social Theory, The State and Modern Society*. Maidenhead, Open University Press.
Martin, B. and Mason, S. (1982). *Leisure and Work*. Sudbury, Leisure Consultants Press.
Marx, K. (1844 (1964)). *The Economic and Philosophic Manuscripts 1844*. New York, New World.
Marx, K. (1858). *Grundrisse*. London, Penguin.
Marx, K. (1867 (1977)). *Capital*, Volume 1. London, Lawrence & Wishart.
Marx, K. (1875 (1971)). *Critique of the Gotha Programme*. Moscow, Progress Publishers.
Marx, K. (1894 (1977)). *Capital, Volume 3*. London, Lawrence & Wishart.
Marx, K. and Engels, F. (1846). *The German Ideology*. London, Lawrence & Wishart.
Marx , K. and Engels, F. (1970). *The German Ideology*. London, Lawrence & Wishart.
Maslow, A. (1973). *Religions, Values and Peak Experience*. New York, Viking Press.
Maxwell, J. (1997) 'The Maxwell Report', *Tobacco Reporter*. http://www.tobacco report.com
Mcfarlane, A. (1978). *The Origins of English Individualism*. Oxford, Blackwell.
McFarlane, A. (1993). 'Louis Dumont and the Origins of Individualism.' *Cambridge Anthropology* **16**(1): 2–21.
McGuigan, J. (2006). 'The Politics of Cultural Studies and Cool Capitalism.' *Cultural Politics* **2**(2): 137–58.
McKay, J. (1991). *No Pain, No Gain? Sport and Australian Culture*. Sydney, Prentice Hall.
Miliband, R. (1969). *The State in Capitalist Society*. London, Quartet Books.
Mill, J.S. (1859). *On Liberty*. Oxford, Oxford University Press.
Moorhouse, H.F. (1989). 'Models of Work, Models of Leisure'. In C. Rojek *Leisure For Leisure*. Basingstoke, Macmillan. pp. 15–35.
Muller-Doohm, S. (2005). *Adorno*. Cambridge, Polity.
Neulinger, J. (1981a). *To Leisure: An Introduction*. Boston, Alyn & Bacon.
Neulinger, J. (1981b). 'Leisure Counselling: A Commentary.' *The Counselling Psychologist* **9**: 69–70.
NSDUH (2004). *National Survey on Drug Use and Health*. www.oas.samhsa.gov/nsduh.htm
OECD (2006). *Employment Outlook*. Paris, OECD.
Office of National Statistics (2000). www.statistics.gov.uk
O'Loughlin, M. (1978). *The Garlands of Repose: The Literary Celebration of Literary and Retired Leisure*. Chicago, University of Chicago Press.
Parker, H., Aldridge, J. and Measham, F. (1998). *Illegal Leisure: The Normalization of Adolescent Recreational Drug Use*. London, Routledge.
Parker, H., Williams, L. and Aldridge, J. (2002). 'The normalization of "sensible" drug use.' *Sociology* **36**(4): 941–64.
Parker, S. (1971). *The Future of Work and Leisure*. London, MacGibbon & Kee.
Parker, S. (1981). 'Choice, Flexibility, Spontaneity and Self Determination.' *Social Forces* **60**(2): 323–31.
Peto, R. and Lopez, A. (2004). 'The Future Worldwide Health Effects of Current Smoking Patterns.' *European Journal of Dental Education* **8**(4): 7–10.
Phoenix, J. and Oerton, S. (2005). *Illicit And Illegal*. Cullompten, Willan.
Pieper, J. (1952). *Leisure: The Basis of Culture*. New York, New American Library.
Popper, K. (1945). *The Open Society and Its Enemies*. London, Routledge & Kegan Paul.

Potter, S. and Bailey, I. (2008). 'Transport and the Environment'. In R.D. Knowles, J. Shaw and I. Docherty (eds) *Transport Geographies*. Oxford, Blackwell.

Poulantzas, N. (1973). *Political Power and Social Classes*. London, New Left Books.

Poulantzas, N. (1978). *State, Power, Socialism*. London, New Left Books.

Presdee, M. (2000). *Cultural Criminology and the Carnival of Crime*. London, Routledge.

Pricewaterhouse Coopers (2008) *Global Entertainment and Media Outlook*. New York, Pricewaterhouse Coopers.

Putnam, D. (2000). *Bowling Alone*. New York, Touchstone.

Qutb, S. (2008). *The Sayyid Qutb Reader*. Abingdon, Routledge.

Roach, J. (2007). *It*. Ann Arbor, University of Michigan.

Roberts, K. (1970). *Leisure*. New York, Prentice Hall.

Roberts, K. (1978). *Contemporary Society and the Growth of Leisure*. London, Longman.

Roberts, K. (1981). *Leisure* (2nd edition). London, Longman.

Roberts, K. (1987). *Leisure and Social Change in the 1980s*. Fifth Canadian Congress on Leisure Research, Dalhouise University, Nova Scotia.

Roberts, K. (2004). *The Leisure Industries*. Basingstoke, Palgrave-Macmillan.

Roche, M. (1992). *Rethinking Citizenship: Welfare, Ideology and Change in Modern Society*. Cambridge, Cambridge University Press.

Rojek, C. (1985). *Capitalism and Leisure Theory*. London and New York, Tavistock.

Rojek, C. (1995). *Decentring Leisure*. London and Thousand Oaks, Sage.

Rojek, C. (2000). *Leisure and Culture*. Basingstoke, Palgrave Macmillan.

Rojek, C. (2005). *Leisure Theory: Principles and Practice*. Basingstoke, Palgrave Macmillan.

Rojek, C. (2007). *Cultural Studies*. Cambridge, Polity.

Rojek, C. and Turner, B.S. (2000). 'Decorative Sociology: Towards a Critique of the Cultural Turn.' *Sociological Review* **48**(4): 629–48.

Rostow, W. W. (1956). ' The take-off into self-sustained growth', *Economic Journal*, 66: 25–48.

Rowe, D. (2004). *Sport, Culture and the Media*. Maidenhead, Open University Press.

Ruck, S.K. (ed.) (1951). *Paterson on Prisons: The Collected Papers of Sir Alexander Paterson*. London, Frederick Mueller.

Runciman, G.W. (1966). *Relative Deprivation and Social Justice*. Berkeley, University of California Press.

Russell, D. (1997). *Popular Music in England*. Manchester, Manchester University Press.

Sage, G. (1998). *Power and Ideology in American Sport*. Champaign IL, Human Kinetics.

Samuel, R. (ed.) (1988). *Patriotism* (3 volumes). London, RKP.

Schor, J. (1992). *The Overworked American*. New York, Basic Books.

Schutz, A. (1967). *Phenomenology of the Social World*. Chicago, Northwestern University Press.

Scottish Office (1999). *Social Inclusion – Opening the Door to a Better Scotland*. Edinburgh, Scottish Office.

Sennett, R. (1999). *The Corrosion of Character*. Norton, New York.

Sennett, R. (2004). *Respect*. Penguin, London.

Sennett, R. (2006). *The Culture of the New Capitalism*. New Haven, Yale University Press.

Shaw, S. (2001). 'Conceptualizing Resistance: Women's Leisure As Political Practice.' *Journal of Leisure Research* **33**: 186–99.

Shiner, M. and Newburn, T. (1997). 'Definiely, Maybe Not: The Normalization of Recreational Drug Use Among Young People.' *Sociology* **31**(3): 511–29.

Simmel, G. (1950). *The Sociology of Georg Simmel*. New York, Free Press.

Siwek, S. (2007). 'The Staggering Cost of IP Piracy.' *Info Tech & Telecom News* January 1, 2007.

Smart, B. (2003). *Economy, Culture and Society*. Milton Keynes, Open University Press.

Snyder, L. B., Milici, F. F., Slater, M., Sun, H. and Strizhakova, Y. (2006). 'Effects of Alcohol Advertising Exposure on Drinking among Youth.' *Archives of Pediatric Adolescent Medicine*, 168: 18–24.

Springhall, J. (1977). *Youth, Empire and Society*. London, Croom Helm.

Stebbins, R. (1979). *Amateurs: On the Margins Between Work and Leisure*. Beverly Hills, Sage.

Stebbins, R. (1992). *Amateurs, Professionals and Serious Leisure*. Montreal, Queens University Press.

Stebbins, R. (2002). *New Directions in Theory and Research of Serious Leisure*. New York, Mellon Press.

Stouffer, S., Suchman, E. A., Devinney, L., Star, S. and Williams, R. (1949). *Studies in Social Psychology in World War II: The American Soldier*. Princeton, Princeton University Press.

Stradling, S., Anable, J., Anderson, T. and Cronberg, A. (2008). 'Car Use and Climate Change.' In A. Park, J. Curtice, K. Thomson, M. Phillips, M. Johnson and E. Clery *British Social Attitudes: 24th Report*. London, National Centre for Social Research/Sage.

Swingewood, A. (1986). 'Review of "Capitalism and Leisure Theory".' *British Journal of Sociology* **37**(4): 608–9.

Taylor, C. (2007). *A Secular Age*. Cambridge, Harvard University Press.

Thompson, E. P. (1967). 'Time, Work Discipline and Industrial Capitalism.' *Past and Present* **38**: 56–97.

Tobacco Warning Labels and Packaging Fact Sheet (2000) 11th World Conference on Tobacco or Health. www.tobaccofreekids.org/campaign/global/docs/warning.pdf

Toffler, A. (1980). *The Third Wave*. New York, Bantam.

Tomlinson, A. (1989). 'Whose Side Are They On? Leisure Studies and Cultural Studies In Britain.' *Leisure Studies* **8**(2): 97–106.

Tomlinson, A. (2006). 'Leisure Studies: Progress, Phases and Possibilities: An Interview.' *Leisure Studies* **25**(3): 257–73.

Tonnies, F. (1957). *Community and Association*. East Lansing, Michigan State University Press.

Touraine, A. (1971). *The Post Industrial Society*. New York, Random House.

Turner, B.S. (1984). *The Body and Society*. Oxford, Blackwell.

Turner, B.S. (1992). *Regulating Bodies*. London, Routledge.

Turner, B.S. (2006). *Vulnerability and Human Rights*. University Park, Penn State University Press.

Turner, B.S. and Rojek, C. (2001). *Society and Culture: Principles of Scarcity and Solidarity*. London and Thousand Oaks, Sage.

Turner, V. (1974). *Dramas, Fields and Metaphors*. New York, Cotnell University Press.

Turner, V. (1982). *From Ritual To Theatre*. New York, PAJ Publications.

UNICEF (2005). *Child Trafficking*. http://www.unicefusa.org/site/apps/s/content.asp

United Nations Office on Drugs and Crime (2007). *World Report*. Geneva, United Nations.

Urry, J. (2002). *The Tourist Gaze* (2nd edition). London, Sage.

Urry, J. (2007). *Mobilities*. Cambridge, Polity.

Urry, J. (not published). *Complexity and Climate Change*. BSA Annual Conference, Warwick University.

US State Department (2005). *International Narcotics Control Strategy Report*. Washington D.C., US Department of State.

Valentine, K., Alison, M. and Schneider, I. (1999). 'The One Way Mirror of Leisure Research.' *Leisure Sciences* **21**(3): 24–46.

Van Moorst, H. (1982). 'Leisure and Social Theory.' *Leisure Studies* **2**(3): 157–69.

Veal, A. J. (1987). *Leisure and the Future*. London, Allen & Unwin.

Veal, A. J. (2004). 'Perspectives on the Leisure–Work Relationship'. In J.A. Veal and A.J. Haworth (eds) *Work and Leisure*. Hove, Routledge. Pp.107–19.

Veblen, T. (1899). *The Theory of the Leisure Class*. London, Allen & Unwin.

Wadsworth, E., Moss, S., Simpson, S. and Smith, A. (2004). 'Factors Associated with Recreational Drug Use.' *Journal of Psychopharmacology* **18**(2): 238–48.

Wallerstein, I. (1974). *The Modern World System*. New York, Academic Press.

Wallerstein, I. (2004). *World-Systems Analysis*. Durham N.C., Duke University Press.

Wallerstein, I. (2006). *European Universalism*. New York, New Press.

Wearing, B. (1998). *Leisure and Feminist Theory*. London, Sage.

Weber, M. (1947). *The Theory of Economic and Social Organization*. New York, Free Press.

Weber, M. (1948). *From Max Weber*. London, RKP.

Weeks, J. (2007). *The World We Have Won: The Remaking of Erotic and Intimate Life*. Abingdon, Routledge.

Wilensky, H. (1960). 'Work, Careers and Social Integration.' *International Social Science Journal* **12**(4): 543–60.

Williams, L. and Parker, H. (2001). 'Alcohol, Cannabis, Ecstasy and Cocaine: Drugs of Reasoned Choice Amongst Young Adult Recreational Drug Users in England.' *International Journal of Drug Policy* **12**: 397–413.

Wilson, W.H. (1994). *The City Beautiful Movement*. Baltimore, Johns Hopkins University Press.

Wimbush, E. and Talbot, M. (1988) *Relative Freedoms: Women and Leisure*. Milton Keynes, Open University Press.

Wittgenstein, L. (1967). *The Blue and Brown Books*. Oxford, Oxford University Press.

Wolfe, S., Higgins, G. and Marcus. C. (2007). 'Deterrence and Digital Piracy.' *Social Science Computer Review* **1**(1): 1–17.

Wolff, M.M.E. (2003). 'The Wealth Divide: The Growing Gap in the US Between the Rich and the Rest: An Interview with Edward Wolff.' *Multinational Monitor* **24**(5): http.multinationalmonitor.org/mm2003/03may

World Health Organization (2004) 'Tobacco Free Initiative.' Geneva, WHO.

World Leisure Organization (1998). 'São Paulo Declaration: Leisure in Globalised Society.' www.worldleisure.org

World Leisure Organization (2000). 'Chater For Leisure.' www.worldleisure.org

Wright Mills, C. (1956). *The Power Elite*. Oxford, Oxford University Press.

Wright Mills, C. (1958). *The Causes of World War Three*. New York, Simon & Schuster.

Wylie, R.W. (2000). *Tourism and Society*. State College, Venture Press.

Yeo, E. and Yeo, S. (eds) (1981). *Popular Culture and Class Conflict 1590–1914*. Brighton, Harvester Press.

AUTHOR INDEX

A

Aitchison, A. 10, 37, 39, 67, 123, 135, 145
Adorno, T. 125
Alterman, E. 163
Althusser, L. 34
Andrew, E. 16, 37, 38, 44
Arendt, H. 112
Aristotle, 91–93, 96, 189
Aronowitz, S. 37

B

Bailey, I. 130
Bailey, P. 133
Bailyn, B. 23
Baudrillard, J. 40
Bauman, Z. 112
Baranowski, S. 144
Bean, P. 150
Beaven, B. 88–9
Beck, U. 49, 77, 125
Bell, D. 31, 36, 37
Bialcheski, D. 113
Blackshaw, T. 10, 39, 124, 126
Blyton, P. 4
Bourdieu, P. 16, 135, 136, 152
Borzello, F. 53, 89
Bowdin, G. 136
Bramham, P. 39
Brewer, D. 69
Burch, W. 36, 47, 109, 110
Burns, T. 180
Bryson, J. 4

C

Campbell, R. 70
Castells, M. 125
Cheek, N. 36, 47, 109, 110
Chick, G. 113
Clark, D. 97
Clarke, J. 10, 16, 37, 38, 44, 67, 120, 144
Clayre, A. 29, 32
Clutterbuck, D. 54
Coalter, F. 54, 110, 113, 133–4, 135
Corrigan, P. 143
Coyle, D. 180
Crabbe, T. 124, 126
Critcher, C. 10, 16, 37, 38, 44, 67, 120, 144

Cross, G. 32, 44, 113
Csikszentmihalyi, M. 5, 28, 29, 86, 111–112, 119

D

Daniels, B. 59–60
De Grazia, S. 27, 63, 68, 72, 93, 94
Deem, R. 38
Dewey, J. 91, 95–7
Di Fazio, W. 37
Donnelly, P. 55
Dunlop, J. 31
Dumazedier, J. 30–1
Dumont, L. 58
Dunning, E. 44, 67, 78-9, 121–2
Durkheim, E. 68, 70, 73, 85, 143, 153, 158
Dustin, D. 113

E

Edington, C. 96, 106, 186
Elias, N. 23, 67, 78–9, 121–2, 132
Eliot, T.S. 134
Engels, F. 141
Eriksen, M. 162, 167
Etzioni, A. 135

F

Ferrell, J. 74, 112
Foucault, M. 39, 67, 145–7
Fuller, F. 133
Frank, R. 17
Frank, T. 45, 46, 160

G

Gartman, D. 44
Giddens, A. 49
Gellner, E. 148
Gershuny, J. 26
Getz, D. 136
Giddens, A. 125, 135
Giulanotti, R. 185
Glanz, A. 167
Glenny, M. 13, 21, 116
Godbey, G. 100
Goffman, E. 85
Goldman, R. 160
Goleman, D. 2, 23
Goodale, T. 100, 107–8, 113

Gorz, A. 37
Gramsci, A. 141–2
Gray, R. 89
Green, E. 38, 121, 144
Green, M. 163
Gruneau, R. 143

H
Habermas, J. 148
Hall, S. 55
Harbison, F. 31
Haregreaves, J. 143
Harmer, P. 51
Harvey, D. 125, 180
Haworth, J. 24
Hayward, K. 74
Headey, B. 12
Hebron, S. 121
Heeley, J. 89
Hemingway, J. 113
Henry, I. 135
Henderson, K. 10, 67, 113, 121
Hill, J. 32, 44
Hirsch, F. 17–18,
Hochschild, A. 3, 22, 23, 37
Horkheimer, M. 125
Horne, J. 184
Hubble, N. 104
Hughes, J. 8, 165
Huizinga, J. 94, 105
Hunnicutt, B. 32, 37, 113
Hutton, W. 135

J
Jackson, E. 105, 107
Jackson, P. 167
Jenkins, J. 4

K
Kammen, M. 44
Kaplan, M. 29–31
Kassof, A. 144
Kasson, J. 44
Katz, J. 5, 51, 76, 112
Kautsky, K. 141
Kelly, J. 99, 113
Kerr, C. 31
Keynes, J. K. 91
Klein, N. 13, 177
Kuhn, T. 118

L
Lash, S. 125
Lau, C. 155

Lim L. 21, 155
Linklater, A. 49
Lopez, A. 162
Lyotard, J. 123
Lyng, S. 76

M
MacCannell, D. 85, 98
McKay, J. 143
MacKay, J. 158, 162
MacKenzie, J. 87
McFarlane, A. 58
McGuigan, J. 45
Madeley, J. 163
Mangan, J. 87
Manning, P. 149
Marcuse, H. 34–5, 79–81, 98, 175
Mares, D. 21, 49, 148, 150
Marks, J. 12
Marx, K. 80, 141
Maslow, A. 112
Merton, R. 82
Meyers, C. 31
Miliband, R. 34, 139–40, 141
Mill, J.S. 167
Mills, C. W. 34
Moorhouse, H.F. 129
Muller-Doohm, S. 111

N
Neulinger, J. 5, 27–8, 29, 86, 119, 153
Newburn, T. 150

O
O'Neill, M. 70
Oerton, J. 70

P
Papson, S. 160
Parker, H. 73, 148, 158-9
Parker, S. 5, 14, 33, 37, 119, 127–8, 129, 153, 167
Peto, R. 162
Phoenix, S. 70
Pieper, J. 27, 72, 93–4, 128
Poulantzas, N. 34, 142
Popper, K. 111
Potter, S. 130
Putnam, D. 135
Presdee, M. 74, 76, 112

R
Roberts, K. 32–3, 37, 44, 99, 125, 139, 160
Roche, M. 134

Rojek, C. 37, 110, 118, 125, 130, 153
Rostow, W. 170
Rowe, D. 184
Ruck, S. K. 89
Runciman, W. G. 18
Russell, D. 44

S
Sage, G. 143
Sanders, C. 74
Sayer, D. 143
Schor, J. 21, 37, 98
Schutz, A. 71
Sennett, R. 23, 37, 45, 85, 161
Shaw, S. 121
Sheard, K. 44
Shiner, S. 150
Siwek, S. 50
Smart, B. 152
Snyder, L. B. 172
Springhall, J. 93
Stalker, G. M. 180
Stebbins, R. 26, 135, 136
Stouffer, S. 18
Stradling, S. 130

T
Talbot, M. 37, 121, 144
Taylor, C. 134
Thompson, E. P. 2
Toffler, A. 31

Tomlinson, A. 53, 124
Touraine, A. 31
Turner, B. S. 134
Turner, V. 60–1, 186

U
Urry, J. 98, 109, 125

V
Valentine, K. 105
Van Moorst, H. 144
Veal, T. 24, 33, 95, 129
Veblen, T. 15, 17, 26, 85, 165

W
Wadsworth, E. 73
Wearing, B. 10, 121, 126
Weber, M. 139
Whitson, D. 143
Wilensky, H. 119, 127, 129
Williams, L. 73
Wilson, W. H. 88, 133
Wimbush, E. 37, 121, 144
Wolfe, S. 50
Wooden, M. 12
Woodward, D. 121
Wylie, R. W. 185

Y
Yeo, E. 143
Yeo, S. 143

SUBJECT INDEX

A
A&B perspectives 17, 154
Academics, in leisure 36–8, 48
Action approach, to leisure 125–126, 130
Air travel 156–7
Alcohol 158, 170–173
Allocative mechanisms 10, 39
Anti-structure 60–1

C
Care for the self 146, 160
Care for the other 146, 160
Cars and leisure 130–131
Cards 76–78
City Beautiful Movement 87–8, 133
Class, and leisure 10, 32, 38–9, 67, 92–3,
    120, 141
Compulsory Competitive
    Tendering 135
Consumption 35–6, 37, 46–7, 79–83
Corporate Social Responsibility 169–170,
    173–5
Corporation 34, 44–46
Counselling, in leisure 28
Cultural criminology 7
Cultural icons 160
Cultural turn 61–2
Crime, and leisure 13, 21, 42, 49–52, 72–76,
    116, 148–51, 155–156

D
Deregulation 21, 27
Disaster Capitalism 175–178
Drugs, and leisure 72–76, 148–51

E
Emotional Intelligence 22, 24–27, 37, 90,
    146–7, 180–1
Emotional labour 22, 37, 95, 146–7, 180–1
Event Management 49, 137–138, 175–176

F
Feminism 39, 120–121, 125–6
Figurational Sociology 121–2
Flow 28, 111–112
Freedom 1–3

G
Gender, and leisure 10
Globalization 21, 27, 34, 42, 145, 153–4, 156,
    159, 180
Governmentality 145–7
Gowers Report 153

H
Habitus 11
Health, and leisure 11–13, 157–8,
    162, 169–70
Hegemony 142
Homo Duplex model 68–70, 73, 85

I
Illegal downloading 50, 56–7, 75,
    151–153
Inequality 12, 14–16
Institutions of normative coercion 68–9
Intentionality 5–9
Islam and leisure 64–67
iTunes 47

K
Kyoto Protocol 43, 154

L
Laissez-faire approach, to leisure 54–5
Leisure Sciences 82–3, 108–9, 110, 113, 124,
    182–3, 187–9
Leisure Studies 29, 33, 34, 38–40, 48, 49,
    82–3, 90, 99, 108–9, 110, 113, 124, 166,
    182–3, 187–9
Life coaching 1, 147
Logic of Industrialization Thesis 31

M
Managerialism 134, 135
Marxism 119–20, 125–6
Mass Observation Studies 104–5
Methodenstreit debate 71, 111
Mimesis 122
Monitoring 23, 27
Moral regulation 144
Motility 122
Multiple equilibria 127–8

N
Neat capitalism 45–6, 49, 62, 173–5, 180

O
Olivennes initiative 153

P
Peak Experience 112
People knowledge 4, 22
Philanthropy, and leisure 15
Pluralist approach to leisure 33, 34
Pollution, and leisure 9, 43, 130–131
Positional goods and leisure 16–19
Post-structuralism 123, 126
Professionalization 97–103
Prohibition 55–6
Prostitution and leisure 69–70, 155–6

R
Rational recreation 87–9, 133, 134
Reconnaissance 23, 27
Relative deprivation 17–18
Religion and leisure 63–67
Repressive Desublimation 79

S
Scarcity 6, 10, 11, 17, 18, 33,
       67, 70, 90
Service Sector 2, 22, 32
Sex and leisure 69

Sociability 122
Social capital 135–6
Social Formalism 119, 125
Social movements 49
Social system approach, to leisure 36, 47
State 33–4, 41–3, 68, 139–41
State-Corporate-Consumer-Academic
       Framework (SCCA) 33–41, 58, 82, 129,
       138, 145, 178–9, 187–189
State-Corporate-Consumer-Academic-Social
       Movement-Illegal Leisure Framework
       41–52, 58–9, 78, 82, 116–117, 129, 151,
       177, 178–9, 181, 187–189
Stateless solutions 83
Sub-politics 49

T
Time-Use Survey 24–25
Tobacco 8, 157, 161–70
Tsunami 46

U
University of Illinois 100–101

V
Voluntarism 1, 5, 19, 29, 30, 68, 181

W
Work ethic 32
Work-life balance 2, 33, 54